Artificial Intelligence and Innovation Management

Series on Technology Management

Series Editor: Joe Tidd (*University of Sussex, UK*)   ISSN 0219-9823

The Technology Management Series is dedicated to the advancement of academic research and management practice in the field of technology and innovation management. The series features titles which adopt an interdisciplinary, multifunctional approach to the management of technology and innovation, and includes work which seeks to integrate the management of technological, market and organisational innovation. All titles are based on original empirical research, and includes research monographs and multiauthor edited works. The focus throughout is on the management of technology and innovation at the level of the organisation or firm, rather than on the analysis of sectoral trends or national policy.

Published

More information on this series can also be found at http://www.worldscientific.com/series/stm

(Continued at the end of the book)

SERIES ON TECHNOLOGY MANAGEMENT – VOL. 38

Artificial Intelligence and Innovation Management

Editors

Stoyan Tanev
Carleton University, Canada

Helena Blackbright
Mälardalen University, Sweden

Published by

World Scientific Publishing Europe Ltd.

57 Shelton Street, Covent Garden, London WC2H 9HE

Head office: 5 Toh Tuck Link, Singapore 596224

USA office: 27 Warren Street, Suite 401-402, Hackensack, NJ 07601

Library of Congress Cataloging-in-Publication Data

Names: Tanev, S., editor. | Blackbright, Helena, editor.

Title: Artificial intelligence and innovation management / editors, Stoyan Tanev,
  Carleton University, Canada, Helena Blackbright, Mälardalen University, Sweden.

Description: Singapore ; Hackensack, NJ, USA : World Scientific Publishing Europe Ltd., 2022. |
  Series: Series on technology management, 0219-9823 ; vol 38 |
  Includes bibliographical references and index.

Identifiers: LCCN 2021042122 | ISBN 9781800611320 (hardcover) |
  ISBN 9781800611337 (ebook) | ISBN 9781800611344 (ebook other)

Subjects: LCSH: Technological innovations--Management. | Artificial intelligence.

Classification: LCC HD45 .A765 2022 | DDC 658.4/063--dc23

LC record available at https://lccn.loc.gov/2021042122

British Library Cataloguing-in-Publication Data

A catalogue record for this book is available from the British Library.

For any available supplementary material, please visit
https://www.worldscientific.com/worldscibooks/10.1142/Q0334#t=suppl

Desk Editors: Nimal Koliyat/Michael Beale/Shi Ying Koe

Typeset by Stallion Press
Email: enquiries@stallionpress.com

Printed in Singapore

About the Editors

Stoyan Tanev is Associate Professor of Technology Entrepreneurship and Innovation Management associated with the Technology Innovation Management (TIM) Program, Sprott School of Business, Carleton University, Ottawa, ON, Canada. Stoyan Tanev's research interests are in the fields of technology entrepreneurship and innovation management, value proposition development, and business analytics. A key research area for him is the application of text analytics for the development of actionable business insights. Before re-joining Carleton University in 2017, Dr. Tanev was part of the Innovation and Design Engineering Section and the Integrative Innovation Management (I2M) Centre at the University of Southern Denmark (SDU), Odense, Denmark. His experience includes also several years of working as a photonics designer for high-tech startups in Ottawa, Canada.

Stoyan has a multidisciplinary background including M.Sc. in Physics (Sofia University, Bulgaria), Ph.D. in Physics (1995, University Pierre and Marie Curie, Paris, France, co-awarded by Sofia University, Bulgaria), M.Eng. in Technology Management (2005, Carleton University, Ottawa, Canada), M.A. in Orthodox Theology (2009, University of Sherbrooke, Montreal Campus, QC, Canada), and Ph.D. in Theology (2012, Sofia University, Bulgaria). Dr. Tanev is one of the leaders of the Special Interest Group on Artificial Intelligence and Innovation Management of the International Society for Professional Innovation Management (ISPIM). He has served for several years as the Editor in Chief of the Technology Innovation Management Review: www.timreview.ca. His broader scholarly interests include the interdisciplinary exploration of epistemological issues on the interface of physics, theology, the natural, and the social sciences.

Helena Blackbright is a researcher in Innovation Management at Mälardalen University, Sweden. At the university, Helena shares her time between research and strategic development at Automation Region, a Center of Excellence with focus on industrial technology and research at the Department of Innovation Management. Her research interest is within support for organizational innovativeness, change in complex adaptive social systems, and the relation between AI and Innovation Management.

Helena has been within the field of innovation management for more than 20 years and with more than 10 years' experience from different intermediary organizations, she finds great interest in multidisciplinary collaboration. She is co-founder of the Swedish think tank addAI.org. Bringing together experts from industry, academia, and society, the goal of addAI.org is to start asking the questions we need to ask ourselves about AI and explore possible answers. Helena also initiated and started the Special Interest Group on Artificial Intelligence and Innovation Management of the International Society for Professional Innovation Management (ISPIM) in 2018 and is since then one of the leaders of the group.

About the Contributors

Maham Aman received the M.Eng. degree in Technology Innovation Management from Carleton University, Ottawa, ON, Canada in 2020 and the B.Sc. degree in Telecommunications Engineering from the National University of Computer and Emerging Sciences Karachi, Pakistan in 2008. Her research interests include Bayesian and statistical machine learning, natural language analytics, and non-stationary distribution learning.

Tony Bailetti holds a faculty appointment in Carleton University's Sprott School of Business and the Faculty of Engineering and Design (carleton. ca). Dr. Bailetti is the past Director of Carleton's Technology Management Innovation (TIM) program (timprogram.ca). He is the founder of the Scale Early, Rapidly and Securely community (globalgers.org), and the *TIM Review* (timreview.ca). He is the lead of the AI for Local Value, a program designed to accelerate the deployment of AI to create value for companies and cities.

Tony's areas of expertise include: (i) technology entrepreneurship; (ii) scaling companies early, rapidly, and securely; and (iii) cross-border ecommerce. He has supervised the completion of 145 theses and projects from students in Masters' programs in engineering and business. Dr. Bailetti earned a Ph.D. and an M.B.A. from the University of Cincinnati, Ohio, USA, where he was a Fulbright Scholar from 1971 to 1975.

Jennifer Barth is Director of Research at Smoothmedia Consulting Ltd. She is an experienced ethnographer and social researcher, with a

D.Phil in Geography (University of Oxford, UK) and an M.A. in Women Studies (York University, Canada) and has previously held a lectureship at Goldsmiths, University of London. Her work is informed by empirical research on the intersections of emerging technologies socio-economic innovation. She provides companies with thought leadership on global issues impacting and shaping our current and future socio-cultural lives.

Jennifer's current research focuses on the human impact of emerging technologies at the leading edge of sustainable growth and competitiveness, digital transformation, and valuing the social and economic impact of less visible technological and cultural change with some of the world's biggest companies and with the third sector. She is skilled at using qualitative and quantitative as well as new emerging methods to bring transformational stories to life.

Navneet Bhalla is an Honorary Research Associate at University College London, in the Department of Computer Science, and a member of the Intelligent Systems Group. Dr. Bhalla is also an Adjunct Research Professor at Carleton University, in the Sprott School of Business, with the Technology Innovation Management Program. Prior to joining University College London and Carleton University, Navneet was a Postdoctoral Fellow at Harvard University (Department of Chemistry and Chemical Biology), at Cornell University (Department of Mechanical and Aerospace Engineering), and Universität Paderborn (Department of Computer Science). He has also worked as a Visiting Researcher at University College London (Department of Computer Science) and as a Scientific Collaborator at Université libre de Bruxelles (Institut de Recherches Interdisciplinaires en Intelligence Artificielle). Navneet has a Ph.D. in Computer Science (University of Calgary), an M.Sc. in Intelligent Systems (University College London), and a B.Sc. in Honors Computer Science (University of Ottawa). Navneet's multidisciplinary research covers artificial intelligence, self-assembling systems, heuristic optimization, mechanical design, soft robotics, and composite materials.

Nina Bozic Yams is a senior researcher in Innovation Management and the Future of Work at the Research Institutes of Sweden (RISE). She drives a collaborative community within the area of sustainable future work which connects more than 40 researchers from across RISE. She is also part of the core teams driving digital ethics and human-centric AI initiatives at RISE. Within the Swedish association of innovation managers Innovationsledarna, she leads a special thematic group on Innovation Management and AI.

Nina's interest is in re-thinking ways of working in time when work is becoming increasingly digital and remote. She is researching how to build organizations for the future, integrating digital technologies (such as AI, IoT, and XR) with new ways of organizing (based on participation and self-management), and innovative mindset and culture. She has been developing methods for exploring possible futures using speculative fiction, artifacts from the future, and embodiment methods to help employees re-think their future work, jobs, and needed skills. Nina is interested in how new technologies, such as AI, can augment humans at work, not only increasing their productivity, but also supporting well-being, creativity, and development. Nina has 17 years of experience working as an innovation enabler and explorer both in companies and public sector organizations. She started her career as a management consultant at Deloitte and then built and run the Centre for Entrepreneurship and Executive Development (CEED) Slovenia. After moving to Sweden, she continued her work as an innovation consultant and pursued a Ph.D. in Innovation and Design. She has been working with organizations, such as ABB, Electrolux, Ericsson, GodEl, various Swedish municipalities, and others.

Chris Brauer is a public intellectual and strategic adviser and is Director of Innovation in the Institute of Management Studies, Goldsmiths, University of London. His analysis are informed by empirical research on the intersections of emerging technologies, human behavior, risk, ethics, governance, productivity, and innovation. His focus is on public and media engagement with global issues impacting and shaping our current and future socio-economic and socio-cultural lives. He works closely in an advisory capacity with a global roster of C-level executives and holds numerous UK-based non-exec, trustee, and board positions. Dr. Chris shares his experiences and speaks regularly at public and corporate events with dispatches from the front lines of innovation and managing risk in the twin ambitions of transformation and sustainable growth for social and economic impact.

Françoise de Viron, now Emeritus, was for 18 years Professor of Knowledge Management in the Louvain School of Management (UCLouvain, Belgium) and Professor of Adult Education at the same university. Previously, she was for 15 years manager in charge of the development of artificial intelligence applications in the power generation and transmission sector within a private company. She is now joint Program Director of the Executive Master in Innovation Management (www. LouvainInnovation.be) and she is a board member and adviser for international companies and networks. Her research fields are intellectual capital management, organizational learning, and adult learning.

Eurydice Fotopoulou is Assistant Professor of Economics at the Institute of Management Studies (IMS), Goldsmiths, University of London. Her research interests include the measurement and management of intangible economic product (healthcare, education, the digital), measurement of productivity of intangible economic product, macroeconomic modeling, social infrastructure, and feminist economics. Her research is largely informed by her experience observing economic inequality in parts of the world she has lived and worked — China, Turkey, the USA and the UK. Eurydice holds a Ph.D. in Economics (University of Greenwich, UK), an M.Sc. in the Political Economy of Development (SOAS, University of London, UK), a B.Sc. in Development Economics (SOAS, University of London, UK). Eurydice also works as an independent consultant and is a board member of the Association for Heterodox Economics and reviewer for several journals.

Benoit Gailly is Professor of Innovation Management and Strategy in the Louvain School of Management (UCLouvain, Belgium) since 2001. He is also joint Program Director of the Executive Master in Innovation Management (www.LouvainInnovation.be). His research focuses on innovation-based strategies and capabilities (see www.Navigating Innovation.org), as well as innovation support systems.

Benoit is the author of numerous scientific publications on innovation and entrepreneurship, as well as of the books *Developing Innovative Organizations* (Palgrave, 2011) and *Navigating Innovation* (Palgrave, 2018). He is a board member and adviser for several innovation networks and international companies, both large industrial firms and technology start-ups. Since 2014 he has also been an associate member of the Board of BiRD (Belgium Industrial R&D) and the Secretary General of the GRD Network (www.GRDNetwork.be).

Amber Geurts is a researcher in Innovation, Technology & Society at the technology assessment organization Rathenau Institute in the Hague, the Netherlands. Before joining Rathenau, she worked as a researcher and consultant at TNO, the Netherlands Organisation for Applied Scientific Research. At TNO, she has been involved in various research projects concerning data-driven foresight, evidence for policy-making, smart industry, and (mission-oriented) innovation policy. Amber is also a visiting research fellow at Aalto University, where she is involved in research projects on AI in material science and on quantum computing.

Amber completed her Ph.D. in Innovation Management at the School of Economics & Business of the University of Groningen in the Netherlands. Her Ph.D. research has won the 2018 ISPIM Innovation Management Best Dissertation Award. Her research has been awarded several grants, and has been published in various journals including *Advanced Science*, *Technological Forecasting and Social Change*, *Technology Analysis & Strategic Management*, and *Journal of Cross-Cultural Psychology*.

Christopher Gustafsson is a Ph.D. student in Innovation and Design focusing on additive manufacturing in the industrial research school Array++, Mälardalen University, Eskilstuna, Sweden. His research interests are in the fields of additive manufacturing, innovation and design, product and process development, and artificial intelligence. A key research area for him is the integration of additive manufacturing in product and process development in the manufacturing industry. Christopher Gustafsson has a multidisciplinary background, including B.Sc in Industrial Design and Product Development (2015, Örebro University, Sweden) and M.Sc in Innovation and Design (2019, Mälardalen University, Sweden).

David Hudson is a technology management professional who has 35 years of experience in industry and academia. He is an executive-in-residence at the University of New Brunswick Technology Management and Entrepreneurship program and an Adjunct Professor in Carleton University's Technology Innovation Management program. Previously, he led new business incubation within the Chief Technology Office at Dell EMC. He has been a Director of Lead to Win (a community/university focused entrepreneurship development program in Ottawa), a board member of a cybersecurity incubator, the chair of the Ontario Centers of Excellence information, communication and digital media sector advisory board, and a consultant to technology firms. And before all that, he was the Vice President of advanced research and development at Nortel and has had an extensive career in technology business management as well as R&D.

David received his Bachelor's and Master's degrees in Systems Design Engineering from the University of Waterloo, Ontario, Canada. His Doctorate is from Carleton University where his research focused on employee innovation on the job. David lives in Ottawa where his wife and their two sons also work in the technology sector.

Peter E. Johansson is Associate Professor in Innovation Science at Mälardalen University in Eskilstuna, Sweden. He is Head of the Division of Innovation Management and a part of the research group Human Organizing in Entrepreneurship, Innovation and Quality Management.

Peter received his Ph.D. in Education in 2011 at Stockholm University; specialized in the fields of workplace learning and organization pedagogics. Peter has been involved in several cross-disciplinary research projects, and his current research interests are positioned in the intersection between operations management and innovation management research. His research deals with the origins of, and conditions for, learning and development of innovation competencies; on an individual and organizational level as well as the relation between those.

Mikael Johnsson is Assistant Professor of Process and Product Development at the Division of Product Development, School of Engineering, Innovation and Design, Mälardalen University, Eskilstuna, Sweden. His research interest is in the field of innovation management.

A key research area for him is the development and implementation of high-performing innovation teams in organizations.

Mikael has a multidisciplinary background, including a B.Sc in Innovation Technology (2006, Mälardalen University, Sweden), Licentiate in Innovation and Design (2014, Mälardalen University, Sweden), and Ph.D. in Mechanical Engineering (2016, Blekinge Institute of Technology, Sweden).

Christian Keen is an Assistant Professor at the Département de Management, Université Laval, Canada. Christian has extensive research and working experience in Europe, Latin America, and North America. Before joining Université Laval, Dr. Keen was Director Graduate Program in Finance at Universidad ORT Uruguay and member of the Department of Marketing & Management at University of Southern Denmark. His professional experience includes being a member of several Boards of Directors of private companies and NGOs. He teaches graduate and undergraduate courses in international entrepreneurship, entrepreneurship, and international business. His research interests are in the areas of international entrepreneurship, entrepreneurship, emerging economies, and rapidly growing firms.

Christian is a member of the editorial board of the *International Journal of Entrepreneurship Small Business*, *European Journal of Family Business*, and associated editor at *TIM Review*. He has presented his research in several international conferences such as Academy of International Business (AIB) and Academy of Management (AOM), and also published papers in those areas.

Manuel Noya has a multidisciplinary background including an M.B.A. Master MDI Dirección de Empresas (Universidad Politécnica de Madrid), M.Sc. in Materials Science and Technology (Universidad de Santiago de Compostela), B.Sc. in Materials Engineering (Universidad Politécnica de Madrid), and B.Sc. Chemical Engineering (Universidad de Santiago de Compostela).

Manuel is an ex-International Fellow at SRI International (Menlo Park, California, USA) and one of the founders and CEO of Linknovate, a start-up founded at Stanford University (Palo Alto, California, USA) and with its main office in A Coruña (Spain). With Manuel as CEO, Linknovate gained access to European funding (seven projects) including the prestigious SME Instrument (EIC Accelerator), to develop its technology. Linknovate has also won multiple competitions: European Open Data start-up contest Finodex, funded by the European Commission; and APORTA National Open Data Contribution Award granted by Red.es, Ministry of Economy in Spain. Since its founding, Linknovate has grown to serve clients (companies and public organizations) in more than 15 countries globally, and with individual users practically all over the world. Linknovate technologies make extensive use of artificial intelligence (machine learning) in the fields of data and text mining. Manuel has served as adviser with Linknovate of multiple calls for Innovative Public Procurement in Spain, assisting as a technological surveillance tool in preliminary market consultations, and in innovation-grade assessment of proposals (pre-award stage) and executed projects (execution stage).

María José Ospina-Fadul is an economic adviser at Public Health England with M.Sc. in Health Economics and Policy (Barcelona Graduate School of Economics, Spain), B.A. in Economics, and B.A. in History (Universidad de los Andes, Colombia). In her previous role as a Manager in consultancy, she gained wide experience in advising national and regional governments in Europe and Latin America to design, monitor, and evaluate demand-side innovation policies. She has published work on the role of innovation procurement in fostering sustainable economic growth in Colombia, Brazil, Uruguay, Spain, and the wider European Union.

María started her career in the Colombian government, where she served as a senior adviser to the Deputy Minister of Defense and to the General Director of Colciencias (Department for Science, Technology and Innovation), developing and managing policies and programs in the areas of defense, health, and innovation.

Erich Prem is chief RTI strategy adviser and CEO of eutema GmbH. He is an internationally renowned expert in research and innovation strategy with more than two decades of work experience in research and innovation management and RTDI policy. Erich Prem is a certified managerial economist and works scientifically in artificial intelligence, research politics, innovation research, and epistemology. He published more than 70 scientific papers and was a guest researcher at the Massachusetts Institute of Technology.

Erich received his Dr.Phil. (epistemology) from the University of Vienna, his Dr.Tech. from TU Vienna where he also completed his Master's in Computer Science (Dipl.Ing). He is a lecturer at TU Vienna in Innovation and in Digital Humanism. He received his M.B.A. in General Management from Donau University.

Galina Esther Shubina is an AI technologist and co-founder of Gradient Descent, a consultancy company dedicated to helping companies become data driven and AI enabled, with focus on actionable strategy and organization. She helped multiple startups as well as bigger companies like Spotify with their data and AI strategy and organizational transformations. Prior to that, she spent 10 years at Google as a software engineer, data scientist, data engineer, and then manager, working on some of Google's core AI applications related to advertising — four of those years in the Silicon Valley. She also built the data and analytics team at Schibsted, then Trinity Mirror (now Reach Plc), and again at an electrical battery manufacturer, Northvolt. She is a co-founder of Women in Data Science, AI&ML Sweden, an organization focused on increasing diversity in the field of AI in Sweden, which includes a community of 1600 technical practitioners. She is currently on the advisory board of the Swedish Agency for Digital Government (DIGG).

Galina Esther Shubina has a B.A. Mathematics and Computer Science (Brandeis University, Waltham, MA, USA), an M.Sc. in Computer Science (Brown University, Providence, RI, USA). She also spent six and a half years in a Ph.D. program in Computer Science, doing research in information visualization, graph drawing, and computational geometry.

Manuel Varela is one of the leading experts in Spain and Europe in public procurement of innovation with B.Sc. in Mechanical & Industrial Engineering (Universidad de Navarra). He has exercised all possible roles in the procurement process, having served first as buyer in his stage as Director of Innovation and Public Health Management in Galicia (Spain), and then for the Galician Innovation Agency (Xunta de Galicia, Spain), leading projects totaling more than 100 million euros. Manuel has also acted as supplier for NATO and the Ministry of Defense, as well as an adviser to public buyers. Finally, on the supply side, and current role as Managing Director of the consulting firm Knowsulting, he has participated in more than 100 projects working for the main Ministries, Autonomous Communities and local entities in Spain, in addition to being the expert in public procurement of innovation at the Cotec Foundation.

Fernando Vilariño is Associate Director of the Computer Vision Centre and Associate Professor at the Computer Science Department of the Universitat Autònoma de Barcelona, Spain. He is currently lecturing in Machine Learning, Robotics, Urban Open Innovation, and Models of Open Innovation and Citizen Science. His research has been linked to diverse areas of computer vision and machine learning, with a particular focus on medical imaging. He has recently led different projects related to the implementation of models of Living Labs in the context of citizen-centric open innovation. He has been invited keynote speaker in different talks in the context of the Social Impact of AI.

Dr. Vilariño has been awarded with the Spanish Government Ramón y Cajal Grant (2010), and Google Academy Award (2014) for his research. He is the current Elected President of the European Network of Living Labs.

Mika Westerlund is an Associate Professor teaching technology innovation management and entrepreneurship at Carleton University in Ottawa, Canada. He previously held positions as a Postdoctoral Scholar in the Haas School of Business at the University of California Berkeley, USA and in the School of Economics at Aalto University in Helsinki, Finland. Mika earned his doctoral degree in Marketing from the Helsinki School of Economics in Finland. Mika has published widely as a scholar and his research interests include emerging technologies, practices, and phenomena that may have major social, economic, ecological, and other implications on our current and future societies.

Sergey Yablonsky is an Associate Professor at Graduate School of Management, St. Petersburg State University in St. Petersburg, Russia with Ph.D. in Computer Science. He is the author of more than 200 publications. He is the co-creator of the Russian WordNet, the Russicon language processor, linguistic resources licensed by Adobe Systems Incorporated, Phoenix Int. (USA), Franklin Electronic Publishers (USA), etc. He has participated in 35 national and international research projects in Russia, and across Europe. His research interests include digital economy, digital business, and entrepreneurship; multisided platforms and markets; artificial intelligence, digital marketing; big data governance; computer linguistics and text mining; semantic and social web. He taught the following courses: Data Governance (Bachelor Program); Digital Marketing & Digital Commerce (Bachelor Program); Digital Business (Master Program); Smart Business Transformation in the Digital Age (CEMS Block Seminar); Multi-Sided Platforms and Innovation in a Global Era (CEMS Block Seminar); Digital Economy (E.M.B.A.).

Sergey is Visiting Professor at WU (Vienna University of Economics and Business) in Austria, Stockholm Business School, Stockholm University in Sweden, Aalto University in Finland, Jaen University in Spain, Lappeenranta University of Technology in Finland, and Häme University of Applied Sciences in Finland.

Contents

Introduction

Stoyan Tanev[*,‡] and Helena Blackbright[†,§]

*Technology Innovation Management Program, Sprott School of Business
Carleton University, 1125 Colonel By Drive, Ottawa, ON K1S 5B6, Canada
†Automation Region, Mälardalen University, IDT, 721 23 Västerås, Sweden
‡stoyan.tanev@carleton.ca
§helena.blackbright@mdh.se

The objective of this book is to contribute to the ongoing debate among innovation scholars and practitioners focusing on the potential impact of Artificial Intelligence (AI) on the ways companies and organizations do business, operate, and innovate. It considers AI as a source of innovation both in terms of innovation within the field of AI itself (AI innovation) and in terms of how it enables or disrupts innovation in other fields (AI-driven innovation). The thematic focus on the relationship between AI and Innovation Management (IM) emerged within the context of the activities of the Special Interest Group on AI and IM of the International Society for Professional Innovation Management (ISPIM), which we happen to represent.[a]

---

[a]ISPIM is a community of members from research, industry, consulting, and the public sector, all sharing a passion for innovation management — how to successfully create new products, processes, and services in a way that could transform new ideas into economic growth and well-being. Formed in Norway in 1983, it is the oldest, the largest, and most active global innovation network: https://www.ispim-innovation.com/.

1

The initial motivation for the book was driven by several realizations that were supported by recent empirical research findings[b]: (a) AI is becoming increasingly present in the field of innovation and reveals great potential but often meets significant challenges; (b) there are different views on how to implement AI for innovation and little agreement, orientation, or guidance on how to do it; (c) AI not only has the potential to produce radically new innovations, but also to rethink IM in general. It is therefore both necessary and timely to explore the different aspects of the relationship between AI and IM.

Deeper knowledge about the innovative impact of AI technologies would be highly relevant to both practitioners and academics within the field of IM. At the same time, different types of AI-related innovation will require different managerial approaches and practices throughout the different phases of the innovation process. The different degrees of novelty, radicalness, and impact will be associated with different challenges, requirements, enablers, and opportunities. However, whether AI is "just another emerging technology" that will drive innovation "as usual" or a technology, which is so revolutionary different that it will fundamentally change the way we design, manage, and study innovations is a question that still remains to be systematically addressed. Highly experienced practitioners and innovation scholars remain divided regarding whether different AI technologies will change the processes and methods with which we innovate and thereby require reconsidering what we know about IM. The discussion of this issue leads to another important question: How will AI transform the ways we do IM research and study innovation in general? It is our belief that the AI impact on the ways we manage innovation will significantly impact the ways we study it.

Our initial presupposition as editors was that the intersection between AI and IM needs to be conceptualized as a dynamic encounter between two fields with a substantial potential to mutually impact each other.

---

[b]Johann Füller and Volker Bilgram, *et al.* Autonomous innovation — How AI and algorithms revolutionize innovation management. Scientific study on the impact of artificial intelligence on innovation management. HYVE Innovation Research GmbH. Munich, Germany, 2019. https://www.hyve.net/en/blog/how-ai-and-algorithms-revolutionize-innovation-management/.

The intersection could be examined with respect to what we innovate, how we innovate it, and the contextual setting within which we innovate. In this sense, AI will be discussed as part of the innovative outcomes, as part of the innovation process and its grounding in the contextual setting within which we innovate, and as part of the IM research process.

The contributors to this book include both scholars and practitioners from multiple countries and different types of institutions. Their selection was done through an open call resulting in the final contribution of 12 chapters. Given the early stage of the knowledge domain, we did not focus on a search for contributors based on a preliminary designed thematic structure, but adopted instead four more generic selection criteria: (a) the ability to provide a relevant distinctive perspective on the relationship between AI and IM; (b) the degree and the quality of professional engagement with the field; (c) the ability to contribute to the thematic and contextual diversity of the contributions; (d) the ability to provide high-quality insights for both innovation scholars and practitioners.

All contributors engaged in the discussion of the relationship between AI and IM in their own specific contexts. The types of contributions include conceptual papers, empirical studies, exemplary cases of the adoption of AI in companies, organizations, and innovation ecosystems, and research studies exploring the applications of AI tools and techniques. The diversity of the contexts could be grouped in four major themes: (a) the innovative role of AI in organizations with a focus on technological and/or organizational management aspects; (b) the potential impact of AI on the innovation management process; (c) the role of AI tools and techniques in innovation management research; (d) the social and ethical aspects associated with the adoption of AI in innovation management. It is clear however, that each of these four themes is a research domain on its own and could become the subject of multiple book publications.

In their chapter "What AI Can Do for Innovation Managers and Innovation Managers for AI," Nina Bozic Yams and Galina Esther Shubina describe a conversation between an innovation manager and an AI technologist, exploring some of the typical misunderstandings and pointing at the need for increased knowledge sharing between representatives of these two professions. The key message of the conversation is that, as organizations move from the early stages of AI maturity toward more advanced levels of integrated AI capabilities, the competences of innovation managers become increasingly important. Innovation managers should enable both building the right mindset for wider adoption of AI in an organization, and supporting other organizational aspects, such as strengthening cross-functional cooperation, agile self-organizing teams and innovative leadership, as well as development of a wider innovation ecosystem for enabling AI integration.

In "A Knowledge-Based Perspective of Strategic AI Innovation Management," Erich Prem points out that, at more than 50 years of age, AI can hardly be called a new or emerging technology, but emphasizes that recent advances have made AI resources and capabilities widely available and applicable to the extent that AI has become a major driver for technology-based innovations. Prem investigates the characteristics of AI technology that are most relevant for IM and discusses some of the key challenges such as data requirements, need for explainability, and ethical considerations. These challenges require a strategic approach to managing AI-related innovation, and a careful consideration of the information flows from the problem domain to the application area stages. The chapter includes a proposal for an epistemic framework for the analysis of AI innovation processes that could help in understanding and improving the dynamic capabilities needed for strategic management of AI-related innovation.

Amber Geurts, in her chapter "Addressing AI Traps: Realizing the Potential of AI for Innovation Trend Spotting, Monitoring and Decision-Making" focuses on the application of AI to the identification and monitoring of innovation and technology trends to support decision-making. According to Geurts, the expectations from the advances in AI in this domain are very high, but there is little knowledge and actual discussion of what it takes to develop such AI-based capabilities, how they could be introduced and affect the decision-making processes. A specific attention is paid to the challenges or "AI traps" of moving toward the adoption of such capabilities. Addressing such traps is important in the evaluation of the promise of AI for innovation trend spotting, as well as in preventing any disappointments with its potential outcomes. The insights developed in this chapter will help innovation managers acquire a more realistic perspective of the potential of AI for innovation trend spotting, monitoring and, ultimately, decision-making.

The chapter "Social Media Video Analysis for Entrepreneurial Opportunity Discovery in Artificial Intelligence" by Mika Westerlund and Maham Aman summarizes the results study which uses topic modeling to analyze the content of expert talk videos on AI, obtained from TEDx Talks channel on YouTube. It examines the feasibility of social media video analysis for entrepreneurial opportunity discovery, identify prominent niches, and suggest potential entrepreneurial opportunities in AI. In this sense, it demonstrates the applicability of AI-based tools in the early stages of the innovation management process. The study identifies six AI application areas based on the results from the analysis and interprets them using relevant scholarly literature. Further, the chapter provides insights into entrepreneurial opportunities within those application areas and concludes with lessons learned. The chapter contributes to the book's theme by examining how AI technologies could enhance the early stages of the innovation management process.

In "AI-Driven Innovation: Towards a Conceptual Framework," Sergey Yablonsky focuses on AI-driven innovations and starts by emphasizing that the links between AI technology, AI usage, and organizational performance remain quite unclear. To improve the efficiency of AI implementation, reduce costs and shape new business opportunities, firms should understand the features, capabilities, and the impact of these innovations on business models, business processes, and employee work practices. To address this gap, an AI-driven value chain framework is proposed, which makes it possible to create a reference model (taxonomy) integrating different types of AI-driven innovation processes and different innovation types. In addition to the taxonomy, an AI organization maturity model and an AI-driven maturity framework are proposed as practical tools for managers interested in adopting AI systems and capabilities.

Navneet Bhalla focuses on "Automating Innovation." He points out that, even though, AI is being used in the context of product innovation, it has been far less explored in the domain of process innovation. At the same time, developing new processes such as, for example, the invention of the moving assembly line, can be highly transformative for both businesses and industry sectors. Bhalla shows how AI algorithms, specifically evolutionary computing, that have been widely used for product innovation can be leveraged for process innovation. The design of self-organizing materials is used as an example demonstrating the role of AI in shifting from a product to a process innovation focus. The chapter describes some of the principles of designing complex systems using AI in an Industry 4.0 context.

The chapter by Françoise de Viron and Benoit Gailly is titled "Artificial Intelligence as a Strategic Innovation Capability." They adopt a knowledge-based perspective of the firm to outline how AI technologies can be seen as new innovation capabilities allowing firms to learn from existing and new knowledge assets. The knowledge-based approach provides a natural way for managers and scholars to adopt a strategic perspective on the development of their AI assets and capabilities. The authors propose a framework of four types of organizational learning strategies (Exploit, Extract, Gather, and Explore) based on the interplay between two key dimensions: (a) building analytic capabilities (both technical and organizational) to best exploit the knowledge embedded in existing data assets; and (b) exploring, identifying, and capturing new sources of knowledge. They emphasize however that the four organizational learning strategies are not exclusive, as an innovation manager may choose or need to combine more than one of them to remain competitive.

In "Disrupting the Research Process through Artificial Intelligence: Towards a Research Agenda," Mikael Johnsson, Christopher Gustafsson, and Peter E. Johansson discuss the potential of AI to disrupt IM research. According to them, the research process has remained virtually unchanged for many decades. However, AI has opened new opportunities that could potentially affect it. For example, there are already AI applications supporting researchers in specific tasks and easing their work focusing on database searching, transcribing, and data management. The authors provide specific examples of AI techniques and applications and discuss their potential for conducting research. They identified three emerging themes with respect to how AI could transform future research: (a) simplification thorough the use of computational power; (b) augmentation of a researcher's capabilities; and (c) replacement by automation. Finally, they identify and discuss some critical questions that could pave a way toward a research agenda.

Stoyan Tanev, Tony Bailetti, Christian Keen, and David Hudson discuss "The Potential of AI to Enhance the Value Propositions of New Companies Committed to Scale Early and Rapidly." They start by emphasizing that a newly developed Value Proposition (VP) is the best expression of a company's innovative capacity — its ability to coordinate the combination of resources to develop new products and services, and shape valuable market offers to address specific customer needs. In their chapter, they address the problem that it is not well known how a new company can use AI to innovate by enhancing its VPs for customers, investors, and other relevant stakeholders. To address this question, the authors reviewed the VP development, business ecosystems, and AI business value literature streams and used the results to develop 182 assertions — statements about what a new company could do to scale its value early and rapidly. Topic modeling was next applied to examine the corpus of assertions and produce a practical framework for VP development in the context new scaling companies. Finally, the authors discuss the explicit link between a new company's resources and capabilities in AI and the seven elements of the framework. The results suggest that AI resources and capabilities can be used to enhance stakeholders' VPs, improve foreign market entry performance, increase customer base, and continuously improve individuals, operations, and infrastructures of new companies. The chapter provides a guide of the business value that AI can offer a new company committed to scale early and rapidly.

In "Fair, Inclusive, and Anticipatory Leadership for AI Adoption and Innovation," Jennifer Barth, Eurydice Fotopoulou, and Chris Brauer focus on the role of management in the process of AI-driven innovation, suggesting that the heart of an AI-enabled organization is the development of a dynamic relationship between leaders and workforce — one based on trust, empathy, and participatory relationships. One of their key points is that the transformation to digitally and AI-enabled organizations necessitates the development of such dynamic relationships. Based on a combination of qualitative and quantitative research insights, the authors suggest that today's organizations should develop proactive learning capabilities, while leaders need to create inclusive cultures that support and invest in such progressive environment. The new relationships between leaders and employees should rest on responsiveness, resilience, empathy, and openness to change. This is particularly relevant in the context of the challenges of our post-COVID-19 world which require a business culture grounded in inclusiveness and the principles of collaborative success.

Fernando Vilariño focuses on "Unveiling the Social Impact of AI through Living Labs." Vilariño points out that, due to its nature, scope, and impact, the digital transformation is a human transformation, not just a new industrial revolution. Social transformations appear at a pace never witnessed before, with challenges that can no longer be tackled by one organization alone. This helps in reinventing the open innovation paradigm in which the integration of multiple stakeholders around a citizen-centric perspective becomes a key element. In this context, according to Vilariño, the impact that AI will bring to society is still to be defined. This task however should be completed prior to the development of new models in which AI-based automation and automatic decision-making will play a fundamental role. As an inherent part of newly emerging IM practices, they will affect strategy, leadership, institutional culture, and processes, going beyond the typical software design area. The author promotes the Living Lab approach as a powerful instrument for this mission. He provides clear examples on how the adoption of the Living Lab paradigm could help in tackling the unveiling of the AI impact.

Manuel Noya, Manuel Varela, and María José Ospina-Fadul focus on the interface of "Innovation Management and Public Procurement of AI." They emphasize that AI technologies have an immense potential to transform the way governments work and innovate at the local, national, and international levels. However, despite the efforts from both governments and supranational organizations, the adoption of this key general-purpose technology has its natural limitations. The chapter lays out the advantages of using innovation procurement to foster the development and deployment of AI technologies for the provision of public services, while also addressing potential bottlenecks. The authors discuss the overarching socio-ethical challenges of real-life procurement cases by focusing mainly on issues related to privacy and accountability. The use cases provide examples of how innovation procurement can support the public sector in spurring and scaling collaborative, inclusive, and human-centric AI innovation. Finally, the authors provide a series of recommendations that could help in avoiding common pitfalls in the innovative procurement of AI.

In conclusion, we would like to express our gratitude to Joe Tidd from the University of Sussex in the UK, Managing Editor of World Scientific Series on Technology Management, and Steffen Conn, Operations Manager of the ISPIM society, for suggesting the idea of publishing a book on AI and innovation management. We have greatly appreciated the cooperation with the Editorial Board of the Technology Innovation Management Review (https://timreview.ca/) for supporting the activities of the ISPIM Special Interest Group in AI and innovation management by publishing several special issues based on selected ISPIM conference publications. The special issues provided us with an opportunity to demonstrate the interest of the international innovation management community in the specific domain and get confident in engaging with the shaping and editing of this book. We would like also to thank all contributors for their efforts, commitment, and discipline in contributing their chapters on time.

Helena Blackbright expresses her deep gratitude to both her husband Mikael and her team at Automation Region. Automation Region is a Center of Excellence at Mälardalen University focusing on industrial technology impact. Helena is grateful to her management for the patient support in the different initiatives that contributed to developing a better understanding of the relation between AI and Innovation Management. Process Manager Catharina Berglund should be especially acknowledged for trusting the team's ability to see the signs of tomorrow in today's explorations.

Stoyan Tanev expresses his gratitude to his wife Maia and his entire family for their patience in dealing with his frequent absences while working on the editing of this book. Stoyan is also grateful to his colleagues — Tony Bailetti, Steve Muegge, Michael Weiss, and Mika Westerlund, from the Technology Innovation Management (TIM) Program at Carleton University, for their encouragement and cooperation in creating and driving the Master of Applied Business Analytics option of the TIM program. The new option has become a great motivation for Stoyan's involvement in the ISPIM Special Interest Group on AI and Innovation Management, as well as in the project focusing on the publication of this book.

Last but not least, the Editors express their pleasure of working together in managing the contributions of so many people across the world who have helped the success of this project.

https://doi.org/10.1142/9781800611337_0002

Chapter 1

What AI Can Do for Innovation Managers and Innovation Managers for AI

Nina Bozic Yams*,‡ and Galina Esther Shubina†,§

*Research Institutes of Sweden (RISE), Sweden
†Gradient Descent AB, Sweden
‡nina.bozic@ri.se
§galina@gradientdescent.com

This chapter is an honest conversation between an innovation manager and an AI technologist, exploring some of the misunderstandings between the two professions and pointing at the need for increased knowledge sharing between the two. In the chapter, different possible similarities, intersections, and benefits of collaboration between AI technologists and innovation managers are covered. As organizations move from early stages of AI maturity toward more advanced levels of integrated AI, the competencies of innovation managers become more important. Innovation managers can help both build the right mindset for wider adoption of AI in an organization and support other organizational aspects, such as strengthening cross-functional cooperation, agile self-organizing teams and innovative leadership, and development of a wider innovation ecosystem for enabling AI integration.

1. Introduction

This is a conversation between Nina, a senior innovation manager and Galina, a senior AI strategist and technologist exploring how innovation management could support organizations on their journey of AI integration, and on the other hand, how AI could support and augment the innovation management practice.

Nina started her career 17 years ago as a management consultant at Deloitte, working with re-organizations of big companies. This is where she became interested in innovation management and started to look at how organizations can create conditions for innovation. She then co-founded and led the Center for Entrepreneurship and Executive Development (CEED) in Slovenia, and later on continued to work as an innovation consultant and trainer in Sweden. She has a Ph.D. in Innovation Management and has in the last 10 years worked with companies, such as ABB, Ericsson, Electrolux, and various Swedish municipalities, exploring how to build more innovative organizations and prepare them for the future of work with new digital technologies. She leads a special thematic group on Innovation Management and AI at the Swedish association of innovation managers (Innovationsledarna). She is a senior researcher at RISE — Research Institutes of Sweden, where she leads a platform on Sustainable Future Work and works with AI transformation and digital ethics.

Galina joined Google in 2004 as a software engineer and spent a decade there working on data science, machine learning, data engineering, and distributed systems problems. After that, she built data and machine learning teams for two media houses and an electrical battery company. Since then, she has spent a few years consulting organizations on data and AI strategy — helping them figure out how to best become data driven and integrate AI into their products and processes. Galina is one of the founders of Women in Data Science (AI&ML) Sweden whose goal is to inspire and support a strong community of female AI technology developers in Sweden. She has a Bachelor's degree in Mathematics and Computer Science and M.Sc. in Computer Science.

2. An Honest Introduction — Could Innovation Management and AI Be Friends?

Nina: I don't know about you, Galina, but I can say that when it comes to the Innovation Management field, I see an increased interest in AI by innovation managers. I guess the fact that both the international community of researchers and practitioners in our field — ISPIM and the Swedish association of innovation managers — Innovationsledarna have special thematic groups on innovation management and AI reflects that. Being a member of these communities, I would honestly say that the level of knowledge, in our community, about AI is still pretty low.

Having conversed with and interviewed some innovation managers, I would say we are also pretty bad at using AI tools in our own work as innovation managers. Although I see many opportunities for how we — innovation managers could augment our work through AI, some of which are highlighted in our article,[1] I think we have a long way to go. What is promising is the curiosity about AI technology in our community and a wish to have a more active role in the journey of AI adoption in organizations. But most innovation managers still see AI as just another technology to be applied to the current product portfolio to make it more efficient and to add some new features or services.

I'm very curious to hear what the perception of innovation managers is in the AI community? Do we have any chance at all to be seen as relevant partners?

Galina: I think the unfortunate truth is that many AI technologists, data scientists, and machine learning engineers think the world is an onion and they can peel it all by themselves. The perception, especially from the folks fresh from school or bootcamps is that what it takes to integrate AI into products and build AI-enabled future is the technology itself. Innovation is us and we're innovation because we have the tools to do the "actual" work.

The hard-won realization that it's not just "if you build it — they will come," that we need to work not just across the technology stack, from front-end to backend, but also ensure that our work is strategically integrated into business comes from experience. With this experience comes not just the recognition that we can't do everything by ourselves, but also, more importantly, the acceptance that multiple perspectives are essential to making more relevant products and better business choices.

The question from AI technologists then is: where do innovation managers fit?

3. Building Bridges, Increasing Diversity, and Crafting a More Holistic Approach

Nina: I think one of the strengths that innovation managers could bring to the table is exactly in bringing these multiple perspectives together around the issues of AI integration in companies. Traditionally, one of the roles of innovation managers is to bring different voices and competences into innovation initiatives in order to create better conditions for new ideas and unexpected connections to emerge. The practice of innovation has simply taught us that if you have 10 people with the same thoughts, background and experience in the room, there will be very little or no innovation happening.

This is why we have become experienced facilitators of complex change processes that often involve both people from different organizational functions and a variety of external stakeholders from the innovation ecosystem. By doing that we've learned how to be translators and bridge builders between people that speak different languages and have different motivations that drive their behavior but still need to find ways to collaborate around a shared purpose and value creation process. I think, since the path of AI integration in organizations is a story that is not only about technology but also about transforming people, culture, organization, and business, this is a relevant competence to bring to the table. I also think that bringing a greater diversity of perspectives into the AI development process would also increase innovation in AI.

Since many companies got stuck in pilot projects experimenting with AI and struggle with a wider adoption and integration of AI in their organizations, including other organizational functions in the AI development would be key to move toward higher AI maturity stages.

Galina: I agree that AI transformation has wider implications for an organization that go beyond technology. I think our AIMI (AI Innovation Maturity Index) nicely shows that (see Fig. 1).[1] It covers the business (strategy and ecosystems), people and organization (mindsets and organization) and technology (data and technologies) aspects. By integrating issues of AI ethics and responsible AI into all dimensions of AIMI, the

Fig. 1. AI Innovation Maturity Index.

model also stresses that the competence in AI ethics will be a crucial part of the AI integration process if we intend to build trust in AI technology, both internally within organizations and among external stakeholders.

Nina: But do you see that happening in practice already or do you feel AI adoption is still predominantly driven by people with technical backgrounds that lack competence in the fields of people, organization, business, and ethics?

Galina: Are we talking about AI adoption or development here? Because when it comes to data scientists, we are predominantly preoccupied with AI development and with providing business insights.

Nina: That's a great point to make when bringing together the management and tech perspectives. I think managers are more preoccupied with the AI adoption in organizations, because it concerns issues they would normally think about, like leadership, people, culture, and organization. But in a way, I was really thinking of both AI development and adoption, maybe we could refer to both as AI integration, because I think we need to increase diversity and bring different perspectives into both. I guess only when other organizational functions, including innovation management become part of the AI development (and not only using off-the-shelf AI solutions), they will start to better understand how AI technology works, the process behind its development, but also what is possible and what is not possible to do with it since there are still a lot of unrealistic expectations about AI from non-AI people.

Galina: If I go back to your question about who is driving AI integration in organizations and whether they have a wider spectrum of competences or not, I don't think the situation is quite so black and white. For many years now, we've been speaking about the "data scientist" role specifically as being a T-shaped with a really wide hat. T-shaped roles have a good depth in the specific skills set, in this case, extracting insights from data and creating machine learning models, while at the same time having also a breadth of shallow soft and hard skills. Data scientists are supposed to be able to communicate complex ideas to the management and business needs to the engineers. They also need to be able to ask the right questions, have an experimental mindset, and curiosity.

Some of these capabilities might remind you of innovation managers, but, at the same time, a data scientist's T "hat" also needs some hard engineering skills that would allow them to work with big data, develop code, integrate their models in the product, integrate new technical tools into their development process, and productionize their models.

While a few of those data science unicorns do exist, we've since come to a realization that this stereotype is largely unrealistic, even more so now that the AI field has matured and requires more specialization. It has also led to unrealistic expectations and quite a few cases of burnout.

Additionally, with the appearance of AutoML — automated machine learning, which allows non-experts to create machine learning models and pipelines — good facilitation of AI integration across everything has also become much more important.

Nina: I think this speaks a lot to how AI development works within organizations. You tend to speak about AI as being something developed and integrated into organizations' products or processes, but all functions like HR, marketing, business, and innovation also need to become AI enabled. They need AI tools to optimize and potentially also innovate their work — but it is also essential that they understand these technologies, how they can impact them and what the possibilities are to become partners in creating and integrating AI processes and products. This is one way of helping organizations to move from small-scale experimental projects with AI toward a wider adoption of AI in organizations.

Galina: That's very true. I think there's a natural duality that AI technologists have in their heads. AI development on one hand and mostly off-the-shelf third-party AI products or tools integrated into processes within the company on the other hand. The latter is often viewed as "not our problem." We tend to over-focus on the first and not pay sufficient attention to the second and the AI adoption issues that come with it.

It's very important to bridge the gap between AI technologists in the organization and all the other functions to enable collaborations that could result in more successful integration of the off-the-shelf AI tools while also creating a feedback loop to improve development and integration of AI technologies developed within the organization. This is where roles like AI change agent and innovation manager come into play.

But at the same time, it's important to know and understand that AI technologists tend to have their head in AI development and might occupy themselves very little with AI adoption.

Nina: Yes, and here I see a problem. We might end up in a situation where we become very tech-driven and fascinated by technology and its capabilities but lose track of why we need this technology in the first place. I'm personally quite worried about this. I think AI is just another technology or tool that should help us, humans, improve our lives and society, and at the same time take care of planet Earth, but not a thing with its own purpose. Especially when AI systems are applied in the public sector and start to seriously affect the lives of citizens, like making decisions about whether they will get social support or not, or whether they will be more likely stopped and harassed by police, ending up in prison, the diversity of perspectives in AI development to avoid bias and discrimination by AI become very important.[2,3] And then there is also a question of whether autonomous systems should have moral agency and the wider question of AI ethics.[4]

Galina: Much as you describe, I see many signs that we discuss societal problems in terms of what Evgeny Morozov calls "technological solutionism."[5] We take complex social problems and try to recast them as something that is well defined and can be solved with technology. For example, lately there are many conversations around AI helping solve gender equality: what AI applications can we develop to make the world less biased? Can we make hiring less biased with AI? Can we make other essential work and life processes more gender equal? In some cases, quite likely.

But I would argue that step one is getting these problems considered and, if necessary, developed by a diverse group of people that includes a lot more women than it currently does — 22% of AI professionals globally are female, compared to 78% who are male,[6] while at AI powerhouses, Facebook, and Google, 15% and 10% of AI research staff respectively are women. This can create a discrimination feedback loop, where developed AI systems perpetuate gender and racial stereotypes.[7]

On the positive side, compared to a few years ago, there's a clearer recognition now that as AI is becoming integrated into many more sensitive contexts like healthcare, finance, industrial quality control, and autonomous cars, a broader engagement is required along many dimensions. Many of those applications are significantly more complex than the features like recommended movies on Netflix or audio-to-text transcription. So, it is now more essential than ever to build and adopt AI in legally compliant and ethical ways, as well as to enable a real transformation and shared storytelling to integrate it into the processes. Cross-functional work is now more essential than ever, and often spans not just one product or one organization, but whole ecosystems. So, I definitely see a bigger role and recognition for innovation managers in the future.

4. The Roles of AI Change Agent and Innovation Manager

Nina: I wonder how the roles of AI change agent and innovation manager can then come together …

Galina: How would you define these roles more precisely? I think it's fair to say that data scientists, machine learning engineers, and other AI technologists sometimes wonder what these roles entail.

Nina: From my perspective, an AI change agent is someone who oversees the integration of AI in an organization and thus needs to think strategically and holistically about it. In the first place, that would mean thinking about how AI can support the overall purpose, values, and strategy of an organization and in what ways it can create new value for organization. But from there on it has to do with everything from what talent, skills, and culture the organization needs to increase its AI maturity, to how integration of AI might transform their ways of working, their business model, and the needed ecosystem of strategic partners, toward more technical issues around data and technical infrastructure that organizations have to build to enable AI integration.

On the other hand, an innovation manager is someone who also has a strategic and holistic perspective, but in this case around how to build conditions for innovation (creating value out of new ideas) across an organization. Innovation can be created through the use of AI but also in many other ways. When I talk about creating conditions for innovation, I think of a very wide spectrum of things, from continuously scanning of what is happening in the environment in order to identify new opportunities for innovation to building an innovation ecosystem with different stakeholders that can strengthen organizational innovation capability. It would also include building culture, leadership, and skillset for innovation across organization, and developing organizational structures that are conducive for innovation. Additionally, it would entail things like managing innovation processes and mastering specific tools for their facilitation, developing a portfolio of innovation projects, and evaluating various innovation initiatives. For a more systematic and comprehensive understanding of the innovation management system and the role of innovation manager one can look into details of the international ISO 56002 standard.[8] Its summary can be found in our article.[1]

In this sense, I think there are many overlaps in the roles of AI change agent and innovation manager, especially when it comes to people, culture and organizational issues. I think the type of mindset and ways of working that are stimulating for innovation are also needed for increased integration of AI in organizations, especially when an organization wants to reach higher AI maturity stages and is not only using AI as a bolt-on technology to optimize existing processes.

Galina: Yes, and I think the more senior managers actually do recognize the need for innovative behaviors and mindset growth when it comes to reaching higher stages of AI maturity, but they often try to assign some of the innovation manager functions to other roles. This commonly happens in smaller companies as well as in highly technical companies. In my experience, it's partly a budgetary issue, which means some people end up overloaded, from wearing too many hats. But it can also mean integrating innovation capabilities within the organization more directly.

My view, as a technologist, is that it is the bigger organizations that are most commonly enabled by innovation managers. There is much more change management required to transform how the organization works and for integrating new tools and technologies and it is immensely helpful to have people who understand this and have the right toolkit to enable this process.

It is important to note that while AI technologists commonly think that people can "just start to use it" ("it" being the AI-enabled products) — adoption rarely works this way in practice. I've been approached by several start-ups who have smart AI products that would clearly solve a specific business problem, but they struggle with sales to their customers. An example is something as clearly useful as receipt scanning that recognizes all parts of all types of receipts and can automatically insert it into an accounting system. Unfortunately, they struggle with sales because they essentially need to become AI change agents for their customers in order to make them comfortable, get their buy-in and integrate it into their process and even strategy.

Nina: That's a good point. So we need this diversity of competences to increase AI adoption and maturity in companies, but maybe instead of focusing on the titles (like innovation manager or AI change agent), we should rather focus on understanding better what competencies are needed by people who are driving AI integration in organizations, realizing that it might be hard for one person to master them all. Maybe we should rather be thinking about a team that covers both tech competence but also competence in people, customers, organization, business models, ethics, and innovation and transformation management.

Galina: I would say, traditionally, either data scientists (as discussed) or product managers (at least in companies like Google) have taken the responsibility for driving AI adoption, while the directors and VPs of product and engineering usually end up responsible for the more organizational aspects of AI integration. Similar to data scientists, I would say that these cross-functional highly context-switching jobs, with ambiguous responsibilities, often lead to burnout and so better organizational models are needed. There is a clear opportunity for innovation managers to improve these processes, increase autonomy for and trust in employees. This can help managers let go of control and create more alignment between different roles which may even improve managers' work/life balance.

At the same time, the data science and machine learning engineering roles have significantly reduced their profile in the last two years to a narrower T-shape and would benefit from expanding it again with more innovation management competencies.

Additionally, as previously mentioned, examples of AI ethics "fails" clearly show that everyone needs to learn about and engage on the questions of ethics. Organizations should ensure that a diverse set of people with different backgrounds are involved in creating, reviewing, and participating in AI products from a very early stage. This ensures that the AI products contain diverse perspectives from the start. Ambiguities involved in predictive technologies mean it is hard to catch any and all problems and ensure they are minimized — one of the best ways is to get many eyes involved in checking these products early on. This will help us avoid "fails" like the one where a healthcare chatbot that, for the same set of symptoms, suggests to men they should be checked for a heart attack and to women that they might suffering from anxiety,[9] or an image recognition software that fails to detect black faces.[10]

Nina: I agree. Additionally, I think where the competence of innovation managers compared to more traditional project or product managers can make a difference is that they can move the mainstream discourse around AI being focused on optimization and automation toward using AI for innovation — creation of value from new ideas stemming from different possible applications of AI. Innovation with AI or AI-driven innovation could both happen in the core business — the products and services the organization offers to customers, but also innovation in internal processes, in collaboration with the wider ecosystem, and in the overall strategy. In that sense, innovation managers, especially in bigger organizations, as opposed to product and project managers, can make sure the AI enables innovation and development (not only optimization) on a more strategic level across the organization, supporting the over-all purpose, values, and strategy of an organization. That would help organizations move from being AI beginners toward higher AI maturity levels.

And since different studies[11] show that one of the main challenges with AI adoption is still peoples' resistance to change and AI, including their fear of AI taking over their jobs, innovation managers could help organizations becoming better at engaging employees in experimentation with possible uses of AI in their work. This might be thinking about which (routine) tasks they want to automate to create more time for creative and strategic work, but also how AI could be used to augment their work and help them make better decisions, become more skillful in detecting changes in environment and in identifying opportunities for innovation. And last but not least, to explore how AI could be used to help them live and work more according to their purpose and values, achieving a better work-life balance and well-being.

Galina: I agree. Another example is how to decide which AI products to develop. These decisions often lay at the intersection of opinions by AI experts and domain experts. AI experts understand what AI can actually do and how complicated it may be, and domain experts understand what is valuable for the business.[12] It is largely at that intersection that magic happens. This is just one trivial example where the results could improve if we have higher quality and more productive cross-functional collaborations, driven by innovation managers. Innovation managers could also help facilitate the dialogue between AI experts and domain experts in a way that would bring up issues around diversity and multimodality of data needed to better capture the complexity of human phenomena in various domains and to stimulate innovation in the AI development process.

But perhaps we're back to our original question. Even if we want to distribute some of the innovation management capabilities across the organization, what roles do we see an AI change agent and an innovation manager play?

Nina: For me, the innovation managers could probably take more responsibility for dealing with changes that are needed in relation to people, culture, and ways of organizing that would be conducive for reaching higher levels of AI maturity and integration in an organization, while traditional AI change agents that often have a more technical background could bring more of the technical expertise to the table. A general competence in business, strategy, UX design, and also AI ethics is still needed to complement the team driving AI integration. I think the competence needs will also change in time depending on the AI maturity level in an organization. This brings us back to the discussion of mindset growth that is needed as we move from AI beginners toward AI leaders.

5. Mindset Growth and Building a Learning Organization

Galina: Yes, mindset growth is something we've been talking a lot about. How do you see innovation management contributing to that?

Nina: I think that one of the core responsibilities of innovation managers in organizations is to nurture innovative mindsets and practices in everyday work. And if we look at what is at the core of an innovative mindset and practice, we see things such as openness and presence, curiosity and experimentation, reflection, and co-creation.[13] These are all important ingredients of organizational DNA that will make employees curious and motivated to engage with new technologies, such as AI, exploring what value they could create in their work and in the pursuit of organizational purpose. An innovative mindset helps employees to not get stuck in the fear of thinking that AI will take away their jobs, and encourages them to be courageous, to try out how it could augment their work and at the same time also enable them to critically reflect about potential challenges with adopting AI in the organization.

In a project where we engaged employees from both industry and the public sector in exploring possibilities and challenges with integrating AI in their future jobs, called DIGI Futures, we saw a clear correlation between mindset growth and openness to AI adoption in the process. The process was designed in a way that encouraged participants to practice core innovative skills — be open, experiment, and critically reflect while they were developing future scenarios and speculative fiction stories about themselves as workers of the future. The more we worked with an explorative mindset, learning about possibilities with AI technology and bringing in different perspectives, the more curious and engaged participants were. A crucial element was also their active participation and a sense of ownership — that they were themselves designing visions of their future jobs with AI and not feeling that the future was decided or imposed on them.

Galina: I can totally see how innovation management can help with AI adoption through development of innovative mindset, but this leads us to the question of the chicken and the egg: while innovative mindset can support employees to be more open to AI adoption, development of AI as technology can also push employees, managers, and the organization as a whole, to grow their mindset and become more innovative.

Having to integrate AI as a technology into the core business requires many elements of the innovative mindset, which can enable not just AI development, but can also create overall improvements elsewhere in the organization. To be able to understand this, we need to understand how working with machine learning affects your mindset as a developer and user.

Machine learning is loosely defined as "a field of study that gives computers the ability to learn without being explicitly programmed." This quote is usually attributed to Arthur Samuel, though it is most likely a reinterpretation from his article.[14] Compared to the traditional software development process, which guarantees production of something specific and deterministic, machine learning produces a model from the "training data" that can make predictions from new data it has never seen. By its nature, machine learning requires a mindset and process where developers cannot fully control or plan the process outcome.

They are forced to open up to uncertainty and get comfortable with it. Like in the practice of action inquiry, where you are making yourself vulnerable to inquiry and continuous transformation by simultaneously conducting action and inquiry to increase effectiveness of your actions.[15]

If we take as an example companies like Google and Spotify which use AI as a core technology in their business, we can see that at any point in time, they are simultaneously running hundreds of experiments with AI.[16,17] Understanding that a ML project doesn't have an end and increasing the number of experiments requires improving innovation capacity and learning mindset. This mindset and focus on experimentation, enables the organization to become data-driven and to democratize decision-making.

Nina: When you are saying that engaging with AI systems can push employees toward developing a more innovative mindset and democratize decision-making, are you thinking also of forcing them to shift from reactive toward a more proactive mode at work? I think that AI can commoditize and democratize both optimization and prediction across an organization.[18] If employees start to use smart analytical tools in their daily work processes, they will start to increase their ability to see patterns and sense change signals in the environment, for example in customers' behaviors. This will help them more quickly identify new customer needs or potential market niches. But then they will also need to proactively respond to these sensed opportunities, having the ability to continuously adapt to changes in the environment. And to build such a culture and mindset, a leadership that encourages and supports such behavioral shift toward being proactive rather than reactive is needed.

Galina: I agree. Even getting more regular access to basic analytical data relevant to their work can kick start this democratization process. Both at Google and at Spotify, I've seen how providing access to fine-grained data in data warehouses that provide no-code visual interfaces causes a "Cambrian explosion" of insights and interest, when supported by learning and by the management. Employees develop a desire to act, and a company that is running dozens or hundreds of experiments can no longer have a completely top-down management approach — it simply doesn't scale.

What kind of leadership then do we need to encourage this process and how is this connected to innovation management? We still see many C-levels being skeptical toward innovation in general. How is this impacting AI adoption?

Nina: Denti and Hemlin, who looked at factors influencing the relationship between leadership and innovation, suggest that leaders giving employees a high sense of autonomy but at the same time supporting them to connect their work with organizational goals, are stimulative of innovation.[19] In that sense we are talking about the importance of servant leadership[20] where managers are ready to let go off control and increase trust in employees. This demands a more shared practice of leadership where employees have a high level of autonomy in their roles and every organizational member is shifting between leading (when it comes to their area of competence) and supporting others in their expertise field.

Making data and information transparent and easily accessible and combining it with predictive tools will only additionally empower all members of the organization to make quicker and more informed decisions. It is about eliminating hierarchies and building flat structures with self-managed teams, moving toward the teal model of organization.[21] Agile ways of working in self-managed teams have been often promoted by innovation managers to create better conditions for distributing innovation across organization and integrating it in everyday practice.

These management principles and leadership style also support openness to and experimentation with new technologies, such as AI.

Galina: I think AI as technology not only demands organizations to be more agile and self-organized but as studies show,[11] organizations which are AI leaders also experience that the further they go in their adoption of AI, the more challenges arise. So, the AI journey is a journey of continuous learning and transformation. Building a capacity for continuous learning is thus an important aspect here. AI as technology can, in my opinion, enable innovation managers to build a learning organization where learning is personalized and adjusted to the interests, needs, and learning styles of each employee. There are already learning platforms, such as Sana (by Sana labs) that help organizations from across sectors use AI-powered learning that accelerates time to mastery and improves employee engagement in learning.

Nina: And here we come back to the inherent nature of continuous learning that is both at the core of innovation culture and process but also as you said at the core of the AI development process or as you call it, machine learning development lifecycle.

6. Machine Learning Lifecycle vs. Iterative Innovation Process

Galina: Yes, let me explain a bit how the machine learning development lifecycle works.

For example, when creating a so-called supervised machine learning model, we would train it on a test data set. A traditional toy example looks at predicting house prices. We acquire a test data set that consists of historical information: a list of houses that have been sold in the last year, their salient features (bedrooms, bathrooms, location), and the prices they sold for. The created model is then used to predict something for which we don't have a known answer in the world. In this same example, that's the price that a house that goes on the market would sell for in the future.

The model a data scientist creates would never give a perfect answer. When creating it, they need to make decisions about what mathematical model to select. Say, logistic regression or deep learning network together with its shape, and several other parameters. They also have to decide how "good" a model is good enough — in mathematical terms, its "error rate," "precision," and "recall." We can often make the model perform perfectly on the test data set, which would invariably make it perform badly on any new data, a concept known as "overfitting." Many parameters and decisions need to be considered during this process and the best of all the imperfect answers must be selected. This model will be integrated into the product and launched. After the launch, the ML model needs to be continuously monitored because the underlying data may change or the conditions in the world may change and make the predictions less relevant: a concept called "model drift." At which point, the model needs to be retrained or sometimes entirely rethought.

Nina: Does this make developers uncomfortable?

Galina: It does tend to make more traditional technologists (like backend engineers) uncomfortable. They tend to deal more in certainties. When dealing with deterministic algorithms, there often exists a so-called optimal solution. I also find that many of us got into the software engineering world because of the feeling of control it gives us. We make precisely the things we want by writing code. For machine learning development, we need to make many decisions and we don't know the final result. For ML developers (but also everyone else in the business), being able to navigate the many uncertainties in the ML lifecycle is crucial.

So, development of ML models requires investigation of data ("playing with data" as we call it), selection of the preferred mathematical model and many associated parameters and many iterations with the test data, before the final selection is done. As someone who transitioned from deterministic algorithms into data science, this process and letting go of certainties while acquiring other goalposts required effort and felt like a transition and a mindset shift.

Nina: It is actually quite similar in the innovation processes. Being in the uncertainty and not being able to predict or control the output is an essential part of any innovation process. Innovation managers often have the role to make sure teams don't jump too quickly for the most obvious. In the beginning of the innovation process, that has to do with not defining too quickly the challenge/problem/customer need, but staying intentionally in the uncertainty as long as it takes to go deeper and explore what the real problem/need is that might lie behind the most obvious one.

To do that, one needs to let go of existing assumptions and open up space for new potentialities to emerge that might need a re-framing of the way we see the challenge. But before that happens, one needs to be in the space of not knowing, a child-like curious mindset that is open and engaging all the senses to let new things come. Later, in the ideation and prototyping phases, it is also crucial to not get stuck too fast with the "best" idea or the "right" answer to the challenge in focus, but rather explore and prototype around several ideas at the same time, doing more cycles of iteration before finding out what works. In this process, one wants to move from re-acting mode in which we keep affirming what we already know, toward re-framing mode, where we can see and sense with a refreshed mind. It is often from there that really new potentialities for innovation emerge.[22]

Galina: This actually sounds most similar to the iteration between experimentation and improvement in the ML lifecycle. Usually, the first ML model created is not particularly good. It takes some extra work to integrate it into the product and start collecting additional data that can be used to retrain and improve this model. In some ways, the journey of a machine learning product only really begins once it goes live and is made available to its users. That's when a "virtuous cycle of data"[12] is activated. A model in operation produces more data that can be used to train a better model and thus acquire more data. Thus, it doesn't have a traditional beginning and end, like a more regular project would, but rather goes into a process of continuous learning.

The business and engineering management needs to understand how this process works and give it space to grow while having an ability to decide when an AI feature is not working out. This requires a more open-ended approach, more trust, being more data driven — but also ensuring that AI products are aligned with the strategic objectives, so there's clarity on what value they might bring to the business.

I've seen several businesses unfortunately that developed their AI feature, but canceled these projects within 12–18 months, usually due to a combination of unrealistic expectations about how easy it would be to get access to relevant data and enable exploration, as well as unrealistic expectations about the quality of the initial results, viewing it as a destination by itself instead of a process of continuous learning and innovation (exploitation).

Nina: I would say that within innovation management, the introduction of design practices popularized fast prototyping and this idea of continuous experimentation through iterative cycles that help an innovation team quickly try out an idea through a fast prototype (that is far from perfect) and then reflect on it and move on to the next cycle to further improve the concept and idea instead of striving for the perfection from the start.

Galina: I guess we could then say that both the machine learning lifecycle and innovation process mimic and require a learning organization process where continuous improvements and learning are extremely important. Having these innovation capabilities would make it easier for new machine learning projects to succeed, while applying effort to develop machine learning projects also develops those same innovation capabilities.

7. From Continuous Improvement and Exploitation Toward Exploration and Innovation: Bolt-on vs. Integrated AI

Nina: Yes. Here we can relate back to the AIMI model we introduced earlier (Fig. 1), which considers two types of AI: "bolt-on" and "integrated." Bolt-on AI is implemented in the existing business processes and products through projects in non-critical areas, relatively independent of other parts. It is focused predominantly on optimization of existing processes, risk management, and short-term return on investment, enabling incremental innovation of the existing business. By contrast, integrated AI considers the company's core domain area and is deeply integrated with overall organizational purpose and strategy. It is more long-term oriented and strategic, focused on the wider ecosystem of the company, creating value across a broader context and closely associated with transformational innovation. Many organizations start their AI journey with bolt-on AI, focusing on optimization of existing business with AI and as they learn more about technology become more explorative, moving from exploitation also toward innovation with AI, progressively reaching higher levels of AI maturity which eventually lands them in the stage of integrated AI.

Galina: We can say that most organizations go through several stages of maturity (Fig. 2) to arrive at the stage where they have become really AI-enabled or, as we say, have Responsible Integrated AI. The first few stages are focused on learning more about AI, developing capabilities to build AI (or machine learning), and operationalizing it (a process that tends to be much more time-consuming than everyone expects). These stages tend to have "bolt-on" use cases.

Once the bolt-on use cases are operationalized, organizations can really move toward more strategic integrated AI, but often have trouble breaking away from their often-hard-won successes in operationalizing the AI use cases within their domain to expand beyond. An innovation manager's toolkit may well be perfect for enabling these organizations to inquire into how and why they should take further steps and move toward

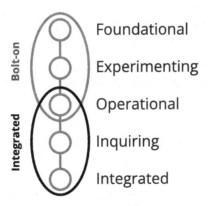

Fig. 2. Bolt-on and integrated AI and AI stages of maturity.

higher maturity levels (inquiring and integrated) that demand, as discussed earlier, mindset growth and more participatory management methods across the organization. Conveniently, this is usually the time when a budget is available for it, though there's usually a push to reap the benefits or reinvest into more bolt-on use cases instead.

Nina: In many ways, the continuous improvement, exploitation, and exploration are demonstrated in miniature in development of a single AI application, but also on a larger scale when we discuss maturity of an organization and their progress toward integrated AI.

Additionally, the integrated stage itself is self-transforming, where an organization is able to learn, evaluate, adjust, and invest in the future. It's the final stage of continuous improvement and reinvention.

8. Ecosystem, System of Systems

Nina: Besides the mindset growth, I guess another capability that is needed to reach higher levels of AI maturity is the ecosystem perspective. And, I think, here again innovation management can help an organization build the wider innovation ecosystem to support AI integration and innovation. This ecosystem might involve shared data infrastructure, testbeds, collaboration with innovative AI start-ups and with universities that have relevant expertise, and access to the pool of future talents (students). It entails also working with training institutions that can help up-skill employees and collaborating with institutions developing policies and regulation related to AI that can have an impact on the organization. Transformative win-win relationships with many different partners, business, academia, start-ups and others is essential for long-term success in the complex world we work and live in.

Galina: This is true and also an area where AI technologists are used to thinking about technology partners, but have little insights into the other partners, which may enable us to more successfully integrate AI.

To turn the coin to the other side, I think when talking about building the innovation ecosystem, AI could also augment innovation managers in this field since AI tools could help them equip organization with smarter foresight, and then, based on predicting what trends might affect organization, identify new opportunities for innovation. Additionally, AI could be used to identify potentially interesting external partners in the ecosystem to collaborate and innovate with based on identified opportunities, supporting innovation managers in the matchmaking process and assessment of potential innovation partners.

As you know, my special pet peeve is that innovation managers often use what we, in the technology, would consider stone age collaboration tools. Enabling collaborative interactions in the cloud that are augmented with smart, AI-enabled features may well be the step number one.

9. Wrapping up

Nina: Ha-ha, yes, we (innovation managers) think we are cool and updated about new technologies, but as you say, we are probably rookies in some fields, like AI. For me, the first step was to start using auto-transcription in the interviews I do in my research.

I think we have covered many dimensions of possible similarities, intersections and benefits of collaboration between AI technologists and innovation managers in this conversation. After this discussion we both feel that I've myself learned more about your field of practice, but also that I was forced to think more about how I as an innovation manager could benefit from AI in my field of work. It also made me reconsider how I could contribute to the AI integration in organizations in different ways.

The first task I will give to myself after this experience is to experiment more with AI-enabled tools in my own work. Furthermore, I would like to engage in some of the many AI development projects in my research institute to test a few ideas about potential contribution of innovation management we explored in this conversation.

What about you, Galina, what are you taking with you from this conversation and how would you wrap it up?

Galina: I think it became embarrassingly obvious to me that I know little about how non-technical people think of innovation and what innovation managers do, despite having participated in several innovation-related programs.

It also gave me many thoughts on the importance of clear communication in any discussions of AI adoption, AI development, and AI integration. There is a very clear focus that I wasn't aware of before starting to collaborate with you on integrating third party off-the-shelf AI into a broad variety of processes.

At the same time, I am also getting a reiteration that as technologists, we often don't spend enough time engaging many non-technical counterparts in development, communication, considerations of what integration of the technologies we develop would look like — whether in our own company or with our customers outside. And likely when we do, we should be engaging twice as much.

I think step one for all of us is to have many candid conversations with people from other functions while asking very honest questions about words and assumptions that seem self-evident — but very likely aren't.

Acknowledgments

We would like to thank Valerie Richardson, Sandor Albrecht, and Kathleen Myrestam for their feedback and suggestions on how to improve our chapter.

References

1. N. Bozic Yams, V. Richardson, G.E. Shubina, S. Albrecht, and D. Gillblad, Integrated AI and innovation management: The beginning of a beautiful friendship. *TIM Review*, **10**(11), 5–18 (2020).
2. K. O'Neil, *Weapons of Math Destruction: How Big Data Increases Inequality and Threatens Democracy*. New York: Crown Publishing Group (2016).
3. S.U. Noble, *Algorithms of Oppression: How Search Engines Reinforce Racism*. New York: NYU Press (2018).
4. V. Dignum, *Responsible Artificial Intelligence: How to Develop and Use AI in a Responsible Way*. Switzerland: Springer Nature (2019).

5. E. Morozov, *To Save Everything, Click Here: Technology, Solutionism, and the Urge to Fix Problems That Don't Exist*. London: Penguin (2014).

6. World Economic Forum, *Gender gaps report 2018 — Assessing gender gaps in Artificial Intelligence*, 2018 [accessed on March 11, 2021]. Available from:https://reports.weforum.org/global-gender-gap-report-2018/assessing-gender-gaps-in-artificial-intelligence/.

7. S.M. West, M. Whittaker, and K. Crawford, *Discriminating systems: Gender, race and power in AI*, AI Now Institute, 2018 [accessed on March 11, 2021]. Available from: https://ainowinstitute.org/discriminatingsystems.pdf.

8. International Organization for Standardization, *ISO 56002 standard, innovation management — Innovation management system — Guidance*, 2019 [accessed on May 15, 2020]. Available from: https://www.iso.org/standard/68221.html.

9. S. Das, It's hysteria, not a heart attack, GP app Babylon tells women. *The Times* [Internet]. October 13, 2019 [accessed on March 11, 2021]. Available at: https://www.thetimes.co.uk/article/its-hysteria-not-a-heart-attack-gp-app-tells-women-gm2vxbrqk.

10. J. Buolamwini and T. Gerbu, Gender shades: Intersectional accuracy disparities in commercial gender classification, in *Proc. Conference on Fairness, Accountability, and Transparency (PMLR'2020)*, 81, 77–91 (2018).

11. Ericsson, Adopting AI in organizations. *The journey towards constant change*, 2020 [accessed on February 20, 2021]. Available at: https://www.ericsson.com/en/reports-and-papers/industrylab/reports/adopting-ai-in-organizations.

12. A. Ng, *AI transformation playbook: How to lead your company into the AI era*, 2018 [accessed on July 10, 2019]. Available at: https://landing.ai/ai-transformation-playbook.

13. N. Bozic Yams, Choreographing innovative practice in everyday work. Mälardalen University Press Dissertations Eskilstuna: Mälardalen University Press (2018).

14. A.L. Samuel, Some studies in machine learning using the game of checkers. *IBM Journal of Research and Development* **3**(3), 210–229 (1959).

15. B. Torbert, S. Cook-Greuter, D. Fisher, E. Foldy, A. Gauthier, J. Keely *et al.*, *Action Inquiry: The Secret of Timely and Transforming Leadership*. San Francisco: Berrett-Koehler Publishers, Inc. (2004).

16. D. Tang, A. Agarwal, D. O'Brien, and M. Meyer, Overlapping experiment infrastructure: More, better, faster experimentation, in *KDD'10*, Washington DC, USA (July, 2010).

17. M. Schultzberg, O. Kjellin, and J. Rydberg, *Spotify's new experimentation coordination strategy* [Internet]. 2021 [accessed on March 11, 2021].

Available at: https://engineering.atspotify.com/2021/03/10/spotifys-new-experimentation-coordination-strategy/.

18. A. Agrawal, J. Gans, and A. Goldfarb, *Prediction Machines: The Simple Economics of Artificial Intelligence.* Boston, MA, USA: HBR Press (2018).
19. L. Denti and S. Hemlin, Leadership and innovation in organizations: A systematic review of factors that mediate or moderate the relationship. *International Journal of Innovation Management* **16**(3), 1240007–1240027 (2012).
20. R.K. Greenleaf, *Servant Leadership: A Journey into the Nature of Legitimate Power and Greatness.* New York: Paulist Press (1977).
21. F. Laloux, *Reinventing Organizations.* Brussels: Nelson Parker (2014).
22. M. Peschl and T. Fundneider, Theory-U and emergent innovation: Presencing as a method of bringing forth profoundly new knowledge and realities, in O. Gunnlaugson, C. Baron, and M. Cayer (eds.), *Perspectives on Theory U: Insights from the Field,* pp. 207–233. Hershey, PA: Business Science Reference/IGI Global (2014).

Chapter 2

A Knowledge-Based Perspective of Strategic AI Innovation Management

Erich Prem

eutema GmbH and TU Vienna
Lindengasse 43, 1070 Wien, Austria
prem@eutema.com

At more than 50 years of age, Artificial Intelligence cannot be called a new technology. However, recent advances in AI have made the field widely available and applicable to the extent that it has become a major driver for technology-based innovations. This chapter investigates the characteristics underlying AI technology that are most relevant for innovation management. It addresses challenges and potential showstoppers, such as data requirements, explainability, and ethical questions. These questions require a strategic approach to managing AI innovation, i.e., a long-term perspective and a careful consideration of the epistemic flow of information from the problem domain to the application. We propose an epistemic framework for the AI innovation process that helps in understanding and improving key dynamic capabilities for strategic AI innovation management.

1. Introduction

Recent advances in AI have made the technology widely available and applicable to the extent that it has become a major driver for technology-based innovations. In this chapter, we take a closer look at the characteristics underlying AI technology that are most relevant for innovation management. We capitalize on the strategic dimension of innovation management, meaning the longer-term capacity and capability-building for AI-based innovation. The aim of this chapter is to set the scene and to clarify the essential steps in building AI models. This should also help to identify major challenges and how to address them.

Following Ref. [1, p. 36], we seek to answer the question of the areas that an AI-innovating company should prioritize in the longer (strategic) perspective. We also inquire about which new skills are needed to address the technological features and challenges of an AI-focused innovation environment. In the following sections, we therefore focus on the *dynamic capabilities to create AI-based technical innovations* and to successfully adopt the necessary changes in the company's operation and resources.

1.1. *Characterizing AI systems*

Given that Artificial Intelligence exists as a discipline for more than 50 years, it is surprisingly hard to define. From the onset, the AI field has been plagued by the problem of specifying what exactly AI means. This has been a challenge for decades and it is still true today.[2,3]

As one possibility, AI can be defined through its objective of building intelligent artificial systems in which case the definition of intelligence is naturally connected to human and in some cases, such as robots and animal intelligence. As another possibility and like other fields of research, it can also be defined through its academic subdisciplines and application fields, i.e., robotics, language understanding, computer vision, automated reasoning, machine learning, neural networks, etc. As a third option with an emphasis on the recent success of machine learning in applications, such as machine translation, image recognition, or medical diagnosis, AI is sometimes defined as the field of systems that learn behavior from data. However, this would exclude traditional AI systems such as expert systems and some types of natural language understanding or language generation systems. It is useful to exclude very simple systems such as thermostats or simple computer programs from the class of AI systems as in practice these have different characteristics from full-scale AI programs. In the following characterization, we therefore speak about "complex" rule-bases and "non-linear" models with many parameters.

In this chapter and by way of definition, AI systems shall be characterized as systems that exhibit a high degree of autonomy in performing tasks in the domains of perception, reasoning, decision-making, language, and speech. These systems work using complex rule-based knowledge bases or learned numeric, non-linear models with large numbers of parameters.

1.2. *Understanding the surge in applications*

There was a massive surge in innovative AI applications after around 2015 when the AI market grew from around US\$5 billion to somewhere between estimated US\$17 billion and US\$34 billion.[a] This is due to a range of independently developed synergistic factors that enabled the application of AI in new problem areas, increased the speed of developing AI models, and generally led to the design of more robust and reliable AI systems compared to those in the 1980s or 1990s. These factors are not just due to recent developments in the field of AI. In fact, it can be argued that with a few exceptions most of the techniques used in AI systems today date back perhaps several decades. The exception concerns the development and refinement of novel learning algorithms including so-called Deep Learning.[4,5] Even though recurrent neural networks have been around for many years,[6] there is now a much better understanding of the algorithms, the necessary data and model structures, the training and evaluation algorithms as well as potential shortcomings and pitfalls.

A first main factor is of course the availability of more data that facilitates the creation of AI models. This data is available from both new types of sensors and from a massively increasing number of sensors that provide nearly ubiquitous measurements of all sorts of phenomena. This also roots in massively reduced costs of sensors that are built not only into smartphones, but can also be found in many devices, machines, or as

---

[a] https://www.statista.com/statistics/941835/artificial-intelligence-market-size-revenue-comparisons/, March 19, 2021.

stand-alone sensor systems that continuously deliver data. Similarly, the massive increase in stored online data including data accessible on the internet has created an abundance of information with huge exploitation potential for AI systems. Automated translators are but one example.[7]

The second key factor is the availability of new and easy-to-use tools for training and developing AI models.[8] Many tools are available online and free of charge, others have become parts of popular or professional toolboxes and software suites.

Thirdly, processing (i.e., number-crunching computation) and memory as well as online storage are available in very high quality at low costs. For many decades, training large neural networks was limited by the fact that it required significant computational resources. While this is still true in many situations where complex neural networks are trained on large amounts of data, the availability of low-cost high-performance computing has made it much easier and faster to train smaller, less complex models. It has also enabled the training of larger, more complex models that simply could not be realized earlier. Figure 1 depicts a simplified AI model development process that was significantly improved given the mentioned factors.

The recent increase in good-quality innovative AI models can be explained with the synergistic combination of many independently developing factors: falling prices for sensors, the increased availability of data, new AI model types and learning algorithms in combination with better and lower-cost computational and memory resources as well as training tools. AI models require intensive testing and validation before they become the basis of innovative applications.

Fig. 1. A high-level perspective of the AI modeling process from the problem domain via sensors to data that implies knowledge but requires pre-processing for training an AI model.

Finally, the surge of AI applications should be framed within the much larger trend toward digitization and digital business models. Even where digitization may initially just concern a single aspect of a business model, it often induces pervasive changes throughout complete business models.[9] In the case of AI, the interest in models that learn from data has itself increased the interest in data as a source for AI-based innovation. Data is thus a driver of AI-based innovation, but these AI models have in turn increased the interest in data as a potential source of innovative AI models.

2. Strategic Challenges of AI for Innovation Management

Can we consider AI a general-purpose innovation technology? It has been argued that AI will revolutionize innovation due to its general-purpose character.[10–12] It not only offers the means to improve existing products, services, and processes, but goes beyond other technologies as it is a general problem-solving approach that — given enough data — facilitates the design of just about any realizable function. While it is certainly true that machine learning exhibits a great potential, such claims are exaggerated. In the following, we will point to some major potential showstoppers that need the attention of strategic decision-makers.

Primary objectives behind the development of novel AI models are process and project innovation.[13] At the process level, the aims are often to increase automation, or to improve resource efficiency and to reduce production costs. Product and service innovations cover a broad range from qualitative innovation, i.e., incremental improvements, to completely new service offerings that can only be achieved with the help of AI models. This implies an extremely broad innovation potential that provides challenges for innovation management in selecting not only the right AI models and technologies, but more fundamentally, the precise character of the targeted AI system. In fact, it can be a huge challenge for innovation management to reliably anticipate what AI can and should be used for. This challenge is aggravated if there is only a poor understanding of how AI models are built and what their technical requirements really are. In the following, we therefore focus on technical requirements for innovative AI models and the modeling process from an information and knowledge perspective.

2.1. *Previous work on strategic AI management for innovation*

Although AI has received significant attention in innovation management, relatively few scholars have explicitly addressed the strategic level. Reference [12] presents an overview of AI and innovation management as well as a framework and research agenda. Starting from the behavioral theory of the firm they assess the use of AI from an information processing perspective. The paper identifies a range of challenges for innovation managers, most notably those related to understanding the potential for innovation, i.e., a process of information collection and sense-making. Our framework in the following focuses on the process of creating an innovation and the related challenges. While AI can help identify important information, the framework also emphasizes the many points at which human innovation managers need to make design decisions. Implicitly, we may thus be more skeptical about the ways in which innovation opportunities can identified automatically.

Reference [14] provides an overview of the opportunities, challenges, and components of AI systems for innovation. It lists six building blocks of AI with the aim to provide an analytic tool for managers. The authors also include a typology of AI-based innovations as either competence-enhancing or competence-destroying which we reconsider in Section 4. This typology can help support managers, including innovation managers, in predicting effects of AI-based innovations on their organizations. This clearly is a case of strategic innovation management as it may influence portfolio decisions, e.g., to give preference to competence-enhancing innovations.

The comprehensive paper of Ref. [15] provides multidisciplinary perspectives of 26 authors on AI, including challenges and opportunities for innovation. From a strategic viewpoint they discuss open research challenges and policy aspects relevant for AI-based innovation. The authors list organizational and managerial challenges of implementing AI-based innovations including the longer-term effect on business areas, the lack of in-house talent, and the question of realism in judging AI solutions. We discuss these aspects from a strategic perspective using our epistemic framework where possible.

Reference [16] discusses empirical findings about how people design AI and machine learning models. It can be considered complementary to the intention of our work here as it underpins aspects of our epistemic framework model with concrete observations of work practices developing AI models. Several of the steps that we also consider essential from a strategic perspective are listed as important work practices, e.g., data curation or tending models.

2.2. *Barriers and challenges of AI innovation*

Despite the impressive progress in AI and its use for realizing innovative services and products, there are significant shortcomings, pitfalls, and potential showstoppers. In previous work[13] we identified a list of specific challenges for Austrian AI companies focusing on developing AI models with the aim of innovating processes and products. The problems range from lack of staff and knowledge to costs, technical aspects such as explaining and validating AI models, to the lack of regulatory frameworks (cf. Table 1).

Many of the challenges require longer-term planning, i.e., strategic thinking and decision-making. In addition to the above listed problems, AI systems have also been criticized because of ethical concerns, potential bias in automated decision-making, de-skilling of staff following the roll-out of AI systems, and a general lack of understanding and hence inability to explain the behavior of AI models. These are potential innovation showstoppers. In the following, we investigate these challenges in relation to the specific technological characteristics of the AI system development process and the flow of knowledge from the problem domain to the AI innovation to identify strategies for managing AI innovation, i.e., those relevant in a long-term perspective.

3. The AI System Building Process: An Epistemic Framework

The broad variety of AI systems and AI technologies ranging from expert systems to neural networks makes it difficult to create a general model that relates the use of AI in the context of innovation management.

Table 1. Barriers and challenges of using AI for innovation listed in interviews with Austrian AI companies.[13]

Barriers and challenges	Examples
Lack of qualified staff	IT experts (general), IT staff with AI expertise, data scientists, specialists and generalists, software developers, AI experts
Costs	Know-how creation, development costs, long development times (trial and error for innovative solutions), hardware costs for robotics
Lack of knowledge	Insufficient information about AI (general), unrealistic expectations, insufficient competence in AI (with not even the definition being clear)
Credibility of AI solutions	Unrealistic claims regarding AI and disappointment
Technical aspects	Lack of explainability for learning systems, lack of data — strong limitation for AI, especially for SMEs
Regulation	Current legal regulation, e.g., in the health sector; unclear responsibilities for overall system behavior
Hesitation	Hesitation of executives, especially with SMEs, but also hesitation of customers
Hype	Risk that the current hype about AI hampers its development, because it blurs the view of real opportunities and creates wrong expectations

Reference [14] proposed a model consisting of four dimensions: input data, processes, and output as well as underlying knowledge base. In this model, inputs are either structured or unstructured data. Processes are pre- (natural language understanding or vision) or main processes (reasoning, learning). Outputs can be generated language, images, or robotic control. The resulting building blocks (cf. Fig. 2) are also connected to an AI inno- vation typology.

In the practice of creating AI-based technological innovation, these components require a process perspective, i.e., how to get from the problem domain to an AI model. The framework presented below, empha- sizes the steps in this process such as sensing, data management, pre-pro- cessing, etc., which can all be challenging steps that requires significant

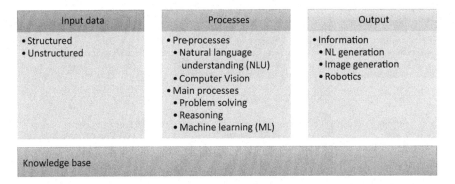

Fig. 2. A general AI model.[14]

expertise and therefore the attention of strategic decision-makers. The proposed framework emphasizes the flow of information from the problem domain to the targeted innovation. As this capitalizes on aspects of information and knowledge, it is an epistemic framework. Our aim will be to clarify the strategic dimensions following these steps from the problem to the AI-based innovation.

3.1. *An epistemic process model from problem to AI-based innovation outcomes*

Figure 3 details the process from Fig. 1 to describe the development steps from the problem domain to an innovation-enabling AI component.

This framework shown in Fig. 3 focuses on the flow of information and knowledge and therefore is an epistemic process model. (In order to not confuse it with the "AI model" we shall henceforth use the term "framework.") Implicitly, the framework focuses on input-heavy AI systems, e.g., in classification, prediction, and decision-making tasks. The suggested framework is less suitable for AI applications that are heavy on the behavior-generating side, such as in robotic systems because of multiple physical feedback loops typically used in autonomous robot design.

The basic epistemic process from the problem domain to the AI system (AI output or AI-based innovation outcomes) and hence, the innovation, could be described as the result of a five-step creative process. Creativity here means that important design choices are required at every

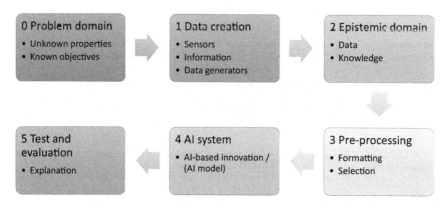

Fig. 3. Representation of the epistemic processes from the problem domain to the AI model. The steps after the epistemologically inaccessible problem domain (0) are (1) the creation of data, (2) understanding (the epistemic domain), (3) pre-processing, (4) AI model creation (tools), and (5) test and evaluation (validation) of the developed AI model.

step. This process model includes steps that are not always considered in the innovation literature as they may only be implicit. They are nevertheless key to understanding and hence managing important challenges for AI innovation management such as dealing with ethics, bias, explanations, or the important aspect of how to get the work done in practice.[16]

We start with the observation that the precise nature of the problem domain is typically inaccessible to the human observer. The system in the problem domain typically lies behind a fundamental "epistemic boundary" (hence "stage 0") and we can only access it through our senses or with the help of sensory systems. As an example, consider a complex process in a production plant. In physics, this fundamental first step involves the creation of observables, for which physicists build sensors, e.g., large telescopes, or particle accelerators. However, we generally assume that the problem domain follows (causal) rules. We further assume that sensory systems interact with the system in the problem domain in a regular fashion (based on natural law) and that it delivers measurements, typically in the form of numbers which can be used as a basis for building a model of the problem domain. In the case of a production plant, we may be able to measure pressure and temperature and assume certain relationships of these parameters to product quality, for example. For a basic yet comprehensive introduction into fundamental aspects of system models, see Ref. [17]. Note that the design of observables is a creative act, especially in physics where sometimes huge efforts are spent on designing and building sensory devices. This is essentially the same in many other areas where sensors are used to inform about a system — the first step. In information systems, the observables (or sensors) may just be text or strings of characters from IT systems, for example when "sensing" replies to questions or when translating text from one language into another. From an information-theoretic point of view, this first step is the only way to ensure that the data at later stages concerns the actual system, i.e., that we collect information about the problem domain. When the connection with the original system is lost (when data is not about the problem domain), it cannot be re-established in any other way than with the means of sensory systems. The challenge of this step is to use sensors that deliver data which is sufficient for an AI algorithm to learn and shape a useful model. Finally, the problem objective, i.e., why a specific model is targeted naturally influences the choice of sensors — and the kind of data required to create an AI model.

Second, there is a step in which it is necessary to make sense of the data or to build a theory about the problem domain (0). This requires human interpretation, understanding, and conceptual decisions. For the creation of a rule-based, symbolic AI system this step is also about formalizing knowledge about the system. This step is all about knowledge, understanding data, and sense-making of the problem domain's representation in data.

Third, sensors deliver raw data in a form that may not be suitable for the creation of an AI model. In addition, many sensory systems will deliver data and information that are not relevant or suitable for the development of a specific AI process. The selection and pre-processing of data are important and often laborious tasks. These tasks can mean an extensive workload, especially in the case of historic data. In many situations, it is not *a priori* clear which sensors or which data carry significant information for a learning AI algorithm. This in fact is why a learning algorithm may have to be used. For supervised learning, there may be steps of manually classifying data, potentially with the help of people which creates the need to oversee and manage this process (Ref. [16, pp. 656–657]).

The fourth step is the actual creation of the AI model. This can be a process of human coding knowledge, e.g., an expert system, or a machine learning process resulting in a trained model. Such models can be numeric or symbolic or both. Apart from key decisions on the general structure of the model, there are important choices about the computational resources, training schemes, cloud services and many other details. The application of a training algorithm may or may not result in a reliable or useful AI model; in some instances the training itself can be unsuccessful and may require different architectures, algorithms, computing environments, etc.

The final step is testing and evaluation of the model properties. This important step at the end of the AI modeling process reconnects the model with the original problem domain (again using sensors of some sort) as described before. In addition, it may be necessary to deliver explanations of the AI system behavior. These explanations should typically refer to assertions about the original problem domain, i.e., they connect steps (5), (4), (2), and (1). The test phase may often be in addition to a more traditional feedback loop with the system users as it mainly concerns just the trained (or designed) AI model as the core of the technical innovation.

There is a lack of predictability in several steps of this framework. It concerns the selection of observables (sensors), coding of data, preprocessing, training, etc. This is a basic problem of machine learning that also impacts on the innovation process. An AI-based technological innovation will nearly always imply a process of trial (training) and error (evaluation). It is therefore inherently difficult to predict quality or to calculate any guaranteed outcomes. Most of the time it will also be impossible to forecast development cycles and, hence, development time.

Moreover, work does not stop once an AI model has been developed successfully. A system containing an AI model will have to be updated and maintained; Ref. [16] refers to this step as *tending models*. In today's practice, this mostly means another training/design and testing/evaluation phase, i.e., retraining of models. It is worth mentioning that an automated (continuous) adaptation of AI models is technically challenging and very rare in practice today even though it would be extremely useful for many practical applications. Sometimes, AI system developers try to reuse components of

AI systems, for example in the field of image recognition. In modular systems, it may be possible to retrain only some of the modules rather than redeveloping the whole system.

3.2. Specific AI modeling challenges for strategic innovation management

This epistemic model allows the identification and description of key challenges in the long-term creation of AI models, hence strategically managing firm resources and dynamic capabilities. It also helps in understanding the specific challenges of AI-based innovations in comparison to other, more conventional IT-based innovations.

3.2.1. *Understanding the modeling process*

The AI model development process is inherently experimental. Until properly tested (5), the relation between the AI model (4) and the problem domain (0) remains often unknown. Although it is advisable to create data (1, 2) that facilitates the creation of a suitable AI model, this cannot be guaranteed before the development (building or learning) of the AI model. Even when there is good reason to assume that the sensors (1) deliver the necessary information and that there is sufficient data (2), it is typically not before a model has been built (4) and evaluated (5) that its precise behavior can be known. To make things worse, many AI (learning) algorithms will create different models even when using the same data in a different order or with different start parameters. This means that two AI models trained with similar data may possess different characteristics — even to the extent that one may be of sufficient quality for the desired task while the other does not work.

It is important that this difficulty is not just an accidental characteristic of an insufficiently developed technology. It is deeply rooted in the fact that — at least for learning systems — the model is only created in the last step and with a certain degree of randomness. As a result, the model design process is necessarily iterative and to some degree uncertain. Obviously, this implies that the costs and qualities of an AI-based solutions may be less predictable than more conventional IT-based solutions. For innovation management, this implies that a high degree of flexibility is needed as the model development may take longer than expected and deliver results of varying quality. Management must commit to an experimental development methodology and plan with reserve budgets.

From a strategic perspective, it is most important that everybody involved in the AI model design understands these challenges. This includes company management who may in many cases not possess expertise in AI model building. It is imperative that the innovation manager and company manager understand the iterative nature to avoid disappointment and false expectation.[18] For many interesting and promising AI innovation projects, it may not even be possible to precisely assess their feasibility before performing at least some initial experiments.

3.2.2. Managing data

The epistemic framework of Fig. 3 clearly shows how the realizability of innovation ideas crucially depends on the availability of knowledge and data about the problem domain. In many cases, given the large amount of data necessary for learning reliable AI models, data about the problem domain needs to be collected long before the start of a concrete innovation project. This thus poses the strategic question of long-term and historic data collection even before knowing anything about the objective or targeted innovation.

With AI, *data becomes potential innovation.* The main challenge is of course that collecting the data before the targeted innovation is known means to simply hope it will be sufficient for future AI models. The important aspect is that the data needs to contain the right information to build a working AI model. The three most important challenges are (i) that there is sufficient data, and (ii) that the right data has been collected, and (iii) that the characteristics of the data — respectively how they were collected — are properly understood. This technical and historical dimension of the data can provide huge challenges and is another key strategic requirement for solid AI-based innovation management. It includes not just data, but also documenting how it was collected and what the data means — information that is typically stored as metadata. In many cases this information is not easily reducible to just a syntactic data description.

Often, understanding historic data requires the availability of experts who have insights into the circumstances under which data was collected. For example, it could mean to know that (and when) one type of sensor was replaced with a new generation. It may include considerations about which cases are represented in the data including for example whether there is any bias in the data collection.

Data is a key challenge for strategically managing a firm's dynamic AI modeling capability. Without proper technical and historical understanding of data, the AI-based innovation modeling process becomes even more trial and error than it already is. The lack of large amounts of historic data can be a challenge for AI-based innovation, especially in small firms where the above-mentioned expertise about the historic data characteristics may not be available. In some cases, data can also be generated for training an AI model. This means that real sensor data is replaced with data that is artificially constructed as if it was collected from real sensor measurements. Such artificial data can only be used with great care and proper evaluation of the resulting AI model is even more important than when real measurements are used.

Figure 4 depicts the overall epistemic framework and shows how domain and modeling expertise relate to the AI modeling process. It also shows the central importance of data curation (as a forward-looking exercise in the direction of future innovation potential) and of data experts that understand the syntactic and semantic data qualities and the data history.

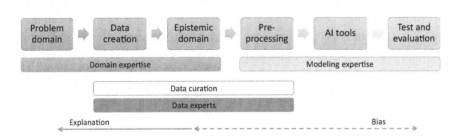

Fig. 4. Key strategic innovation capabilities for AI models: domain expertise, modeling expertise, and data curation — the area for data experts. Questions of bias and explanation should connect the AI model (i.e., tested features of the model) with data and knowledge about the problem domain and with the original problem domain.

3.2.3. *Ethical issues*

Innovative AI models generate a great deal of discussion because they raise important ethical questions. The epistemic process model also helps to understand the challenges of bias and explanation. Improper bias in an AI model can emerge from many sources. It can arise from a bias in the training algorithm, even from the pre-processing steps, and an inadequate consideration of the understanding of the problem. However, in many cases bias roots in an inadequate choice of measurements so that certain types of situations are represented differently from others. A frequent example is an underrepresentation of women in a data set while the application would in fact require an equal representation of men and women.

Similarly, explanations of the AI system behavior may require the establishment of references between the AI model output, its input, and an understanding of the problem domain. In many learning systems, the statistical nature of the model construction makes it very difficult to understand precisely how certain models were created and thus why a certain output results from the model. Nevertheless, many applications of AI systems would benefit from precisely such explanations, especially when the models aim at improving human decision-making.

The strategic challenge here lies in properly understanding the problem domain, the data characteristics, and the features of the developed AI model. While it may still be difficult to provide clear explanations in many cases, a proper understanding of data and problem domain will be helpful in the analysis of an AI model.

In addition to bias and explanation, there are often ethical concerns about privacy, i.e., about personal data used for building AI models. In the epistemic model, privacy aspects concern the relation of the problem domain (i.e., people and their behavior) to how data is generated and used in later steps of the process.

The information flow process model suggests that proper constraints on personal data should happen early in the epistemic process if it is desirable to maintain the privacy of personal data. This means that the sensors (1) need to be designed such that only minimal personal information suffices for the creation of the AI model. In the case of statistical modeling, it may be sufficient for many applications to create artificial data

((1) to (2)) that does not contain actual personal information and only mimics the statistical properties of measurements. Such privacy-preserving techniques can mean strategic advantages for innovation in sensitive, privacy-related application domains.

Other ethical issues include how AI systems should and should not be used and what their potential effects are on humans operating with such systems. This ranges from automated decision-making to de-skilling of staff, i.e., the question as to whether an AI innovation destroys or enhances human (or company) competencies.

3.2.4. *Competence-enhancing versus competence-destroying AI-based innovation*

A useful distinction for strategic decision-making on AI-based innovations is between competence-enhancing versus competence-destroying AI innovations.[1,14,19] An innovation can be said to be competence-enhancing when it significantly improves a product or process. If an AI innovation creates a completely new service or product class, or substitutes an existing good or service, it may result in destroying an existing competence. In the cases of processes, the latter can mean that previous knowledge required for a production process is no longer required and is replaced with an automated process. Replacing drivers with autonomous vehicles can be considered competence-destroying within the mobility sector. A range of (semi-) autonomous driver support technologies are examples of AI-based innovations that are enhancing the product offering without fundamentally changing the set of relevant competencies in the automotive industry.

The distinction between competence-enhancing and competence-destroying innovations is, however, far from straightforward. Reference [14] uses the example of predictive maintenance as a competence-enhancing service innovation that can improve service quality while at the same time still requiring the intervention of technicians. Predictive maintenance can even improve the service quality further by pointing maintenance workers to the precise point of the potential problem or by forecasting the precise parts that require replacement or maintenance. However, it is easy to imagine situations in which predictive maintenance leads to de-skilling of maintenance workers. If their work schedule becomes primarily driven by AI-based forecasting, they may see fewer cases of systems that are about to fail which can impair their learning from real-world cases. Similarly, autonomous driving can lead to significant reduction of driving capabilities. This is the reason why train engine drivers, for example in automatically operating underground systems, are often scheduled to manually operate their trains. This phenomenon has led to a surge of publications addressing de-skilling through autonomous driving. Interestingly, some authors suggest that initial high levels of skilled driving are more important than regularly driving.[20] The classification of an innovation as competence-enhancing or competence-destroying depends on the time frame for judging the impact of the system. Moreover, it also depends on decisions about where to draw the system boundary. In any case, the proper ethical assessment of an AI-based innovation can help prevent innovation failures and public relation catastrophes caused by AI-products and services that are publicly perceived as unethical.

4. Strategic Resources Supporting Dynamic Capabilities for Successful AI Innovation

Following our discussion of the epistemic AI model we identify five key strategic resources necessary to manage the dynamic capabilities necessary for successful AI innovation. They are knowledge, i.e., human resources or talent, data, ethics, process and expectation management, and regulation.

4.1. *Knowledge and human resources*

The long-term capability to develop AI-based innovation relies on the availability of the right competencies and skills in the firm. As can be seen from the framework (Figs. 3 and 4), domain experts are vital for any AI-based model. Typically, such domain experts are available if the AI innovation addresses aspects that lie within a company's core competence areas. More challenging — and generally a significant problem for companies — are capabilities on the AI modeling side. Not only are very few AI experts readily available from the labor markets, but it is also difficult to hire IT experts without specific AI expertise. As discussed before, AI modeling requires a solid understanding of the AI tools, data pre-processing, and evaluations, steps (3), (4), and (5) in our model. Skilled staff therefore require an understanding of mathematics (analysis, gradient-descent methods), statistics, physics, engineering, or computer modeling. In addition, it may be helpful to have at least a basic understating of linguistics for text-based AI, logic for rule-bases and expert systems, computer graphics, or robotics.

A particular longer-term challenge is to ensure competencies and capabilities in the field of ethics. There are today very few experts that understand the challenges of data privacy, automated decision-making, explanations, etc. and the rules and expectations from the side of users and regulators. As Ref. [21] points out, an *industry AI ethicist* also must be able to communicate ethical principles within a corporate structure. Such competencies can be tricky for smaller enterprises in that a dedicated AI ethics expert is neither readily available nor can it usually be financed. From a strategic perspective it is therefore important to develop such competencies in-house or build partnerships with organizations that have both an interest in the ethical aspects as well as an understanding of the business side. The latter, however, is often even challenging for research institutes and university departments given the traditional separation of engineering and scientific disciplines from the humanities. Effective ethical frameworks include issues of company culture, governance, and controls.[18,22]

4.2. *Data curation capabilities*

It is often said that large amounts of data are a prerequisite for success with AI innovation and should thus form the basis of strategic decisions in digital businesses. While this is true in many cases, it is not sufficient. The epistemic model clearly demonstrates the importance of data curation that goes far beyond simple collection. Reference [16] describes curation more in line with what we describe as pre-processing and selection. However, the term *curation* in this paper was chosen to emphasize the need to choose and pick data — much like a museum curator chooses objects for a collection. Just like the museum curator, a data curator must choose and pick before the object or data are actually put to use — in an exhibition or an AI model for innovation. From a strategic perspective, data is curated without yet having a concrete application innovation in mind.

It first concerns the understanding of data history, technical characteristics, and its potential meaning in the application domain. This requires proper selection of data, its metadata information and means to capture significant changes in the data collection history.

Secondly, there may not be sufficient data to train an AI model as planned. In such cases, there is a need to cleverly produce data in strict alignment with the statistical properties of the problem domain. Creating or manipulating artificial data and ways of specially treating personal data are also vital for addressing the important issue of privacy. These topics are related as artificial data can be created with the main aim to avoid the use of personal data.[23]

Thirdly, understanding data characteristics is also important for avoiding unwanted bias, for improving explanation and thus increased trust in an AI-based innovation.

4.3. *Process and expectation management*

We have seen that the development of AI-based technological innovations typically follows a trial-and-error methodology. This is an inherent feature in the process of AI model development. It also requires a solid evaluation and validation of the created AI model. As a result, AI-based innovation development is inherently unpredictable. Before an AI model is evaluated, it is practically impossible to decide whether it is sufficient for the targeted application. This makes it nearly impossible in many cases to predict how long its development will take or how much the development will cost, or whether it going to work in principle.

As a result, innovation managers need to manage not just the development process, but also the expectations of company management as well as those of potential customers. For users, explainability of an AI model may only be possible to a limited extent. For managers, there is an inherent unpredictability of the development process and its cost.

The lack of explainability and proven correctness of some AI models also means that AI-based innovations are more difficult in areas where such expectations are either typical, e.g., in engineering, or even suggested from regulation, e.g., in automated decision-making that impacts on user rights.

Managing these expectations on the user side thus can mean to exclude certain types of innovations or application areas from AI-based approaches. It can also mean to target users with dedicated information that explicitly explains what an AI-based innovation can and cannot do. The false attribution of qualities to relatively simply AI systems has its own history, for example as in the case of Weizenbaum's ELIZA system. ELIZA was an extremely simple text generator that users mistook for a computer therapist.[24] Strategic expectation management in this case means to inform users about the limits of the systems, warn about potential failures and misinterpretation.

A sub-task of managing expectations and understanding ethical implications consists in properly identifying the long-term impacts of AI-based innovations. This requires at least some degree of impact assessment, for example as regards the impact on de-skilling of the workforce. Such technology assessments can be performed using scenario analysis, studying technology trajectories and by focusing on the contextual embedding of the targeted AI-based innovation, i.e., social, environmental, or political factors, and by using tools such as a PESTLE-analysis.[25]

4.4. *Regulation*

A final strategic dimension relevant for AI-based innovation is the regulatory environment. For many AI-based innovations it is important to understand the rules governing the area of application. Unfortunately, the precise rules applicable to an AI-based innovation are often very unclear, e.g., in the health industry or are quickly developing, such as is the case with privacy regulation. Companies interested in developing AI-based models therefore need to monitor the regulatory environment closely even when they have no intention to drive the regulatory developments.

Regulation is by no means a showstopper to AI-based innovations. In fact, more clarity including standards and clear norms have the potential to facilitate innovation using AI. Examples include the challenging regulatory environment for automated decision-making and personal data in the European Union. It is often far from clear how to design a system that uses an AI-based model so that it properly aligns with existing regulation.

Similar to other areas of technology or business regulation, smaller companies may not be able to devote experts just to the monitoring or influencing of regulatory frameworks. However, the development of regulatory competencies is a necessity for successful AI-based innovation in the long run.

5. Conclusion

This chapter focused on a set of strategic challenges that need to be addressed in AI innovation management. The epistemic framework presented in this chapter helps to identify the challenges at different steps of the AI model development process which require the attention of strategic decision-makers. These challenges can easily turn into potential showstoppers for AI-based technological innovations when not given sufficient consideration.

The proposed framework emphasizes those aspects of the AI modeling process that relate to data and knowledge. While AI models are sometimes presented as a kind of "miracle solution" to innovation, the framework presented in this chapter underlines that the decisive factor for successful AI modeling is the proper consideration of the information flow from the problem domain to the targeted innovation at all steps. These steps are required for any AI modeling, but they become essential for organizations aiming to create more than just a single AI-based innovation. The framework shows the essential role played by properly managing information creation through sensors, data curation, knowledge management, competent tool application etc. Each of these steps also entails strategic decision-making at organization level. In fact, in managing expectations of customers it may even addresses aspects outside the innovating organization.

At the current state of development of AI technology, we have barely scratched the surface of what may be possible in the future — despite the long history of AI already. It is likely that we will see an even stronger shift towards mainly data-driven models for realizing IT functionality. Hence, all the steps in our framework are likely to receive much more attention in the future, even in situations where the creation of technological innovation may not be the primary focus of AI model development. This should create ample opportunities for organizations that decide to strategically manage their dynamic capabilities for AI-based technological innovation from an epistemic perspective.

References

1. J. Tidd and J. Bessant, *Strategic Innovation Management*. UK: Wiley (2014).
2. R. Brooks, Intelligence without reason, in R. Chrisley (ed.), *Artificial Intelligence: Critical Concepts*, Vol. 3, 107–163. London and New York: Routledge (2000).
3. P. Wang, On defining artificial intelligence. *Journal of Artificial Intelligence*, **10**(2), 1–37 (2019).
4. L. Deng and D. Yu, *Deep Learning: Methods and Applications*. Hanover, MA: Now Publishers (2014).
5. Y. LeCun, Y. Bengio, and G. Hinton, Deep learning. *Nature*, **521**, 436–444 (2015).
6. J. Schmidhuber, A local learning algorithm for dynamic feedforward and recurrent networks. *Connection Science*, **1**(4), 403–412 (1989).
7. Y. Wu, M. Schuster, Z. Chen, Q.V. Le, M. Norouzi, W. Macherey *et al.*, Google's neural machine translation system: Bridging the gap between human and machine translation, arxiv.org/abs/1609.08144 (2016).
8. M. de Prado, J. Su, R. Saeed, L. Keller, N. Vallez, A. Anderson *et al.*, Bonseyes AI Pipeline — Bringing AI to you. End-to-end integration of data, algorithms and deployment tools, arxiv.org/abs/1901.05049 (2019).
9. E. Prem, A digital transformation business model for innovation, in *Proc. ISPIM Innovation Summit*, 1–11, Brisbane, Australia (December 2015).
10. I. Cockburn, R. Henderson, and S. Stern, The impact of artificial intelligence on innovation, Working Paper No. w24449. National Bureau of Economic Research, Cambridge, MA (2018). Available at: https://www.nber.org/papers/w24449 (accessed on April 14, 2021).

11. J. Liu, H. Chang, J. Forrest Yi-Lin, and B. Yang, Influence of artificial intelligence on technological innovation: Evidence from the panel data of China's manufacturing sector. *Technological Forecasting & Social Change*, **158**(2), 120142 (2020).

12. N. Haefner, J. Wincent, V. Parida, and O. Gassmann, Artificial intelligence and innovation management: A review, framework, and research agenda. *Technological Forecasting & Social Change*, **162**, 120392 (2021).

13. E. Prem, Artificial Intelligence for innovation in Austria. *Technology Innovation Management Review*, **9**(12), 5–15 (2019).

14. U. Paschen, C. Pitt, and J. Kitzmann, Artificial intelligence: Building blocks and an innovation typology. *Business Horizons*, **63**, 147–155 (2020).

15. Y.K. Dwivedi, L. Jughes, E. Ismagilova, G. Aarts, C. Coombs, T. Crick *et al.*, Artificial intelligence (AI): Multidisciplinary perspectives on emerging challenges, opportunities, and agenda for research, practice and policy. *International Journal of Information Management*, **57**, 101994 (2021).

16. C. Wolf, AI models and their worlds: Investigating data-driven, AI/ML Pecosystems through a work practices lens, in Sundqvist *et al.* (eds.), in *Proc. iConference 2020*, LNCE 12051, 651–664, Borås, Sweden (March 2020).

17. J. Casti, *Reality Rules*, Vols. 1 and 2. Wiley-Interscience (1992).

18. A. Kerr, M. Barry, and J. Kelleher, Expectations of artificial intelligence and the performativity of ethics: Implications for communication governance. *Big Data & Society*, **7**(1), 1–12 (2020).

19. M. Tushman and P. Anderson, Technological discontinuities and organizational environments. *Administrative Science Quarterly*, **31**(3), 439–465 (1986).

20. S. Trösterer, A. Meschtscherjakov, A. Mirnig, A. Lupp, M. Gärtner, F. McGee *et al.*, What we can learn from pilots for handovers and (de)skilling in semi-autonomous driving, in *Proc. of the 9th International Conference on Automotive User Interfaces and Interactive Vehicular Applications*, 173–182, Oldenburg, Germany (2017).

21. O. Gambelin, Brave: What it means to be an AI ethicist. *AI Ethics*, **1**, 87–91 (2021).

22. C. Cath, Governing artificial intelligence: Ethical, legal and technical opportunities and challenges. *Philosophical Transactions of the Royal Society A*, **376**(2133), (2018).

23. R. Torkzadehmahani, R. Nasirigerdeh, D. Blumenthal, T. Kacprowski, M. List, J. Matschinske *et al.*, Privacy-preserving artificial intelligence techniques in biomedicine, arXiv:2007.11621 (2020).

24. J. Weizenbaum, *Computer Power and Human Reason: From Judgment to Calculation.* New York: W. H. Freeman and Company (1976).

25. M. Vallati and A. Grassi, AI to facilitate legal analysis in the PESTLE context, in *Proc. Emerging Technology Conference (EMiT)*, 66–68, Huddersfield, UK (April 2019).

https://doi.org/10.1142/9781800611337_0004

Chapter 3

Addressing AI Traps: Realizing the Potential of AI for Innovation Trend Spotting, Monitoring and Decision-Making

Amber Geurts

TNO, The Netherlands Organisation for Applied Scientific Research
Department of Strategic Analysis & Policy
PO Box 96800, 2509 JE The Hague, The Netherlands
a.geurts@rathenau.nl

This chapter focuses on the utilization of AI to identify and monitor innovation and technology trends to support decision making. There are high expectations from the advances in AI to provide better, more timely and more complete information and insights on innovation and technology trends to support decision making. There is, however, less discussion of what it takes to develop such AI-supported monitoring of innovation, and how such new ways are introduced and affect decision-making processes. We pay specific attention to the challenges of moving towards the adoption of such AI-supported innovation monitoring capabilities. We refer to these challenges as "AI traps." Addressing such traps is important in the evaluation of the promise of AI for innovation trend spotting, as well as in preventing any disappointments with its potential outcomes. The insights developed in this chapter are therefore meant to help innovation managers realize the full potential of AI for innovation trend spotting, monitoring and, ultimately, decision-making.

1. Introduction

Led by recent improvements in big data, computing power, and machine learning technologies, Artificial Intelligence (AI) has become a topic of increasing importance within society, science, and business. Among the many possibilities of AI within the field of innovation and management, we pay specific attention to the utilization of AI to identify and monitor innovation and technology trends to support decision-making by managers (in short: AI-supported innovation monitoring). The detection of innovation and technology trends has been a central point of research for years,[1] but today's cycle of innovation, characterized by fast technological change, increased dynamisms and complexities, has heightened the importance and interest in it.[2]

To provide insights into innovation and technology trends and monitor them, companies can already utilize so-called innovation scanning services, such as Itonics Trend Radar, TrendWatching, Thought Works Technology Radar, the EU Innovation Radar Platform, or Google trends.[a] Although such radars have started to incorporate AI to identify innovation and technology trends, their use to detect emerging technologies or innovations is often inadequate. That is, for novel and emerging technologies or innovations the dominant terminology might not yet have appeared (divergence of terminology).[3] Combined with the aforementioned accelerating pace of technological innovation, decision makers face the challenge of identifying relevant topics as early as possible[4] in order to support decision-making. To address such information and intelligence needs, improved search strategies are still required. Such search strategies should rely on different types of data and have the ability to learn and build up knowledge over time. AI represents an opportunity to explore such new strategic possibilities for innovation and technology trend spotting, monitoring and decision making.[3]

In this chapter, we start by briefly discussing the many opportunities of AI to detect and monitor innovation trends and their trajectory over time to support decision making. Next, we build upon our experiences in two recent projects focusing on developing such AI-supported innovation monitoring to highlight the challenges innovation managers face to realize the potential of AI for innovation trend spotting, monitoring and decision

---

[a]Websites of such innovation and technology trend radars include: www.itonics-innovation. com/trend-radar, https://www.innoradar.eu/, https://www.thoughtworks.com/radar/faq, https://trendwatching.com/.

making without ending up with disappointing results. We refer to those challenges as *AI traps*. By highlighting the opportunities of AI-supported innovation and technology trend spotting in combination with addressing the AI traps that stand in the way to realize the promise of AI, we develop insights that could help innovation managers realize the potential of AI for innovation trend spotting, monitoring and, ultimately, decision making.

2. The Potential of AI for Innovation Trend Spotting, Monitoring and Decision-Making

As emerging technologies like AI, Virtual/Augmented Reality (VR/AR), Internet of things (IoT), blockchain, or quantum computing technologies, have an increasing impact on the way we live and the way we do business, the topic of technology emergence is of increasing scholarly interest. However, the evolution and (future) impact of such emerging, potentially disruptive, technologies on existing industrial sectors is highly uncertain and equivocal[5]: it remains a challenge to trace emerging technologies and innovations over time, or to identify related enablers, inhibitors, weak signals, and/or tipping points surrounding such technologies that could inform decision makers. The accelerating pace of technological innovation and social change further exposes firm to an increasingly complex space of strategic options.[6] As a result, innovation managers increasingly struggle to examine trends in such new and emerging technologies — even though today's high-paced cycle of innovation places more emphasis than ever on the management of innovation and technology.

Despite organizations' strong incentive to look for and detect emerging innovation and technology trends at an early stage to develop relevant organizational responses and courses of action, a major part of such decision-making activities is still performed relying on manual labor from experts and managers. Nevertheless, over the years, increasingly more data has become available for analysis and interpretation. Furthermore, the recent renewed interest in AI appears to create an opportunity for innovation managers to explore new possibilities to identify trends around new and emerging technologies and innovations.[3] AI algorithms can reveal patterns in data and are uniquely capable to help identify and trace emerging innovation and technology trends. We discuss this potential in more detail in Sections 2.1 and 2.2.

2.1. *The potential of AI*

AI has been established as an academic discipline within computer science in the 1950's. Initially, it was defined as the process of *making a machine behave in ways that would be called intelligent if humans were so behaving*.[7] Nowadays, AI encompasses efforts ranging from building a general-purpose technology (*broad AI*) to AI's that perform narrow classification, prediction and optimization tasks (*narrow AI*).[8]

Over time, AI research has gone through many cycles of popularity.[9] The current renewed interest in AI has been triggered by advancements in *machine learning* (ML), the computer science field that focuses on how to construct computer programs that automatically improve with experience.[10] The field of ML can be further divided into different subfields, which include *supervised machine learning* (ML algorithms are trained on input-output pairs from a real process to produce optimal outputs for unseen inputs) and *unsupervised machine learning* (ML algorithms are only given input data but no output and tasked with a learning objective).[11] Algorithms to analyze patterns in unstructured data sources include, among others, text mining, Natural Language Processing (NLP), topic-modeling via Latent Dirichlet Allocation (LDA), unassisted Hierarchical Dirichlet Process, and Deep Learning (DL) methods based on artificial neural networks.[6,12–14] There is an increased interest in the application of such algorithms within the field of innovation trend spotting, monitoring, and decision-making.

2.2. *The potential of AI for innovation trend spotting, monitoring and decision making*

AI is poised to create unprecedented possibilities to develop data-supported and meaningful insights in future technology and innovation trends in order to support the management of technology and innovation.[3,14,15] ML algorithms can reveal patterns from both labeled/structured and unstructured datasets.[11,13,16] As a result, emerging technology and innovation trends or relations between trends could be identified even before they have recognizably been established within a certain domain. Furthermore, it is possible to detect changes in a trend, such as trend growth/decline or trend shift/stability. The continuous input of new data can make this process also more "real-time" than before, identifying shifts and changes in emerging patterns before humans might do so.

Still, although AI is said to present the possibility to make predictions or decisions more timely and adaptive to changes in context than before, applying AI for new and emerging innovation trends is challenging: it is difficult to grasp the relationships among innovation ideas that consist of unknown dimensions that constantly change over time in ways that can be difficult to anticipate or measure.[3,17] Nevertheless, an increasing number of studies take up the challenge to utilize AI for innovation trend spotting, monitoring and decision making. For instance, studies have started to explore the possibilities introduced by AI to spot innovation trends around topics such as AI or Mobility-as-a-Service (MaaS)[6,12] or innovative companies.[18] Furthermore, studies have started to explore the possibilities of AI to detect the rate and direction of innovation to identify, for instance, early convergence around emerging innovation topics.[17,19,20] The study of Ref. [17, p. 1], for instance, shows how the utilization of an unsupervised machine learning algorithm *provides a leading indicator of shift in innovation topics and enables a more precise analysis of movement in ideas space. Working with such measures is important because it enables more accurate estimates of the direction of innovation.* Furthermore, the study described in Ref. [20] not only shows the rate and direction of shift in innovation topics, but also contrasts the shifts in the academic field from shifts in the private sector. By doing so, the study shows that AI research in private sector organizations tends to be less diverse than research in academia. In addition, AI researchers from the private sector also tend to focus mostly on deep learning, with limited attention for the societal or ethical implications of AI.

3. Realizing the AI Innovation Potential and Addressing the AI Traps

As mentioned, there is great excitement about the advances in AI, and the opportunities AI introduces for improved, data-driven decision making.[14,15] AI is set to provide better, more timely and more complete information and insights to support decision making. There is, however, less discussion of what it takes to develop AI-supported innovation monitoring and how such new ways are introduced and affect decision-making processes.

We base our insights on our experiences from two recent innovation trend spotting and monitoring projects (see Box 1). Based on these two projects, we argue that the implementation and operationalization of AI within organizations introduces specific *challenges* that hamper or even slow down the process of utilizing AI for decision making. Addressing such challenges is important as it might result in disappointing results when those challenges are left unaddressed. The realization of the promise of AI, requires emphasizing these challenges of moving toward AI-supported innovation monitoring to detect innovation trends and/or their directionality and trajectory. We refer to those challenges as *AI traps*.

Our research — see Box 1 — points to four key challenges or AI traps associated with moving toward AI-supported innovation monitoring.

Box 1: Utilizing AI for innovation trend spotting, monitoring and decision making in two projects

We have developed insights based on reflections on two recent innovation trend spotting projects — renamed for this chapter as follows:

(1) *The future outlook project (FO-project)* in which AI algorithms have been used to identify emerging innovation and technology trends in the field of Mobility-as-a-Service (MaaS),[b] and

(2) *The innovation monitor of AI project (IMAI)* in which the aim has been to utilize AI algorithms to identify emerging trends in the field of AI in the Netherlands, and to show the findings of this novel identification method in an innovation dashboard with compelling visuals.

---

[b]MaaS brings together the planning, booking and payment of all possible transportation options via apps. Such transportation options are not limited to trains, trams and taxis, but also includes shared bikes, cars, and scooters. MaaS then enables the smart combination of all these types of transport so that journeys can be customized according to the traveller's wishes.

In both projects, the aim has been to explore the use of AI (specifically Natural Language Processing — a subfield of AI focused on processing human language) to strengthen innovation trend spotting and monitoring activities regarding emerging technologies. To do so, a domain ontology[c] has been created through a structured knowledge elicitation process in which both expert knowledge and data sources have been consulted. The resulting knowledge model is used as input for a rule-based classifier, which classifies results according to a preferred output.

Both projects have been undertaken in close collaboration with innovation managers and innovation policy makers, who have been involved throughout the entire process to reflect on and evaluate the (intermediate) results and their relevance for decision making. During the run-time of these projects, the role of AI in managerial decision processes has been explored in more depth. The analysis of these processes has resulted in the identification of four key challenges for organizations when moving towards AI-supported innovation monitoring.

The AI traps that were identified are as follows.

(1) *Overreliance on easily accessible quantitative big data: data looking for a strategic issue.* Overreliance on easily accessible quantitative data is a challenge that popped-up early in the research process. At the start of the project, the key objective focused on utilizing AI to address a specified strategic issue. For instance, in the IMAI-project the aim was to identify innovative companies that produce AI technologies. In the FO-project, on the other hand, the aim was to not only identify trends around MaaS technologies, but also to identify the impact on job market transitions. While the aim was clear, soon the following question arose: how the issue at hand can be addressed with the data that is (easily) available. Rather than question-guided data collection, the issue at hand was reformulated to match the data the research team had easy access to. As a consequence, the question what

---

[c]Ontologies originate from the semantic study of concepts and relations and incorporate and formalize domain knowledge through graphical structures that link concepts through semantically motivated relations.[11]

type/kind of data is best suited to address specific types of questions was neglected. To address this AI trap, more attention should therefore be given to the possibility of collecting different types of data and their suitability for answering different types of questions. Ultimately, this comes down to the need of methodological discipline in pursuing the initial project objective, i.e., the need for an alignment between the project objective, the methodology and the data that would provide the best way to meet the objective.

(2) *High demand for dashboards: acquiring insights in just a few clicks.* Dashboards that include enticing graphics are almost an integral part to any AI-supported innovation trend spotting project. The key aim of dashboards is to display the insights from the AI-supported analysis in the form of "insightful" and "visual" graphs on an easily accessible site, making the information available in "just a few clicks." As a result of this emphasis on displaying results on dashboards, the translation of data-driven results to meaningful insights for strategic innovation management issues is often ignored. In the IMAI project for instance, the aim was to identify innovative companies that produce AI algorithms in the Netherlands. The first result was, indeed, a very interesting looking graph of the Netherlands, divided by provinces, that showcased the number of companies working on the production of AI algorithms. For strategic decision making, however, knowing the number of innovative companies is nice but not necessarily insightful. Rather, information is needed on what type of company is this (e.g., incumbent/new entrant, large/SME/start-up, sector, etc.) and on which AI technologies those firms focus including what the trend is in those topics (e.g., increasing/decreasing attention). Based on such insights, innovation managers and policy makers can make strategic decisions about the emerging technology. To address the AI trap of missing the potential of AI, it is necessary to include sufficient time and resources to the formulation of the information needs of innovation managers and policy makers early in the process, and the refinement of the AI-supported insights so that they start to provide answers to those information needs later on in the process. This requires a research team that includes innovation professionals next to computer and data scientists. The challenge therefore refers to need for companies to reconsider

their talent development and management practices with a focus on integrating innovation, information technology and data management skills.

(3) *Overemphasis on AI algorithms: spending 80% of your budget on something that is 20% of interest.* Our experience shows that 80% of the project time and resources could be easily spent on getting the data in the right structure for analysis and, subsequently, getting the AI algorithm to run and produce results that are meaningful. This could be even more challenging as, in our experience, few organizations that ask for AI-supported innovation insights actually have a technological infrastructure, metadata structure or data sharing facility ready. As a result, there are often barely any resources nor time left to actually start addressing the strategic issue that was the reason for initiating the project in the first place. In the case of the FO-project, this particular trap resulted in disappointment regarding the results that had been obtained during the project. In the end, the project didn't proceed beyond a first identification of trends and the strategic questions that the innovation managers were keen to address remained largely unaddressed. As most strategic issues are time-sensitive, the trap of an overemphasis on setting up and running AI algorithms can thus result in a slow process and disappointment in the results obtained in the end. There thus remains a challenge for organizations to be prepared for the need for AI-supported insights for innovation management and take steps to ensure that they have all the necessary prerequisites.

(4) *Undervaluation of biases: too much "faith" in AI-supported insights for innovation management.* Any analysis of data is subject to bias. Even when identifying trends in innovation — a topic that perhaps doesn't elicit question over fairness right away — biases should be considered seriously. For instance, during the two projects we have discussed how biases might affect our results and identified the following sources of bias during the run-time of the projects: (a) confirmation bias (the tendency to provide (illicit) arguments that are based on ill-selected data, mental models or experience a trend "exists"); (b) recency bias (the tendency to assign greater value to recent events than to historical ones); (c) availability or selection bias (the tendency

of AI researchers to be selective in the selection of data for further processing and training); or (d) human bias (when data or algorithms are labeled or designed by humans that come with idiosyncratic knowledge, experience or mental models or trainings). Fully relying on and trusting AI-supported insights for innovation management may thus be dangerous due to such biases. To address this AI trap to realize the potential of AI managers should discuss the assumptions and biases inherent in the search process to identify innovation and technology trends and their implications for the findings. When presenting the results of AI-supported trend spotting, such limitations should be clearly indicated as assumptions under which the model works.

4. Conclusion

This chapter has highlighted the opportunities of AI to help in decision-making support, enabling fresh perspectives on the detection of innovation trends and their directionality and trajectory. There is great excitement about the advances AI, and the opportunities it introduces for improved (i.e., better, more timely, more complete) data-driven insights for decision-making. Rather than delving deeper into the many opportunities of AI for innovation management, we circumvent the allure of AI to address the challenges or AI traps that appear when moving towards AI-supported innovation monitoring to detect innovation trends and/or their directionality and trajectory.

This chapter has shown that in the practical implementation of such AI-innovation monitoring, innovation managers are often confronted with very similar AI traps: (1) overreliance on easily accessible quantitative big data; (2) high demand for dashboards; (3) overemphasis of AI algorithms; and (4) undervaluation of biases. Our discussion of these AI traps or challenges when moving toward AI-supported innovation monitoring to detect innovation trends and/or their directionality and trajectory point to the crucial role managers play in this process. That is, managers must decide on the most relevant strategic issue to address, the data and appropriate forms of analysis that could be used to address that issue, and the conclusions that can be drawn based on the analysis and in light of the issue at hand. After all, strategic issues are messy, interdependent and ill-structured and thus require not only AI-supported insights, but also expert judgment, experience, intuition and other sources of knowledge. As such, when AI is used well, it can complement, rather than substitute for, those sources of knowledge. Thus, AI can be used for innovation management, but only when technological infrastructure is in place, and awareness has grown towards the limitations of AI.

References

1. J.M. Utterback, *Mastering the Dynamics of Innovation: How Companies Can Seize Opportunities in the Face of Technological Change*. Cambridge, MA, USA: Harvard University Press (1994).
2. J.M. Coccia, Sources of technological innovation: Radical and incremental innovation problem-driven to support competitive advantage of firms. *Technology Analysis & Strategic Management*, **29**(9), 1048–1061 (2017).
3. A. Geurts, R. Gutknecht, P. Warnke, A. Goetheer, E. Schirrmeister, B. Bakker, and S. Meissner, New perspectives on data-supported foresight: The hybrid AI-expert approach. *Futures & Foresight Science* (2021). DOI: https://onlinelibrary.wiley.com/doi/full/10.1002/ffo2.99.
4. C. Mühlroth and M. Grottke, A systematic literature review of mining weak signals and trends for corporate foresight. *Journal of Business Economics*, **88**(5), 643–687 (2018).
5. Y. Ben-Haim, *Information-Gap Decision Theory: Decisions under Severe Uncertainty*, 2nd ed. New York: Wiley (2006).
6. C. Mühlroth and M. Grottke, Artificial intelligence in innovation: How to spot emerging trends and technologies. *IEEE Transactions on Engineering Management*. DOI:10.1109/TEM.2020.2989214 (2020). Available at: https://ieeexplore.ieee.org/document/9102438.
7. J. McCarthy, M. Minsky, N. Rochester, and C. Shannon, A proposal for the Dartmouth summer research project on artificial intelligence, August 31, 1955. *AI Magazine*, **27**(4), 12–14 (2006). https://doi.org/10.1609/aimag.v27i4.1904.
8. S. Russell and P. Norvig, *Artificial Intelligence: A Modern Approach*, 3rd ed. USA: Pearson (2009).
9. M. Boden, *AI: Its Nature and Future*. New York, NY: Oxford University Press (2016).
10. T. Mitchell, *Machine Learning*. New York: McGraw-Hill (1997).

11. L. Himanen, A. Geurts, A. Foster, and P. Rinke, Data-driven materials science: Status, challenges, perspectives. *Advanced Science*, **6**(21) 1900808 (2019).

12. B. Braaksma, P. Daas, S. Raaijmakers, A. Geurts, and A. Meyer-Vitali, AI-supported innovation monitoring, in *Proc. First International Workshop, TAILOR 2020, Trustworthy AI — Integrating Learning, Optimization and Reasoning*, Virtual Event, September 2020.

13. Y. LeCun, Y. Bengio, and G. Hinton, Deep learning. *Nature*, **521**(7553), 436–444 (2015).

14. A. Porter, Data Analytics for better informed technology & engineering management. *IEEE Engineering Management Review*, **47**(3), 29–32 (2019).

15. M.J. Mazzei and D. Noble, Big data dreams: A framework for corporate strategy. *Business Horizons*, **60**(3), 405–414 (2017).

16. G. Von Krogh, Artificial intelligence in organizations: New opportunities for phenomenon-based theorizing. *Academy of Management Discoveries*, **4**, 404–409 (2018).

17. F. Teodoridis, J. Lu, and J. Furman, Measuring the direction of innovation: Frontier tools in unassisted machine learning (May 8, 2020). Available at SSRN: https://ssrn.com/abstract=3596233; http://dx.doi.org/10.2139/ssrn.3596233.

18. P. Daas and S. van der Doef, Detecting innovative companies via their website. *Statistical Journal of the IAOS*, **36**, 1–13 (2020).

19. J.L. Furman and F. Teodiridis, Machine learning could improve innovation policy. *Nature Machine Intelligence*, **2**(2), 84–84 (2020).

20. L. Klinger, J. Mateos-Garcia, and K. Stahoulopoulos, A narrowing of AI research? (September 24, 2020). Available at SSRN: https://ssrn.com/abstract=3698698; http://dx.doi.org/10.2139/ssrn.3698698.

Chapter 4

Social Media Video Analysis for Entrepreneurial Opportunity Discovery in Artificial Intelligence

Mika Westerlund* and Maham Aman[†]

Technology Innovation Management Program
Sprott School of Business, Carleton University
1125 Colonel By Drive, Ottawa, ON K1S 5B6, Canada
*mika.westerlund@carleton.ca
[†]mahamaman@gmail.com

This study uses topic modeling to analyze contents of 159 "expert talks" videos on artificial intelligence (AI), obtained from TEDx Talks channel on YouTube, in order to examine the feasibility of social media video analysis for entrepreneurial opportunity discovery, identify prominent niches and suggest potential entrepreneurial opportunities in AI. The study identifies six AI application areas based on the results from the analysis and interprets them using relevant scholarly literature. Further, the chapter provides insight into entrepreneurial opportunities within those application areas and concludes with lessons learned. The chapter contributes to the book's theme by examining how AI technologies could help the early stages of the innovation management process.

1. Introduction

Entrepreneurial opportunity discovery is vital for new ventures.[1] While opportunity discovery often relies on "internal factors," including the entrepreneur's prior knowledge and experience,[2] various "external factors" such as technological advances, changes in political or regulatory climate, and major demographic shifts contribute to the emergence and detection of potential opportunities.[3] For instance, artificial intelligence (AI) as an emerging technology provides entrepreneurs with ample business opportunities. The global spending on AI is expected to grow from US$50 billion in 2020 to over US$110 billion in 2024, with an increasing emphasis on various AI services.[4]

In the 2020s, AI will become as much part of our everyday life as the Internet and social media did in the past.[5] However, AI's rapid growth can leave entrepreneurs baffled about what could be prominent application areas. Research and development of AI are driven by industrial demands,[6] because industries including healthcare, transportation, and manufacturing will benefit from AI in numerous ways.[7] Companies can use AI to optimize, automate and transform the nature of their business and innovation processes, provide better services, and constitute higher quality and lower costs.[8–10] However, research on AI from the application perspective has focused on specific business functions such as marketing,[11,12] customer relationship management,[13] human resource management,[14] and technology-assisted decision-making.[15]

The identification of entrepreneurial opportunities in AI can benefit from the use of external insight, including expert opinions, forecast of novel business trajectories, and comparison of different future visions.[16] Recent research has proposed the mining of social media as means to discover entrepreneurial opportunities.[17] Machine learning applications such as topic modeling have been hailed useful with social media data.[18] At the same time, it has become increasingly easy to scrape contents of videos published on social media platforms, which has enabled scholars and firms to use publicly available videos to gain valuable insight.

This chapter uses topic modeling on a sample of "expert talks" videos from TEDx Talks channel on YouTube to (1) examine the feasibility of social media video analysis for entrepreneurial opportunity discovery and (2) identify prominent niches and potential entrepreneurial opportunities in AI. The approach is method-driven, meaning that we first analyze the social media video data using machine learning to find relevant topics in expert talks. Then, we use scholarly literature to interpret the topics and gain insight into entrepreneurial opportunities within the topics. The benefits of this method include that it is faster and takes less effort than conventional methods. Further, entrepreneurial opportunity discovery in this method is guided by expert opinions, providing relevance, and the interpretation is enriched with emerging research, providing rigor.

The chapter is organized as follows: we will start by explaining the obtained social media video data and our method of analysis. Then, we will interpret and report the results from the analysis. Thereafter, we discuss potential entrepreneurial opportunities for AI applications related to specific application domains and as part of the early stages of the innovation management process in general. Finally, we conclude by discussing the key lessons learned.

2. Method

This study applies a machine-learning based content analysis method "topic modeling" on a sample of TEDx "expert talks" videos on YouTube to identify what AI experts consider as prominent application areas in AI. The contents and metadata of 159 "expert talks" videos were found and obtained in September 2019 using YouTube's search engine on TEDx Talks channel. We used "artificial intelligence" and "AI" as keywords. The criteria for including an expert talk into our data set were threefold: the objective criteria that (1) the expert talk was given in English and (2) YouTube's auto-captioning option provided a transcript of the content, as well as the subjective criterion that (3) the title of the video suggested the talk was relevant from the perspective of our study.

All of the videos in our data set were published between June 2013 and September 2019. Only a few "expert talks" on AI were published in the first years of this timeframe, and the majority (83%) of them dated from 2017 to 2019 (Fig. 1). This was quite expected, given that the topic of AI has only recently grown in popularity, the number of videos uploaded to YouTube annually is growing at a rapid speed, and the TEDx concept has grown in recent years. The average length of videos in our data set was 14 minutes and 27 seconds, and the combined number of views of those videos exceeded 9 million at the time of data collection. While 129 (81%) of the expert talks were provided by a male presenter, only 30 (19%) were provided by a female presenter, suggesting a gender bias in AI experts.

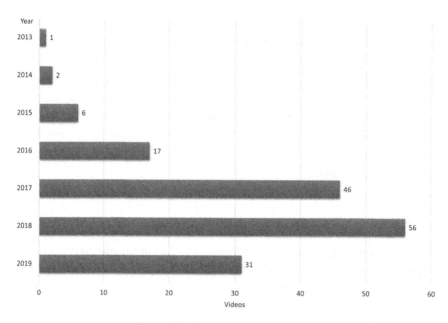

Fig. 1. Distribution of videos by year.

In order to further understand the "expert talks" chosen for our study, we saved and analyzed metadata for each video. This metadata included the title of the video, URL, presenter's name and gender, upload date, length of the video, as well as the number of views, comments and likes and dislikes. First, we categorized the 25 most viewed videos based on their upload date to understand how popular expert talks have evolved over time. Based on the video titles, the topics of the oldest "popular expert talks" in our data set had generic focus on explaining the audience what AI is in general and what it means for the future of humanity. This was unsurprising, given that only a while ago, most people probably knew little about the topic. Recent "popular expert talks" were more focused on specific areas, for example, how AI and other emerging technologies such as blockchain can be merged to create societal and business value.

Second, we categorized the top 25 "popular expert talks" by their number of comments. Interestingly, videos whose title reflected negative sentiment of AI, suggesting for example that humans should be concerned about AI because it will destroy the humanity, received more comments as

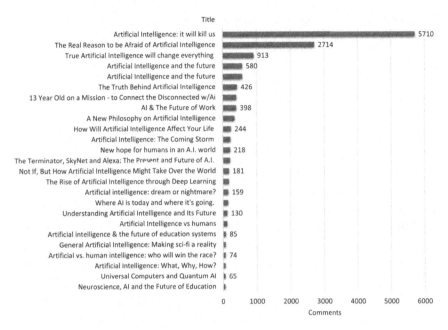

Fig. 2. Number of comments for the 25 most viewed videos.

well as likes and dislikes compared to talks whose title reflected a more positive tone or addressed AI's role in a specific domain such as healthcare or education (see Fig. 2). These findings are aligned with Ref. [19] who found that the majority of comments from internet users focus on the apocalyptic and destructive nature of AI rather than AI application areas. That said, this chapter does not present further analysis of the metadata but rather focuses on the video content to identify opportunities.

The transcripts of video contents were acquired using YouTube's auto-generated captions. While automated captions provide an easy method to capture the video contents in a text format,[20] the accuracy of captioning varies by audio quality, background noise, accents, and the complexity of words. A recent study using captions from university commencement speeches found an average of one error occurring every 26 seconds.[21] TEDx Talks are recorded with high audio quality and minimal background noise, thus we deemed the accuracy acceptable. A clean transcript of each video was obtained by using the YouTube's "toggle timestamps" option, which allowed us to copy-paste the transcript onto a blank document and use word processing software to format the text. The formatted text was transferred to a spreadsheet to create a corpus for topic modeling.

Topic modeling is an automated content analysis technique designed to infer hidden topics in text corpora.[22] The text can be sourced from anywhere including emails, book chapters, blog postings, social media posts such as tweets, journal articles, news articles, open-ended survey responses, and any other kind of unstructured text. While topic modeling began as a field about finding structure in written texts, it has since become a method that can exploit grouped data in many settings.[23] It can also be applied for the analysis of images, video content, sound features, generic markers, computer source code, and so on, as long as the data can be converted into applicable text format.[22,23] As speech on the "expert talks" videos were available as transcripts, topic modeling was deemed highly suitable method for the analysis.

In specific, our study relies on Latent Dirichlet Allocation (LDA). LDA is hierarchical probabilistic model used to decompose a collection of documents into a number of topics,[22] and it provides a quick and automated way to summarize large document collections. LDA discovers abstract topics in the corpus based on clusters and frequency of words found in each document. We used Orange 3.22 software package[24] with text mining widget to analyze the corpus of video transcripts. During the analysis we inputted a number of stop words to exclude noise from the model.[23] Of note, researchers have to select the number of topics to be generated.[25] After trying various number of topics, we considered six topics providing the best model. The chosen model avoided overlap in topics and allowed a good interpretability of the topics. Each topic had ten characteristic keywords that helped us to interpret and label the topic.

3. Results

The topic modeling analysis revealed six topics in the investigated "expert talks": (1) saving biodiversity, (2) automation, (3) diplomacy, (4) quantum computation, (5) healthcare, and (6) societal impacts (see Table 1). These topics were labeled based on their keywords and interpreted to provide

Table 1. Topic labels based on their keywords.

Topic	Keywords	Label
1	Biodiversity, nutrients, revolutionary, ecological, universities, sightings, conservation, memorize, forests, preceded	Saving biodiversity
2	Trades, industrialized, specialist, craftsmen, mindset, repeatable, cautioned, guilds, tossed, cautioning	Automation
3	Diplomacy, intensive, polarization, negotiation, ambassador, negotiating, European, attract, coalition, disrupting	Diplomacy
4	Entropy, celled, organism, combust, nano, wires, slime, mold, choosing, creatures	Quantum computing
5	Recovery, addiction, opioid, substance, Monday, epidemic, phobia, misuse, relapse, finished	Healthcare
6	Time, right, need, learning, world, know, data, human, work, years	Societal impacts

insight about entrepreneurial opportunities within each topic. In order to interpret and gain insight into potential entrepreneurial opportunities within the topics, we referred to video transcripts associated with each topic, as well as relevant scholarly literature on AI. That is, the six topics were used as "keywords" to look for related scholarly articles that could better explain the topic and suggest entrepreneurial ideas. The topics from the analysis of "expert talks" helped us to browse and organize the emerging literature on AI more efficiently and gain research-based rigor to support our interpretation and opportunity discovery.

3.1. *Saving biodiversity*

The first topic discusses how AI can contribute to environmental sustainability by helping protect the nature and save biodiversity. Whereas biodiversity ensures a balance in earth's ecosystem and gives ecological communities the ability to withstand stress, saving biodiversity is a top priority for many conservation biologists. An effective way to protect the biodiversity is to make use of relevant data. AI can analyze large volumes of environmental data to help making better decisions and taking concrete action. Advances in AI technologies, particularly "deep learning" enable automated classification of visual, spatial and acoustic data in the context of environmental conservation.[26] They unlock the ability to process huge amounts of data that signal extinction of species, identify environmental risks, and provide alerts to nature conservationists.[27]

As an example, AI can spot endangered species from aerial video taken by drones.[27] While analyzing aerial video showing animals or plants in a landscape, deep learning algorithms can distinguish endangered species from cattle, domestic animals, and least-concern animals or plants, and thus identify concentrations of vulnerable species. Further, AI can be used to classify the meaning and sentiment of social media posts to track illegal wildlife trade, including live animals and animal products sold at online marketplaces.[28] Deep learning can also help in the protection of marine biodiversity by distinguishing invasive alien species from native species based on the sounds they produce.[29] Invasive alien species are one of the most alarming threats to marine biosafety, and thus developing sound recognition to spot them is a leap towards the protection of biodiversity.

3.2. *Automation*

The second topic discusses how AI will transform the industrial landscape as a consequence of rapidly increasing automation. Recent evolution of automation is characterized by various autonomous and semi-autonomous systems such as industrial robots getting more intelligent and increasingly sophisticated thanks to technological advances in AI. In developed economies, smart automation can offer means to fight offshoring of production, as it enables economically competitive local sourcing.[19] The downside of this evolution is that automation has already eliminated a number of repetitive tasks that were previously performed by people.[30] On the other hand, while AI-based advances in automation will reduce the need for human labor in repetitive tasks, they may also provide people with new types of occupations that do not even exist today.[31]

Automation does not only apply to manufacturing industries. AI is increasingly used as part of new generations of goods and services that serve customers across the globe. For instance, connected and autonomous vehicles make one of the most highly anticipated AI-based technological developments of the present time.[32] Self-driving cars will likely radically change the way people move one place to another, as the need for a driver becomes obsolete and the autonomous vehicle can serve a large number of people rather than remain unused and parked in a garage while the owner is not riding it. Similarly, fleets of autonomous trucks can disrupt the commercial transportation industry by enabling logistics companies to have platoons of trucks with tight distances and synchronous driving capabilities, thus achieving fuel cost savings.[33] Similarly, autonomous drones can disrupt small parcel delivery in urban areas.

3.3. *Diplomacy*

The third topic is about the potential of AI to provide assistance in various areas of diplomatic interest. AI impacts diplomacy particularly in two ways; first, by changing the environment in which diplomacy is practiced; and second, by offering new tools for diplomats to aid them in their activities.[34] Such tools can help staff at embassies and consulates to better understand other people or the nature and gravity of various events in real-time, streamline their decision-making processes, track and manage the public's expectations locally and globally, and facilitate crisis handling. AI can assist diplomats in times of crisis by helping them understand what is happening (descriptive analytics) and identify possible developments of ongoing events[35] based on historical data (predictive analytics).

For instance, AI can be useful in negotiations, by helping diplomats to analyze past negotiations and predict the outcome of current negotiations or other diplomatic processes.[35] On the flipside, AI also raises potential challenges for state sovereignty.[36] The integration of AI into military operations and weapon systems can facilitate state-led cyberattacks, fake news, and deepfake campaigns against foreign states, organizations and citizens to achieve political goals[37] or create a fear-factor. Advanced AI weapon systems can change the nature of warfare. The use of "killer robots" in armed conflicts is appealing because autonomous weapons are faster, safer, and more effective than only human soldiers, and because such robots can carry out lethal missions without feelings of guilt or fear.[19]

3.4. *Quantum computing*

The fourth topic discusses how AI links with quantum computing, an emerging field that relies on the quantum behavior of subatomic particles to provide superior computation and information processing capacities.[38] The development of quantum computers is a tremendous advancement and the anticipated benefits of quantum computing to business, technology and society may finally be realized.[39] Quantum technology also contributes to the development and application of more effective machine learning applications that can deal with massive parallel processing of high dimensional data.[40] In other words, powered by the superior information processing capacity of quantum computing, AI and machine learning applications are expected to become significantly more efficient and applicable to analyzing larger and more complex data sets.

Quantum computers have the potential to make a significant impact on businesses across industries as well as public sector organizations. For example, quantum computing-backed AI could reduce the time used for option pricing or risk-assessment calculations, optimizing a national-level power grid, developing more accurate environmental models, real-time optimization of traffic flows in populous cities, and discovering new chemicals and materials.[39] Other application areas include air traffic systems for aviation, space mission planning and scheduling, fault diagnosis of complex technical systems, and robust system design.[39] Further, quantum algorithms can be used to identify abnormalities in diagnostic images with high precision[40] and can thus be used as computational aid in diagnostic reasoning and neural problem-solving.[41]

3.5. *Healthcare*

The fifth topic considers the impact of AI on healthcare. Novel AI tools for diagnosis, monitoring and treatment could dramatically improve quality of care and patient outcomes, and re-balance clinician workload in psychiatry and healthcare.[42] There are numerous application areas within the healthcare sector. For example, AI could play a major role in reducing the negative impacts of opioid painkillers in pain management by providing efficient methods for risk screening, guiding patients to treatment, and matching patients with appropriate treatment resources.[43] Further, behavioral interventions, whether for the management of chronic pain, overeating, medication adherence, or substance abuse, may be ineffective outside of the clinic environments in which they are conducted. This shortcoming has sparked an interest in developing technologies that are capable of monitoring, detecting and predicting changes.[44]

National healthcare systems can benefit from AI, stretching all the way from resource allocation to complex disease diagnostic, and result in preventive, predictive, personalized and precise care.[45] AI and machine-learning solutions can improve the patient-care bond in multiple ways, including better accuracy, productivity, and workflow, thus contributing to a health system that, rather than just curing disease, can promote wellness and prevent disease before it strikes. For example, finding a clinically objective signature of opioid abuse would assist physicians in offering the proper treatment to those patients who attempt to hide their addiction. Such a composite biomarker can be detected using AI.[43] While there are many opportunities for AI in healthcare, they require ethical consideration to ensure the successful implementation of the technology.[46]

3.6. Societal impacts

The sixth topic discusses the impacts that AI will have on our society as a whole. The role of societal impacts of AI is noted in previous studies, suggesting that 70% of public discussion on AI is about its societal impacts in terms of social, economic, and environmental effects.[19] AI can bring unprecedented benefits to our society through faster, more efficient, and more meaningful analysis of data. For instance, AI allows for a low-cost, accessible way to gain insight from environmental data,[47] thus enabling farmers to analyze soil fertility and predict local weather conditions. Also, AI can help businesses to analyze complex big data to improve their operational efficiency, customer relationships, and decision-making capability, and provide customers with hyper-personalized service.[48]

Nonetheless, there are also negative impacts such as the deepening of the socio-economic divide as companies are adopting AI and robotics to replace human workforce. Also employees could benefit from the robotic process automation taking care of repetitive, dull, dirty and dangerous processes,[19] thereby allowing for humans to focus on physically safer and more motivational tasks. However, debate on AI repeatedly puts forward that AI will lead to the accumulation of wealth and power to even fewer people and cause a growing underclass of permanently unemployed and technically unskilled.[19] The topic also explores the effects that AI will have on the value of human life. Not only people gradually lose their skills as AI takes care of tasks on their behalf, but without proper safeguards in place AI may someday exceed humans in terms of physical and cognitive capabilities. AI could then perceive humans as inferior to technical systems or even as a threat, and thus enslave or destroy the humanity.

3.7. *Insight into entrepreneurial opportunities*

After interpreting the six identified topics based on the results from the topic modeling analysis and scholarly literature, we can now summarize their key points and provide some insight into potential entrepreneurial opportunities in AI regarding those topics (see Table 2).

3.7.1. *Environmental applications*

In the area of "saving biodiversity," there are numerous entrepreneurial opportunities for AI-based environmental applications. Such applications can help save the biodiversity by spotting, counting, and predicting the movement of endangered species in real-time. They make it easy for social entrepreneurs and nature conservationists to protect certain plants and animal species from danger. Thus, various environmental organizations may adopt such applications for their own use as well as sponsor a company in order to develop and make such applications public and freely available at least in developing economies.

3.7.2. *Industrial applications*

As to "automation," there is need for various industrial applications such as robotics designed for industrial production and assembly to support manufacturers in their automatization of work processes. Further, various

Table 2. Entrepreneurial opportunities in AI.

Topic	Label	Opportunities
1	Saving biodiversity	Environmental applications for social entrepreneurs and environmental organizations to protect nature and endangered species across the globe
2	Automation	Industrial applications for firms and consumers, including manufacturing robotics, autonomous systems and vehicles, digital assistants, and novel services such as roboethical consultation
3	Diplomacy	Analytical applications for governments and embassies to support maintenance of diplomatic relationships, aid in intercultural negotiations, and identify and prevent harmful disinformation
4	Quantum computing	Quantum computing applications for companies and research organizations to crunch complex data, including drug development, cybersecurity, financial modeling, and route and flow optimization systems
5	Healthcare	Medical applications for physical and mental health organizations such as clinics and hospitals to help them provide patients with preventive, predictive, personalized and precise care
6	Societal impacts	Educational applications for schools, other education sector organizations, and individuals to help citizens achieve skills to apply AI systems in everyday life and maintain their employability

autonomous systems such as autonomous vehicle solutions and service robots such as commercial and household cleaning robots, as well as smart assistants and AI chatbots in digital environments provide ample opportunities. Also, there is an emerging demand for services that do not exist today, such as roboethical consultation to ensure that a client's smart, self-learning systems embrace legally and morally righteous values.

3.7.3. Analytical applications

In regard to "diplomacy," there is need for analytical applications aimed at governments and embassies to support the creation and maintenance of diplomatic relationships, aid in intercultural negotiations, and identify and prevent disinformation. Such applications could focus on conversational aid such as real-time speech-to-speech and speech-to-text translation, or real-time sentiment analysis of speech. Further, AI could be used to analyze historical data from past negotiations to predict the outcomes of ongoing negotiations. Also, governments need tools that can identify and prevent fake news and deepfake campaigns in the online environment. Finally, there are opportunities related to cybersecurity and intelligent warfare solutions both online and in the traditional battlefield.

3.7.4. *Quantum computing applications*

"Quantum computing" provides the potential for offering a variety of quantum computation-based applications for companies and research organizations that need to analyze large amounts of complex data. AI and machine learning algorithms and tools empowered by powerful quantum computers can help companies and organizations across the globe enter a new era of drug development or create novel cybersecurity solutions and encryption models, enable more accurate and complex financial modeling, and provide solutions and systems for various route and flow optimization problems across multiple industries, for example, transportation, aviation and space industries, as well as in the public sector such as smart cities.

3.7.5. *Medical applications*

In the "healthcare" sector, physical and mental health organizations such as clinics and hospitals would benefit from AI-based medical applications that help them provide patients with preventive, predictive, personalized and precise care. For example, physicians would need analytics to help their patients maintain long-term sobriety and promote a healthier recovery process. AI could track patients' heart rate, stress levels, physical location and biomarkers and alert the doctor. Pattern detection AI and intervention technology can help empower individuals to change any unwanted behavior. Smart alert and response systems could help patients prevent addictions, depression, suicidal ideation or obesity. AI embedded with wearable technologies is a new field for solutions with human-centered design to keep people more engaged in their recovery process.

3.7.6. *Educational applications*

Finally, the topic of "societal impacts" reflects that there is need for educational applications for schools, other education sector organizations, and individuals. AI will bring a new dimension to many occupations, a fact that needs to be addressed in future education. For example, sales and customer account managers will increasingly require AI skills. Educational applications help people cope with the changes that AI may bring to our everyday lives by letting them achieve new skills needed to apply AI systems and maintain their value in the shifting employment market. Educational applications that are available to everyone can also exacerbate inequality and reduce the socio-technical divide by allowing for diverse and underrepresented populations and socio-economic groups learn how to make use of the ubiquitous AI technology.

4. Conclusion

This chapter used topic modeling to analyze 159 "expert talks" videos on AI, obtained from TEDx Talks channel on YouTube. Our objectives were to (1) examine the feasibility of social media video analysis for entrepreneurial opportunity discovery and (2) identify prominent niches and suggest potential entrepreneurial opportunities in AI. In so doing, we gathered some key lessons that should be shared for other to learn and that could be used to discuss how we met the above two objectives.

4.1. *Social media video analysis aids opportunity discovery*

Based on our experience from the application of social media video analysis for entrepreneurial opportunity discovery, we believe that the method is equally applicable to other business domain as part of the early stages of the innovation management process. Further, we suggest that it can be used for research and practice on the subject. These notions contribute to the literature on entrepreneurial opportunity discovery using social media data[7,17] by illustrating that machine-learning tools, namely topic modeling on publicly available videos of expert opinions can help in the identification of opportunities for AI applications.

Our method of starting with the machine-learning based data analysis and using the results from the analysis to look for scholarly literature that can provide support and help in interpreting the topics is different from the conventional research approach that begins with extensive literature review. Our method is faster and takes less effort, thereby providing benefits when the researcher or entrepreneur lacks time and resources to perform a thorough review of emerging literature.

There are however several limitations that anyone applying the method should keep in mind. First, they need to be able to scrape the video contents in text format. We noticed that not all TEDx "expert talks" videos were available as a transcript, even if the talk was provided in English, which is the language that probably has the best auto-captioning support on YouTube. This limitation may lead to excluding potentially interesting and relevant videos from the corpus. This is especially relevant if the corpus is small or many found videos on the subject lack transcripts.

Second, the accuracy of the auto-captioning algorithm is relevant from the perspective of data quality. Although we deemed the quality of TEDx video captions as acceptable because the "expert talks" were recorded with high audio quality and minimal background noise, we observed some obvious errors in the transcriptions. Auto-captioning is sensitive to noise and poor audio, and using the method on other than TEDx videos might result in reduced accuracy and more problems in analysis. We recommend that anyone using auto-captions would pay attention to this aspect.

Third, our examination of metadata suggested that certain kind of topics received more views, comments and (dis)likes. This suggests that even if we focus on expert opinions in the analysis, social media video analysis would significantly benefit from adding more in-depth analysis of viewers' comments and reactions. Those comments and likes might provide important insight on the topics and whether the large audience agrees with the expert opinion. Further, a sentiment analysis of "expert talks" and viewers' comments would further clarify the tone and help in understanding what topics could provide the best opportunities.

4.2. *AI presents numerous entrepreneurial opportunities*

Our topic modeling analysis of "expert talks" videos revealed six areas where AI can make a contribution and provide entrepreneurs with opportunities. We used scholarly literature on AI to provide richer interpretation of the topics. Expert opinions provided relevance whereas scholarly literature provided rigor in terms of details and researched information, suggesting that the identified application areas should be considered viable options when looking for entrepreneurial opportunities.

Based on the analysis, we suggested six entrepreneurial opportunities for AI applications, namely: (1) environmental applications, (2) industrial applications, (3) analytical applications, (4) quantum computing applications, (5) medical applications, and (6) educational applications. There are several aspects that need to be highlighted regarding them. First, some of these areas are more established than the others. For example, contemporary research and development in AI is heavily driven by industrial needs, and there are already firms on the market focusing on industrial robotics, AI-driven business support systems, and autonomous vehicles. Conversely, quantum computing is barely leaping out of the lab,[49] suggesting the area is in very early stage of development with little competition. That said, both areas have ample opportunities.

Second, the analysis revealed some opportunities that are less obvious and provide interesting niche areas. We believe that the "expert talks" video analysis helped us to track such niche areas and identify somewhat unusual opportunities. For example, while environmental applications are an unsurprising area, using AI to specifically distinguish endangered marine species from others by the sounds they produce is less obvious to many. Also, analytical applications that are specifically designed for use in diplomacy make an unexpected niche. Thus, the results contribute to our understanding on AI advancements by revealing application areas that have not been central to the attention of public discussion.[50]

Third, although we suggested application areas and entrepreneurial opportunities, they remain at somewhat superficial level. Entrepreneurs can benefit from this study as it may help them identify areas that AI experts have noted and get ideas for specific application types. However, there are numerous other factors that matter when choosing an opportunity to focus. These include entrepreneur's experience in the area, access to market, current state of competition, and regulatory, legal and ethical aspects, among others. Nevertheless, we believe that our method and findings provide AI scholars and entrepreneurs with useful ideas. Opportunity discovery is a key component of the early stages of innovation management. Thus, the chapter contributes to the book's theme on how AI technologies could help in enhancing innovation management practices.

References

1. H. Guo, J. Tang, Z. Su, and J.A. Katz, Opportunity recognition and SME performance: The mediating effect of business model innovation. *R&D Management*, **47**(3), 431–442 (2016).
2. S.F. Costa, M.L. Ehrenhard, A. Caetano, and S.C. Santos, The role of different opportunities in the activation and use of the business opportunity prototype. *Creativity and Innovation Management*, **25**(1), 58–72 (2016).
3. R. Suddaby, G.D. Bruton, and S.X. Si, Entrepreneurship through a qualitative lens: Insights on the construction and/or discovery of entrepreneurial opportunity. *Journal of Business Venturing*, **30**(1), 1–10 (2015).
4. S. Soohoo, R. Membrila, T. Manabe, A. Minonne, and J. George, Worldwide Artificial Intelligence Spending Guide (V2 2020). International Data Corporation (2020). Available at: https://www.idc.com.
5. M. Haenlein and A. Kaplan, A brief history of artificial intelligence: On the past, present, and future of artificial intelligence. *California Management Review*, **61**(4), 5–14 (2019).
6. Y. Pan, Heading toward artificial intelligence 2.0. *Engineering*, **2**(4), 409–413 (2016).
7. C. Vocke, C. Constantinescu, and D. Popescu, Application potentials of artificial intelligence for the design of innovation processes. *Procedia CIRP*, **84**, 810–813 (2019).
8. V. Gherheş, Artificial intelligence: Perception, expectations, hopes and benefits. *Romanian Journal of Human — Computer Interaction*, **11**(3), 220–231 (2018).

9. S. Russell, D. Dewey, and M. Tegmark, Research priorities for robust and beneficial artificial intelligence. *AI Magazine*, **36**(4), 105–114 (2015).
10. I.M. Cockburn, R. Henderson, and S. Stern, *The impact of Artificial Intelligence on innovation*. NBER Working Paper No. w24449, Cambridge, MA (2018).
11. G. Overgoor, M. Chica, W. Rand, and A. Weishampel, Letting the computers take over: Using AI to solve marketing problems. *California Management Review*, **61**(4), 156–185 (2019).
12. N. Wirth, Hello marketing, what can artificial intelligence help you with? *International Journal of Market Research*, **60**(5), 435–438 (2018).
13. J.K.-U. Brock, and F. von Wangenheim, Demystifying AI: What digital transformation leaders can teach you about realistic artificial intelligence. *California Management Review*, **61**(4), 110–134 (2019).
14. P. Tambe, P. Cappelli, and V. Yakubovich, Artificial intelligence in human resources management: Challenges and a path forward. *California Management Review*, **61**(4), 15–42 (2019).
15. Y.R. Shrestha, S.M. Ben-Menahem, and G. von Krogh, Organizational decision-making structures in the age of artificial intelligence. *California Management Review*, **61**(4), 66–83 (2019).
16. S.L. Jarvenpaa, and L. Välikangas, Opportunity creation in innovation networks: Interactive revealing practices. *California Management Review*, **57**(1), 67–87 (2014).
17. N.Ko, B. Jeong, S. Choi, and J. Yoon, Identifying product opportunities using social media mining: Application of topic modeling and chance discovery theory. *IEEE Access*, **6**, 1680–1693 (2018).
18. B. Jeong, J. Yoon, and J.-M. Lee, Social media mining for product planning: A product opportunity mining approach based on topic modeling and sentiment analysis. *International Journal of Information Management*, **48**, 280–290 (2019).
19. M. Westerlund, The ethical dimensions of public opinion on smart robots. *Technology Innovation Management Review*, **10**(2), 25–36 (2020).
20. M. Westerlund, D.A. Isabelle, and S. Leminen, A machine-learning analysis of videos on entrepreneurial fear of failure, in *Proc. from the ISPIM Connects Global 2020 Conference*, December 2020.
21. J.-H. Lee and K.-W. Cha, An analysis of the errors in the auto-generated captions of university commencement speeches on YouTube 2020. *Journal of Asia TEFL*, **17**(1), 143–159 (2020).
22. D.M. Blei, Probabilistic topic models. *Communications of the ACM*, **55**(4), 77–84 (2012).

23. T. Schmiedel, O. Muller, and J. vom Brocke, Topic modeling as a strategy of inquiry in organizational research. *Organizational Research Methods*, **22**(4), 941–968 (2018).
24. Orange 3.22 (2019). https://orangedatamining.com/.
25. D. Maier, A. Waldherr, P. Miltner, G. Wiedemann, A. Niekler, A. Keinert, *et al.*, Applying LDA topic modeling in communication research: Toward a valid and reliable methodology. *Communication Methods and Measures*, **12**(2–3), 93–118 (2018).
26. A. Lamba, P. Cassey, R.R. Segaran, and L.P. Koh, Deep learning for environmental conservation. *Current Biology*, **29**(19), R977-R9822019 (2019).
27. A. Bhattacharyya, L. Jansen, M. Kleinke, and R. Hartanto, Toward automated biodiversity research on the tropical ecosystem using artificial intelligence, in *Proc. from the Tropentag 2019 Conference on International Research on Food Security, Natural Resource Management and Rural Development*, Kassel, Germany (September 2019).
28. E. Di Minin, C. Fink, T. Hiippala, and H. Tenkanen, A framework for investigating illegal wildlife trade on social media with machine learning. *Conservation Biology*, **33**(1), 210–213 (2019).
29. K. Demertzis, L.S. Iliadis, and A. Vardis-Dimitris, Extreme deep learning in biosecurity: The case of machine hearing for marine species identification. *Journal of Information and Telecommunication*, **2**(4), 492–510 (2018).
30. S. Makridakis, The forthcoming artificial intelligence (AI) revolution: Its impact on society and firms. *Futures*, **90**, 46–60 (2017).
31. A. Agrawal, J. Gans, and A. Goldfarb, The Economics of Artificial Intelligence: An Agenda. The University of Chicago Press, Chicago, IL (2019).
32. D. Bissell, T. Birtchnell, A. Elliott, and E.L. Hsu, Autonomous automobilities: The social impacts of driverless vehicles. *Current Sociology*, **68**(1), 116–134 (2020).
33. S.E. Shladover, Connected and automated vehicle systems: Introduction and overview. *Journal of Intelligent Transportation Systems*, **22**(3), 190–200 (2018).
34. S. Grottola, Artificial intelligence and diplomacy: A new tool for diplomats? DiploFoundation (2018). https://www.diplomacy.edu/blog/artificial-intelligence-and-diplomacy-new-tool-diplomats.
35. C. Bjola, Diplomacy in the age of artificial intelligence. EDA Working Paper, January 2020, Emirates Diplomatic Academy (2020).

36. D. Kim, Artificial Intelligence in East Asia: An Overview from the Canadian Perspective. Asia Pacific Foundation of Canada, Canada, BC (2019).
37. M. Westerlund, The emergence of deepfake technology: A review. *Technology Innovation Management Review*, **9**(11), 40–53 (2019).
38. Y. Wang, Quantum computation and quantum information. *Statistical Science*, **27**(3), 373–394 (2012).
39. Y. Kanamori and S.-M. Yoo, Quantum computing: Principles and applications. *Journal of International Technology and Information Management*, **29**(2), article 3 (2020).
40. V. Dunjko and H.J. Briegel, Machine learning & artificial intelligence in the quantum domain: A review of recent progress, *Reports on Progress in Physics*, **81**(7), 074001 (2018).
41. A. Wichert, *Principles of Quantum Artificial Intelligence*. Singapore: World Scientific Publishing (2014).
42. D. Solenov, J. Brieler, and J.F. Scherrer, The potential of quantum computing and machine learning to advance clinical research and change the practice of medicine. *Missouri Medicine*, **115**(5), 463–467 (2018).
43. R.J. Ellis, Z. Wang, N. Genes, and A. Ma'Ayan, Predicting opioid dependence from electronic health records with machine learning. *BioData Mining*, **12**, 3 (2019).
44. E.W. Boyer, R. Fletcher, R.J. Fay, D. Smelson, D. Ziedonis, and R. W. Picard, Preliminary efforts directed toward the detection of craving of illicit substances: The iHeal project. *Journal of Medical Toxicology*, **8**(1), 5–9 (2012).
45. A. Meiliana, N.M. Dewi, and A. Wijaya, Artificial intelligent in healthcare. *Indonesian Biomedical Journal*, **11**(2), 125–135 (2019).
46. C.A. Lovejoy, V. Buch, and M. Maruthappu, Technology and mental health: The role of artificial intelligence. *European Psychiatry*, **55**, 1–3 (2019).
47. S. Russell, D. Dewey, and M.E. Tegmark, Research priorities for robust and beneficial artificial intelligence. *AI Magazine*, **36**(4), 105–114 (2015).
48. N. Ameen, A. Tarhini, A. Reppel, and A. Anand, Customer experiences in the age of artificial intelligence. *Computers in Human Behavior*, **114**, 106548 (2021).
49. D. Castelvecchi, Quantum computers ready to leap out of the lab in 2017. *Nature*, **541**(7635), 9–10 (2017).
50. OECD, *Artificial Intelligence in Society*. Paris: OECD Publishing (2019).

Chapter 5

AI-Driven Innovation: Towards a Conceptual Framework

Sergey Yablonsky

St.-Petersburg State University, Graduate School of Management
IT in Management Department
Volkovskiy per., 3, St. Petersburg, 199004, Russia
s.yablonsky@spbu.ru

The main purpose of this chapter is to discuss AI-driven innovations. Generally, the links between AI technology, AI usage, and organizational performance remain unclear. To improve the efficiency of artificial intelligence implementation, reduce costs and shape new business opportunities, firms should understand the features, capabilities, and the impact of these innovations on business models, business processes and employees. This area however is very little studied. To address this gap, an AI-driven value chain framework is proposed, which makes it possible to create a reference model (taxonomy) of AI-driven innovation processes and innovation types. Finally, an AI organization maturity model and an AI-driven maturity framework are discussed.

1. Introduction

Artificial intelligence (AI), with its sub disciplines machine learning (ML) and deep learning (DL), has been widely discussed in fundamental and information technology (IT) literature.[1-6] Since its first mentioning in 1951,[7] AI has become an essential component of the IT paradigm and a contributor and prerequisite to overall organizational success.[8,9] Therefore, AI has gained steadily increasing managerial and scientific attention.

Over the time, the role of AI and its impact have progressed and become an organizational capability of strategic importance.[3,10,11]

AI needs large amounts of data. With the adoption of digital platforms in the context of organizational forms that have become significant over the past decades,[12] data has become a kind of raw material and basis for a new infrastructure used to generate revenue. Nowadays, a digital platform together with its related ecosystems (industrial, data or otherwise), is positioned to create and capture value in digital economies.[12-19] With billions of consumers and providers connected through digital platforms and engaging with other users almost continuously, digital platforms record and analyze enormous amounts of user-generated data, tracked via cookies and other services.[19] Where there is data, there is value. Data and analytics are central to success in the platform business. But successful platform growth and scaling requires more data, more complex data, more variables, and more sophisticated analysis by more business people, beyond what can be done manually. Therefore, the use of artificial intelligence can solve such problems.

The vast array of available Big Data (BD) and the rapid evolution of AI insights and services have given rise to some visibility of technology abundance. This virtuous cycle between BD and AI will initially have the greatest impact on different types of AI applications. However, while most organizations have enough data processing solutions, products, and vendors, they are typically lacking a single view into what AI-driven innovation(s) and transformation services they need to use.

AI reshapes companies and how innovation management is organized. Enterprise AI-driven innovation involves not only advanced machine learning (ML) and deep learning (DL) but also symbolic AI (SAI), advanced analytics (AA), natural language processing (NLP), and decision optimization (DO), to enable automated actions, robotics, and other application areas, to optimize existing business processes and to implement new use cases.[20] AI-driven innovation in the enterprise aims to discover organizational knowledge, incorporate analytical insights into decision processes and accelerate them by orders of magnitude. To be more effective, businesses require a broad overall view of the design and development of its enterprise architecture[9] including all related AI-driven innovations.[21,22] However, along this transition it might not be enough to deploy new AI digital technologies in the enterprise to demonstrate a suitable AI technology readiness. Enterprises need to be able to adequately employ these kinds of technologies in value-added processes for exploiting their full potentialities and reaching a suitable AI maturity. In this context, connected AI systems can interact between each other using standard Internet-based protocols and can analyze data to predict failure, configure themselves, and self-adapt to changes, in other words, being sustainable and resilient.

Generally, the links between AI-driven innovations, technology, AI usage, and organizational maturity remain unclear. Furthermore, there are methodical gaps in the design process of the AI-driven innovations regarding the theoretical foundation of the innovation model and the fundamental understanding of AI-driven innovation management. To address the above-mentioned gaps, our research goal is to develop a methodically sound AI-driven value chain model and AI-driven innovation reference framework which guides its users how to design AI-driven innovations to contribute to their overall organizational maturity.

The remaining of this chapter is structured as follows. Section 2 examines the main definitions and conceptual background of AI-driven value chain and ML life cycle based on literature review. Section 3 describes the methodology. In Section 4 the AI-driven value chain is developed and described, which makes it possible to create the reference model (taxonomy) of AI-driven innovation processes and innovation types in Section 5. Finally, the AI organization innovation and AI-driven maturity framework are discussed in Section 6. Section 7 discusses the results of this study.

2. What Is AI?

Mentioned as early as 1951,[7] AI was coined as a collective term referring to the data science domain and the different tools employed within it. But still, there is no universally accepted definition of AI. Despite the growing research interest in AI, most of the studies on AI look at it from a technical, architectural, or information system perspective,[23,24] rather than from a managerial and business platform perspective. In the context of this chapter, the following AI definitions have been adopted from a report by the Joint Research Centre (JRC), the European Commission's science and knowledge service,[25] OECD, and some of the international standards.

2.1. *Definitions*

"Artificial intelligence (AI) systems are software (and possibly also hardware) systems designed by humans that, given a complex goal, act in the physical or digital dimension by perceiving their environment through data acquisition, interpreting the collected structured or unstructured data, reasoning on the knowledge, or processing the information, derived from this data and deciding the best action(s) to take to achieve the given goal. AI systems can either use symbolic rules or learn a numeric model, and they can also adapt their behavior by analyzing how the environment is affected by their previous actions."[25]

"AI is a generic term that refers to any machine or algorithm that is capable of observing its environment, learning, and based on the knowledge and experience gained, taking intelligent action or proposing decisions. There are many different technologies that fall under this broad AI definition. At the moment, ML techniques are the most widely used."[25]

"An AI system is a machine-based system that can, for a given set of human-defined objectives, make predictions, recommendations, or decisions influencing real or virtual environments. AI systems are designed to operate with varying levels of autonomy."[3]

AI system lifecycle phases involve[3]: (i) "design, data and models"; which is a context-dependent sequence encompassing planning and design, data collection and processing, as well as model building; (ii) "verification and validation"; (iii) "deployment"; and (iv) "operation and monitoring." These phases often take place in an iterative manner and are not necessarily sequential. The decision to retire an AI system from operation may occur at any point during the operation and monitoring phase.

AI knowledge refers to the skills and resources, such as data, code, algorithms, models, research, know-how, training programs, governance, processes, and best practices, required to understand and participate in the AI system lifecycle. AI actors are those who play an active role in the AI system lifecycle, including organizations and individuals that deploy or operate AI. Stakeholders encompass all organizations and individuals involved in, or affected by, AI systems, directly or indirectly. AI actors are a subset of stakeholders. Trustworthy AI refers to AI that respects the values-based principles.

Reference [26] defined AI as a digital innovation that offers solutions to transform enterprise products, service and business using AI, Big Data (BD) and Advance Analytics (AA). So, AI is powered by BD that involves collecting from of a wide variety of inputs, including publicly available data, information, or knowledge, human intelligence, and active gathering, then processing the resulting inputs to better understand and predict competitor strategies and actions. In several ways, AI anticipate interest in BD domains more than other disciplines do.

Reference [27] stated that AI is still a surprisingly fuzzy concept. They suggested that AI is not one monolithic term but instead needs to be seen in a more details. Authors argue that this can either be achieved by looking at AI through the lens of evolutionary stages (artificial narrow intelligence, artificial general intelligence, and artificial super intelligence) or by focusing on different types of AI systems (analytical AI, human-inspired AI, and humanized AI).

The absence of a formal commonly agreed AI definition demanded in this chapter the usage of AI term inclusively with sub disciplines ML, DL, AA, NLP, SAI, and DO.[5,27,28]

2.2. *Ways of AI usage*

Reference [21] discussed three ways through which a business can use AI: assisted intelligence, augmented intelligence, and autonomous intelligence. Numerous AI services are BD-driven machine learnt. As more and more machine-learnt services make their way into software applications, which themselves are part of business processes, robust life cycle management of such machine-learnt models becomes critical for organizational business processes.[29]

Machine learning models' training is a data intensive effort and real-world BD is often messy and must be cleaned and prepared to make it usable for training AI models. Recent studies show that curating BD contributes to more than half the time in the lifecycle management of AI models.[29] Since BD plays a pivotal role in AI, managing the BD pipeline effectively, and aligning BD curation efforts with the business goals and requirements can be key differentiators for organizations. Thus, the lifecycle of machine learning models is significantly different from that of the traditional software (Table 1).

ML and, increasingly, DL approaches are having a substantial effect on many industries.[10] Over the past few years, DL has made tremendous

Table 1. Difference between traditional and machine learning approaches.

Main concepts	Traditional [software] applications	Machine learning models
Software applications	Deterministic	Probabilistic
Data processing	Programmed to behave as per the data requirements and specifications	Learn from data
Data structure	Data tends to be transactional in nature and mostly of structured type	Data for machine learning models can be structured, semi-structured or unstructured. Unstructured data can further come in multiple forms such as text, audio, video and images
Data pipeline	Limited number of liner stages	Multiple stages, namely data acquisition, data annotation, data preparation, data quality checking, data sampling, data augmentation steps — each involving their own life cycles thereby necessitating a whole new set of processes and tools
Pipeline roles	Traditional software engineering roles	New set of roles, such as data managers, data annotators, data scientists, fairness testers, etc.
New features	Does not always have to deal with	Must deal with fairness, trust, transparency, explainability
Result	Accurate barring defects	Typically need multiple iterations of improvements to achieve acceptable accuracy, and it may or may not be possible to achieve 100% accuracy

progress, achieving or surpassing human-level performance for a diverse set of tasks including image classification,[30] playing games such as Go,[31] safety-critical systems such as self-driving cars,[32] text generation,[33] and aircraft collision avoidance systems.[34] This extensive adoption of DL techniques presents new challenges as the predictability and correctness of such systems are of crucial importance. Unfortunately, DL systems, despite their striking capabilities, often demonstrate unexpected or incorrect behaviors in corner cases for several reasons such as biased training data, overfitting, and underfitting of the models.[35] Reference [35] defines a DL system to be any software system that includes at least one Deep Neural Network (DNN) component. The development process of the DNN components of a DL system is basically different from traditional software development. Unlike traditional software, where the logic of the system is specified directly, the DNN components learn their rules automatically from data.[35] The developers of DNN components can indirectly influence the rules learned by a DNN by modifying the training data, features, and the model's architectural details (e.g., number of layers) as shown in Fig. 1. As a DNN's rules are mostly unknown even to its developers, testing and fixing of erroneous behaviors of DNNs are crucial in safety-critical settings.

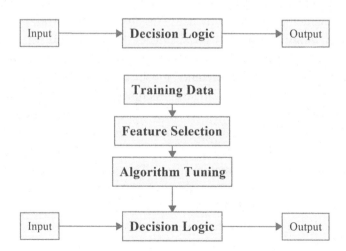

Fig. 1. Comparison between traditional and ML system development processes.

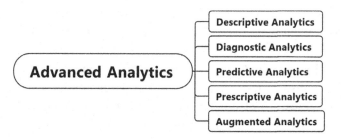

Fig. 2. Advanced analytics.

Advanced analytics has gained increasing interest from business and IT professionals looking to exploit huge amounts of internally generated and externally available BD. As it is shown in Fig. 2 the field of analytics is broken down into five categories.[17] AA is heavily related with AI, ML, DL, and BD.

3. Research Design and Approach

As it was mentioned before, AI is not one monolithic term and needs to be considered in a more details. The objective of this chapter is to address the AI-driven innovation characteristics that elucidate the assembly of main innovation notions into several concepts composing an AI-driven innovation reference model. A reference model is an abstract framework or domain-specific ontology (taxonomy) consisting of an interlinked set of clearly defined concepts produced by an expert or body of experts to encourage clear communications.[36] A reference model can represent the component parts of any consistent idea, from business functions to system components, if it represents a complete set. This frame of reference can then be used to communicate ideas clearly among members of the AI community. Reference models are successfully used in different fields of innovation management[37,38] and AI reference architecture.[20] Therefore, this study contributes to the design phase of the reference model of AI-driven innovation.

To fulfill that purpose, the following conceptual-to-empirical approach was adopted. First, the literature was extensively reviewed to identify the potential dimensions of AI-driven innovations. In recent years, there has been a growing interest in using more than one methodology and method, possibly from different areas of thought, in solving a single multidimensional problem.[39] Reference [40] points out that enormously complex, multidimensional, and ill-structured problems, made up of social, behavioral, coercive, exploitative, and manipulative components, require such contrivances that perennially preoccupied contemporary systems thinkers' need to develop different and independent endeavors and competing orientations. Thus, the design of the requirements of the AI-driven innovation artifacts is built upon sources of justificatory knowledge across three domains: (1) value chain; (2) innovation management; and (3) AI innovations. We chose a design science research approach for our study; our intended artifact was a framework for an AI-driven innovation. Our approach was also inspired by methodologies for the conceptual analysis of innovation management. More specifically, we place certain demands on our conceptualizations[41]:

- they must fill the empirical and theoretical need for concepts
- they should be capable of being operationalized, qualified, typologized and used as concepts for taxonomies
- they must be syntactically and semantically compatible with common conceptualizations of related concepts, i.e., the concepts of system, innovation, and AI.

The concept of AI-driven value chain that describes the full range of AI activities needed to create a product or service was proposed. The primary AI-driven value chain, its relations with AI and components/ dimensions of an established AI innovation conceptualization were defined. For companies that produce AI-driven goods and services, such value chain comprises the steps that involve bringing a product from conception to distribution, and everything in between. The data reliability and internal validity of the initial AI-driven innovation reference model conceptualization was then triangulated with a range of additional data, consisting especially of publicly available global and local government AI strategic documents and policies, the EU, US, Asian, Russian venture's white papers and annual reports, research papers and cases. Primary research was carried out in the form of semi-structured thematic interviews with different types of AI specialists to evaluate how much of the AI-related concepts identified in the literature review are being used in practice.

Summing up, in this chapter we address the following research questions:

- What is AI-driven value chain?
- How the AI-driven innovation reference model (taxonomy) can be defined and described?

4. AI-Driven Multidimensional Value Chain

The real value of AI could be determined through the multidimensional life cycle of AI, BD and AA. This life cycle allows to examine the value of AI over [Big] Data life cycle as a framework to consider how an enterprise might determine the value of enterprise data[17,18] and machine learning.[29] Reference [42] defines "data value chain" as follows (p. 31): "A value chain is made up of a series of subsystems each with inputs, transformation processes, and outputs ... As an analytical tool, the value chain can be applied to information flows to understand the value creation of data technology. In a Data Value Chain, information flow is described as a series of steps needed to generate value and useful insights from data."

The focus here is mostly on the BD enterprise micro-level value chain as defined by Ref. [42]. Micro-level value chains are used to model the high-level activities that comprise an enterprise. The proposed AI data-driven value chain identifies the following key activities/dimensions (Fig. 3).

(1) *AI awareness.* Big Data Acquisition is the process of gathering, filtering, and cleaning data before it is put in a data warehouse, data lake, or any other storage solution on which data analysis can be carried out, meaning the availability of BD and access to BD sources. There are a variety of BD types and sources. Value is created by acquiring and combining data from different sources. BD pre-processing, validating, and augmenting, as well as ensuring data integrity and accuracy add enterprise value. ML Data Pipeline — data collection and preparation. Data collection and preparation is a key step in training an AI model. The model needs to see enough instances of each kind that organization is trying to detect/predict. This stage involves many activities such as identifying right type of data in right distributions, sampling the data to guide the model performance, enriching the data

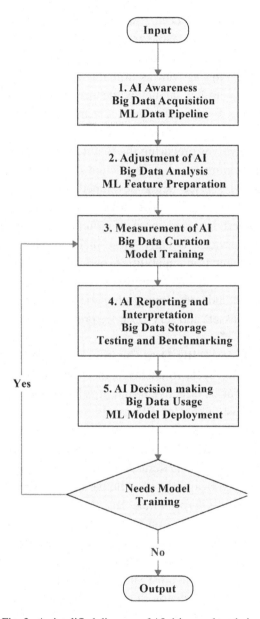

Fig. 3. A simplified diagram of AI-driven value chain.

via labeling, storing the lineage of the data, checking the quality of the labeled and prepared data, establishing specific metrics for measuring the quality of the data, storing, and analyzing the data.[29]

(2) *Adjustment of AI.* Big Data Analysis is concerned with making the raw data acquired amenable to use in decision-making as well as domain-specific usage. Value is referred to using the raw data acquired in decision-making as well as domain-specific usage and providing access to data with low latency while ensuring data integrity and preserving privacy. Evaluation, machine learning, information extraction and data discovery of intangible BD assets add value. ML Feature Preparation involves preparing the features from the collected data to initiate the training models. The actual preparation steps depend on the type of AI service being developed. For example, preparatory steps might involve in text processing and audio signal processing for building natural language processing/understanding and speech-to-text type of services. Usually, these include, developing tokenizers, sentence segmentation capabilities, part-of-speech taggers, lemmatization, syntactic parsing capabilities etc. In the case of audio data, these things include developing phonetic dictionaries, text normalizers etc. These assets and services once prepared are then used in training algorithms.[29]

(3) *Measurement of AI.* Big Data Curation is the active management of data over its life cycle to ensure it meets the necessary data quality requirements for its effective usage. It is based on the active management and measurement of BD assets over a life cycle to ensure it meets the necessary BD quality requirements for effective usage. ML Model Training includes making decisions about what frameworks to use (TensorFlow/Pytorch/Keras, etc.), for deep learning (GPT-3) how many hidden layers and the specific parameters at each layer etc.

(4) *AI reporting and interpretation.* Big Data Storage is the persistence and management of data in a scalable way that satisfies the needs of applications that require fast access to data. Testing and Benchmarking refers to the finalized model which is tested against multiple datasets that are collected and against various competitor services, if accessible and applicable. Decision Support and Descriptive Analytics refer to the examination of data to answer the question "What happened?" or "What is happening?" characterized by traditional business intelligence (BI) and visualizations such as pie charts, bar charts, line graphs, tables, or generated narratives.

(5) *AI decision-making*. Big Data Usage covers data-driven business activities that need access to data, its analysis, and the tools needed to integrate data analysis within the targeted business activity. It covers the main BD assets used in business decision-making that can improve competitiveness through reduction of costs, increased added value, or any other parameter that can be measured against existing performance criteria.

ML Model Deployment and Automation refer to the critical decisions that are made on the deployment configuration of the model. Significant engineering might be required to make the feature extraction steps production-grade and wrap the trained model into a software package that can be invoked from the larger business application. Decision Support and Decision Automation includes Diagnostic Analytics, Predictive Analytics and Prescriptive Analytics.

5. AI-Driven Innovation Taxonomy

The AI-driven innovation reference model (taxonomy) is shown in Fig. 4.

The proposed AI data-driven value chain model can be applied to data, information, and knowledge flows of different types of innovation processes[a] to understand the following AI-driven value creation (see Fig. 4 — type of AI innovation process):

- *Business model innovation*: Innovating the AI-driven Value Proposition, Customer Segments, Channels, Relations, Key Resources and Key Activities to reduce costs, to create new Revenue Streams or optimize existing ones.
- *Open innovation*[43]: Innovating with stakeholders' AI-driven ecosystem: Big Data, ML and DL models, API (Application Program Interfaces), AI platforms, etc.
- *Marketing and branding*: Innovating the customer experience using AI services and products.

---

[a]https://openinnovation.eu/14-09-2016/8-types-of-innovation-processes/.

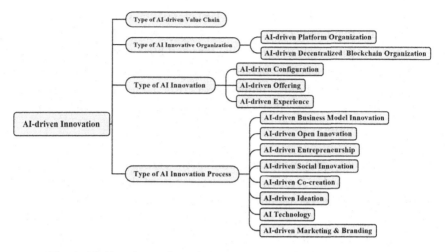

Fig. 4. AI-driven innovation reference model (three levels of taxonomy).

- *Ideation*: Innovating the product idea & concept using AI services for modeling, simulation, decision making, etc.
- *Technology*: Innovating the AI-driven product functionality.
- *Co-creation*: Innovating the AI-driven customer involvement.
- *Social innovation*: Innovating the Artificial-Human relationship corporate culture.
- *Entrepreneurship*: Innovating through AI-driven entrepreneurial thinking.

Epicenters of AI-driven Business Model Innovation are Resource-driven (e.g., OpenAI GPT-3), Offer-driven (for example, IBM Watson, Google AI, RapidMiner), Customer-driven (e.g., Amazon GO), Finance-driven (e.g., AI + Blockchain).

Reference [44] identified ten basic types of innovations that form three main groups: configuration, offering, and experience innovations (see Fig. 4 — type of AI Innovation). The proposed reference model of AI-driven innovation contains expanded matrix of 120+ subtypes of possible AI-driven innovations. For business model patterns from configuration-profit subgroup there are suggested AI-driven innovation frameworks (e.g., AI-driven platform innovation[18]).

The proposed AI data-driven value chain is an approach suited, for example, to Open innovation. AI applications can be developed using components like open APIs, JSON streams and services from available open sources. The open innovation proposed by Ref. [43] is a solution where a firm uses both internal and external ideas (in the case of AI — Bid Data and ML/DL models with open API access) that can result in faster product-to-market, lower cost and higher firm sustainability. This is supported by an increasing trend toward external resources of BD and ML/DL. In AI it makes sense to have open innovation and indulge in collaborative development and vise verse. The AI-driven Open Innovation can be reformulated from the Open Innovation principles[43] as follows.

- Not all internal Data and ML/DL models work for enterprise, so we must find and tap into the Big Data and ML/DL models outside our company.
- External ML/DL models can create significant value. Internal AI-driven innovation is needed to claim some portion of that value.
- We do not have to originate the research to profit from it. We need only an API (Application Program Interface) to connect and benefit from the knowledge.
- Our Enterprise has no facilities to create and train ML/DL models, so we must access them through the API.
- Building a better AI-driven business model is better than getting to the market first without it.
- If we make the best use of internal and external Big Data and ML/DL models, we will win.
- We should profit from others' use of our API, [Big] Data and ML/DL models, and we should buy others' Big Data, ML/DL models and API access whenever it advances our business model.

6. AI-Driven Organizational Innovation and Maturity

Organizations now employ AI in data-rich aspects of their operations. The AI-driven organizational maturity framework allows the evaluation of AI dynamic nature by placing focus on data-driven human-machine

Table 2. Multidimensional data-driven AI maturity framework (updated from Ref. [17]).

Stage of AI maturity	Who produces insights?	Who decides and how?	Who acts based on decision?	AI-driven value chain level
1. Human led	Human analyzers and produces insights using limited technology	Human decides based on experience and rules	Human acts or executives	Partly[*] 1, 2
2. Human led, machine supported	Human analyzers and produces insights using a portfolio of tools	Human analyzers based on optimized machine prescriptions	Human acts or executives	Partly[*] 1, 2, 3, 4
3. Machine led, human supported	Machine analyzers and produces insights with human review	Human decides based on optimized machine prescriptions	Human acts or executives with machine oversight	1, 2, 3,[**] partly[*] 4, 5
4. Machine led, human governed	Machine analyzers and produces insights without human review	Machine decides within a framework of human governance	Machine acts or executes with human oversight	1, 2, 3, 4,[**] partly[*] 5
5. Machine (machine led and machine governed)	Machine analyzers and produces insights	Machine decides	Machine acts or executes	1, 2, 3, 4, 5[**]

Notes:
[*] — levels of the AI-driven value chain.
[**] — the specific completeness of the AI-driven implementations are determined by the size of the organization, domain-specific usage and industry.

relationships, and the application of AI at various levels of data-driven automation scope, as shown in Table 2.

The AI-driven organizational maturity framework can be used in different ways as follows:

• For identification: it helps in identifying the level of AI maturity for the enterprise. It helps in explaining differences between organizations and in understanding why some companies mature in AI-driven innovations and others do not. It creates a common language.

- For analysis: it helps in analyzing the AI strengths and weaknesses of organizations.
- For discussion: it helps in understanding and discussing the strengths and weaknesses of AI-driven organizations in R&D marketing research.

7. Conclusion

Organizations worldwide must evaluate their vision and transform their people, processes, technology, and data readiness to unleash the power of AI and thrive in the digital era.[24] To help with strategic innovation planning and investment decisions related to AI-based automation, this chapter have advocated the value of the AI-driven innovation conceptual framework.

The AI-driven value chain (Fig. 3) allows to create new ways to reuse and extract value from BD/ML/DL assets through AI-driven platform innovation. Since AI comes in different shapes and sizes, the AI-driven innovation reference model (taxonomy) can be adopted and utilized in a range of AI-driven frameworks that embrace the different industries and a local context. AI innovators can use the reference model to define the conceptual layout of an AI-driven organizations and describe the AI innovation characteristics in each of the dimensions.

BD is an increasingly important concept to better understand the complex reference model of AI-driven innovation. Open collaboration researchers with Big datasets accessed through APIs that span different contexts, as well as novel ML/DL models and analytical techniques influence innovation processes and organization structure of all types of AI-driven innovation (see Fig. 4).

References

1. S. Lucci and D. Kopec, *Artificial Intelligence in the 21st Century: A Living Introduction.* Mercury Learning and Information; 2nd Edition (8 December, 2015), ISBN-13: 978-1942270003, ISBN-10: 1942270003.
2. E. Brynjolfsson and A. McAfee, *The Second Machine Age: Work, Progress, and Prosperity in a Time of Brilliant Technologies.* New York: W.W. Norton and Company (2016).

3. K. Perset, N. Nishigata, and L. Aranda, *Artificial Intelligence in Society*. Paris: OECD Publishing (2019).
4. R. Girasa, AI as a Disruptive Technology. Ch 1 in *Artificial Intelligence as a Disruptive Technology*. pp. 3–21, Cham: Palgrave Macmillan (2020). https://doi.org/10.1007/978-3-030-35975-1_1.
5. D. Zhang, S. Mishra, E. Brynjolfsson, J. Etchemendy, D. Ganguli, B. Grosz, T. Lyons, J. Manyika, J.C. Niebles, M. Sellitto, Y. Shoham, J. Clark, and R. Perrault, *The AI Index 2021 Annual Report*, AI Index Steering Committee, Human-Centered AI Institute, Stanford University, Stanford, CA (March 2021). Available at: https://aiindex.stanford.edu/report/ (accessed 14 December, 2021).
6. B. O'Sullivan (ed.), *Artificial Intelligence: Foundations, Theory, and Algorithms*. Book Series, 9 volumes. Cham: Springer, (2015–2021).
7. H. Bruderer, The birth of artificial intelligence: First conference on artificial intelligence in Paris in 1951? in *Proc. International Communities of Invention and Innovation (HC 2016)*. IFIP Advances in Information and Communication Technology, Vol. 491. Cham: Springer (2016).
8. H. Benbya, T. Davenport, and S. Pachidi, Special issue editorial: Artificial intelligence in organizations: Current state and future opportunities, *MIS Quarterly Executive*, **19**(4), 9–21 (2020).
9. M. Iansiti and K. Lakhani, *Competing in the Age of AI: Strategy and Leadership When Algorithms and Networks Run the World*. Harvard Business Review Press, Boston, MA (2020).
10. T. Sejnowski, *The Deep Learning Revolution*. MIT Press, Cambridge, MA (2018).
11. H. Karjaluoto, A. Shaikh, J. Kietzmann, and L. Pitt, Artificial intelligence and machine learning: What managers need to know, *Business Horizons*, **63**, 131–133 (2020).
12. P. Evans and A. Gawer, *The Rise of the Platform Enterprise. A Global Survey*, New York: Center for Global Enterprise (2016). Available at: http://www.thecge.net/wp-content/uploads/2016/01/PDFWEBPlatform-Survey_01_12.pdf (accessed April 2, 2021).
13. K. Boudreau, Open platform strategies and innovation: Granting access vs. devolving control, *Management Science*, **56**(10), 1849–1872 (2010).
14. G. Parker, M. Van Alstyne, S. Choudary, *Platform Revolution: How Networked Markets are Transforming the Economy, and How to Make Them Work for You*. London: W.W. Norton (2016).
15. M. De Reuver, C. Sørensen, and R. Basole, The digital platform: A research agenda, *Journal of Information Technology*, **33**(2), 124–135 (2018).
16. S. Yablonsky, A multidimensional framework for digital platform innovation and management: From business to technological platforms, *Systems Research and Behavioral Science*, **35**(4), 485–501 (2018).

17. S. Yablonsky, *Multi-Sided Platforms (MSPs) and Sharing Strategies in the Digital Economy: Emerging Research and Opportunities*. IGI Global (2018). Hershey, PA.
18. S. A. Yablonsky, AI-Driven Digital Platform Innovation. Technology Innovation Management Review, **10**(10), 4–15 (2020). http://doi.org/10.22215/timreview/1392.
19. M. Cusumano, D. Yoffie, and A. Gawer, The future of platforms, *MIT Sloan Management Review*, **61**(3), 46–54 (2020).
20. F. Hechler, M. Oberhofer, and T. Schaeck, *Deploying AI in the Enterprise. IT Approaches for Design, DevOps, Governance, Change Management, Blockchain, and Quantum Computing*. Berkeley, CA: Apress, (2020).
21. A. Rao, A strategist's guide to artificial intelligence, *Strategy + Business*, **87**, 46–50 (2017).
22. J. Bjorkdahl, Strategies for digitalization in manufacturing firms, *California Management Review*, **62**(4), 17–36 (2020).
23. K. Lyytinen, Y. Yoo, and J. Boland, Digital product innovation within four classes of innovation networks, *Information Systems Journal*, **26**(1), 47–75 (2016).
24. R. Jyoti, N. Ward-Dutton, P. Carnelley, S. Findling, and S. Marshall, *IDC MaturityScape: Artificial Intelligence 1.0*, Doc # US44119919 (2019).
25. S. Samoili, M. López Cobo, E. Gómez, G. De Prato, F. Martínez-Plumed, and B. Delipetrev, *AI Watch. Defining Artificial Intelligence. Towards an Operational Definition and Taxonomy of Artificial Intelligence*, EUR 30117 EN. Luxembourg: Publications Office of the European Union (2020).
26. A. Annoni *et al.*, *Artificial Intelligence: A European Perspective*, Craglia, M. (ed.), EUR 29425 EN. Publications Office of the European Union, Luxembourg (2018).
27. A. Kaplan and M. Haenlein, Siri, Siri, in my hand: Who's the fairest in the land? On the interpretations, illustrations, and implications of artificial intelligence, *Business Horizons*, **62**(1), 15–25 (2019).
28. S. Loureiro, J. Guerreiro, and I. Tussyadiah, Artificial intelligence in business: State of the art and future research agenda, *Journal of Business Research*, **129**, 911–926 (May 2021).
29. R. Akkiraju *et al.* (2020) Characterizing Machine Learning Processes: A Maturity Framework. In: D. Fahland, C. Ghidini, J. Becker, and M. Dumas. (eds.) *Business Process Management. BPM 2020. Lecture Notes in Computer Science*, Vol. 12168. Cham: Springer (2020). https://proxy.library.spbu.ru:2060/10.1007/978-3-030-58666-9_2.
30. K. Simonyan and A. Zisserman, Very deep convolutional networks for large-scale image recognition, https://arxiv.org/pdf/1409.1556.pdf (2015).

31. D. Silver, A. Huang, C. Maddison, A. Guez, L. Sifre, G. van den Driessch *et al.*, Mastering the game of Go with deep neural networks and tree search, *Nature*, **529**, 484–489 (2016).
32. M. Bojarski, D. Del Testa, D. Dworakowski, B. Firner, B. Flepp, P. Goyal, *et al.*, End to end learning for self-driving cars, https://arxiv.org/abs/1604.07316 (2016).
33. T. Brown, B. Mann, N. Ryder, M. Subbiah, J. Kaplan, P. Dhariwal, *et al.*, Language models are few-shot learners, https://arXiv preprint arXiv:2005.1416 (2020).
34. K.D. Julian, J. Lopez, J.S. Brush, M.P. Owen, and M.J. Kochenderfer, Policy compression for aircraft collision avoidance systems, in *2016 IEEE/AIAA 35th Digital Avionics Systems Conference (DASC)*, 1–10 (2016).
35. K. Pei, Y. Cao, J. Yang, and S. Jana, DeepXplore: Automated whitebox testing of deep learning systems, https://arxiv.org/abs/1705.06640 (2017).
36. R. Poli, M. Healy, and A. Kameas, (eds.), *Theory and Applications of Ontology: Computer Applications.* New York, NY: Springer Dordrecht Heidelberg (2010).
37. I. Zolotová, P. Kubičko, L. Landryová, and R. Hošák, Innovation processes — Reference model, collaboration via innovative zone and integration into enterprise environment, in J. Frick and B. Laugen, (eds.), *APMS 2011, IFIP AICT*, Vol. 384, 567–577 (2012).
38. S. Zygiaris, Smart city reference model: Assisting planners to conceptualize the building of smart city innovation ecosystems, *Journal of the Knowledge Economy*, **4**, 217–231 (2013).
39. W. Ziniel, Empirical approach and conceptual models, in *Third Party Product Reviews and Consumer Behaviour.* Wiesbaden: Springer Gabler (2013).
40. R. Flood and M. Jackson, *Creative Problem Solving: Total Systems Intervention.* Wiley (1991).
41. O. Granstranda and M. Holgerssonb, Innovation ecosystems: A conceptual review and a new definition, *Technovation*, **90**, 12 (2020).
42. S. Sun, R. Law, J. M. Cavanillas, E. Curry, and W. Wahlster (eds.), New horizons for a data-driven economy: A roadmap for usage and exploitation of big data in Europe, *Inf. Technol. Tourism* **17**, 245–247 (2017).
43. H. Chesbrough, *Open Innovation: The New Imperative for Creating and Profiting from Technology.* Harvard Business School Press (2003).
44. Doblin (A Deloitte Business), The ten types framework — The discipline of building breakthroughs (2013). Available at: https://doblin.com/ten-types (accessed April 14, 2021).

https://doi.org/10.1142/9781800611337_0007

Chapter 6

Automating Innovation

Navneet Bhalla

Department of Computer Science, University College London
Gower Street, London WC1E 6BT, UK
Sprott School of Business, Carleton University
1125 Colonel By Drive, Ottawa, ON K1S 5B6, Canada
n.bhalla@cs.ucl.ac.uk
navneet.bhalla@carleton.ca

Artificial intelligence is changing the way we invent. Although it is not commonplace today, artificial intelligence is being used for product innovation, for example, in the design of physical objects and software. However, a far less explored area is applying artificial intelligence to process innovation. Developing new processes can be transformative, such as the invention of the moving assembly line. This chapter presents how the same artificial intelligence algorithms, specifically evolutionary computing, used for product innovation can be leveraged for process innovation. The design of self-organizing materials is used as an example to guide the reader through topology optimization (product innovation) to the creation of complex systems (process innovation). The principles from designing complex systems using artificial intelligence are abstracted — constraints, time, and noise — and discussed in the context of Industry 4.0.

1. Introduction

We are in the midst of the fourth industrial revolution,[1] driven by artificial intelligence (AI). These revolutions are not just defined by innovative products, but also by the innovative processes that lead to these new technologies in the first place.[2] The evolution of the assembly line serves as an example to illustrate this point.[3]

Prior to the first industrial revolution, single artisans would craft artifacts by hand or using simple tools and machines. The first industrial revolution introduced mechanical production equipment powered by water and steam, which lead to new divisions of labor and assembly lines. One of the defining inventions of the second industrial revolution was the invention of the moving assembly line, introduced by the Ford Motor Company.[4] The third industrial revolution was defined by the use of electronics and information technology to further automate production.[5]

In the case of automobile manufacturing, computers and robotics enabled the development of the Toyota Production System (TPS). TPS is a management system, which organizes manufacturing and logistics (including interaction with suppliers and customers).[6] TPS is an important precursor to the more generic management practice of lean manufacturing.[7]

AI, broadly defined as intelligence displayed by machines,[8] and Machine Learning (ML), computer algorithms that improve automatically through experience,[9] have started to be integrated into manufacturing processes.[10] For example, ML is used to detect anomalies in the operating parameters of machines based on past behavior data. The benefit is that ML can often predict when a machine is about to fail in advance, which reduces costs by allowing for preventive maintenance of a machine or the replacement of a machine in a production system.

However, can AI/ML be used to invent new manufacturing processes? Abstractly, can AI/ML be used to revolutionize process innovation? Can AI/ML be used to (semi-)automate innovation management? The aim of this chapter is to provide initial answers and foundational information, which can serve as a starting point to using AI/ML for process innovation.

Specifically, Evolutionary Computing (EC)[11] — a branch of AI (Fig. 1) that is inspired by Charles Darwin's theory of evolution by means of natural selection[12] — is used to demonstrate how AI can be used for process innovation. Self-assembly — a process by which a disordered system of pre-existing components, in a particular environment, form an

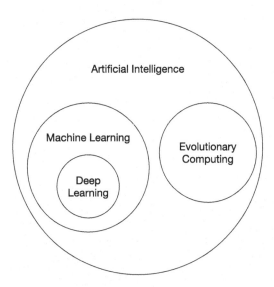

Fig. 1. Venn diagram showing the relationship between artificial intelligence, machine learning, deep learning, and evolutionary computing.

organized structure or pattern as a consequence of specific, local interactions among the components themselves, without external direction[13] — is used as a case study.

Although we see the results of self-assembly in the natural world,[14] from snow crystals to sand dunes, and as the foundation of biological development,[15] from bacteria to blue whales, the design of artificial, complex, self-assembling systems remains an elusive task.

This chapter presents how AI has shown tremendous promise in addressing the above design problem.[16] Section 2 introduces the fundamentals of EC and presents a few notable examples of how EC has been used for product innovation in the recent past. Next, an overview of self-assembling systems is given, followed by the way EC has been used to generate the designs of components to self-assemble into a target artifact.[17] Section 3 starts by explaining how a more complex target artifact can be achieved by simply dividing the self-assembly process into time stages.[18] Next, the author outlines a novel approach to how EC can be used to generate staged self-assembling systems, which serves as the basis for a thought experiment in which AI can be used to innovate the self-assembly process through the use of more sophisticated components and environments.

Finally, this chapter concludes by comparing and contrasting the use of AI for product innovation versus process innovation. The concepts from Section 3 are abstracted from EC and self-assembly to provide generic attributes for how AI can be used in innovation management, to help guide us forward from the early stages of this fourth industrial revolution.

2. Background

Natural evolution, it can be argued, is the most creative process in the universe[19]: Biological organisms evolve and adapt to their environment through iteration. Universal Darwinism extends the original theory beyond its domain of biological evolution on Earth, with the aim to formulate a generalized version of the mechanisms of variation, selection, and heredity.[20] This process has been abstracted and codified into a class of algorithms called EC.

One of the remarkable characteristics of evolution is that it is an autonomous process. This same characteristic distinguishes self-assembly from other methods of construction. In general, how to design self-assembling systems is a computationally intractable problem.[21] However, AI, and specifically EC, are well suited to solve or approximate solutions to this problem.[17]

2.1. *Evolutionary computing*

In EC, an initial set of candidate solutions, referred to as a population of individuals, is generated and iteratively updated. Each new iteration, called a generation, is produced by stochastically removing less desired solutions by introducing small, random changes over time. In biological terminology, a population of individuals is subjected to natural selection (or artificial selection) and mutation. As a result, the population will gradually evolve to increase in fitness. In EC, the fitness of an individual is calculated using a mathematical function.

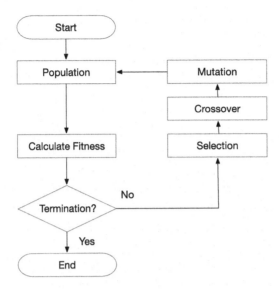

Fig. 2. Genetic algorithm flowchart.

There are numerous, specific algorithms that belong to EC, varying in the representation of individuals for example. Here, we use the term Genetic Algorithms (GAs) as an all-encompassing term for these types of algorithms.[11] Figure 2 shows a flowchart that represents a canonical GA.

The first step is to randomly generate an initial population of individuals. The second step is to evaluate the fitness of each individual in the population, by applying a fitness function. The third step is to determine if a stopping criterion has been achieved. Two such criteria are if the maximum number of generations has been met or if an individual in the population has achieved the maximum fitness for a maximization function (or likewise the minimum fitness for a minimization problem). If the stopping criterion is met, then the algorithm exits, else it continues in a loop. The first sub-step in the loop is to apply a selection method to individuals in the current generation. The second sub-step in the loop is to apply variation. Variation consists of crossover (sexual or asexual reproduction in biology) and mutation (making small changes to the representation of an individual). Variation is applied to create a new set of individuals until a population of equal size to the original population is achieved. Sometimes elitism is used in GAs, where an individual is copied directly from the current population to the next population, as a technique to help reduce genetic drift (particularly when the population size is small).[22] The new population replaces the old population, and the loop in the algorithm is completed by evaluating the fitness of the new population.

The following scenario is used to further explain the parts of a GA, and to serve as a precursor to self-assembly (Section 2.2) and topology optimization (Section 2.3). Given a set of cubic building blocks with colored faces (one color per face, from a predefined set of colors), randomly glue matching color faces together to construct a structure. A target structure is specified. The difference between the constructed structure and the target structure serves as the fitness function (a mathematical definition of spatial difference is provided in Section 2.3). This is an example of topology (i.e., shape and connectivity) optimization. As the number of blocks increases (as the size of target structure increases) and the number of colors increases, this becomes a very difficult problem to solve, akin to finding a "needle in a haystack."

In this scenario, an example of an individual's representation (genotype) and representational mapping (phenotype) is provided in Fig. 3.

Each block is represented by a string of six characters (each character representing a color for a specific face of a cube). Each individual is represented by a set of six-character strings. This results in each individual's

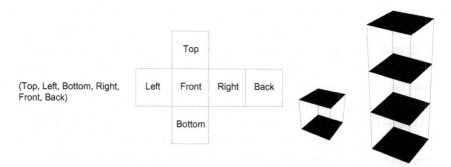

Fig. 3. From left to right: Positional notation (genotype), unfolded square representation, single cube with top and bottom faces in black, and a linear structure (phenotype) created from three of the former cubes.

P1: (I, I, -, P, Q, -) (J, J, T, S, -, -) (-, L, -, S, N, I) (M, -, -, -, T, S)

P2: (R, S, S, -, -, Q) (I, J, I, J, -, -) (M, N, Q, -, T, T)

C1: (I, I, -, P, Q, -) (I, J, I, J, -, -) (-, L, -, S, N, I) (M, -, -, -, T, S)

C2: (R, S, S, -, -, Q) (J, J, T, S, -, -) (M, N, Q, -, T, T)

Base: (I, I, -, P, Q, -) (I, J, I, J, -, -) (-, L, -, S, N, I) (M, -, -, -, T, S)

Addition: (I, I, -, P, Q, -) (I, J, I, J, -, -) (-, L, -, S, N, I) (M, -, -, -, T, S) (M, N, Q, -, T, T)

Deletion: (I, I, -, P, Q, -) (I, J, I, J, -, -) (M, -, -, -, T, S) (M, N, Q, -, T, T)

Point: (I, I, -, P, Q, -) (I, J, I, J, -, -) (**Q**, -, -, -, T, S) (M, N, Q, -, T, T)

Fig. 4. In this example, each letter maps to a unique color and "-" represents no assembly. Top: Parent 1 (P1) and parent 2 (P2) are selected to create child 1 (C1) and child 2 (C2) by variable length crossover. Bottom: Base line genotype, that undergoes the mutation operations of addition, deletion, and point (where the character that is mutated is in bold).

genotype to possibly be of different lengths. Therefore, a variable length, sexual crossover operator is needed (Fig. 4), where two individuals (parents) are chosen to create two new individuals (children). Each child is subjected to mutation (addition, deletion, and point), where the occurrence of a mutation is based on probability values (specified as parameters to the GA).

There are many methods of selecting the parents to populate the next generation. In this work, the method of selection is called fitness proportionate selection or roulette wheel selection.[11] The fitness of each individual in the population is calculated. A probability is associated with each individual based on the fitness score (Equation 1). If f_i is the fitness of individual i in the population, then its probability of being selected is p_i, where N is the number of individuals in the population.

$$p_i = \frac{f_i}{\sum_{j=1}^{N} f_j} \tag{1}$$

It should be noted that the individual(s) with the best fitness are not always selected. This promotes genetic diversity. Furthermore, it helps balance the exploration versus exploitation tradeoff in GAs.[23] Finally, as the algorithm iterates, the system evolves, and the population converges to an optimal or near optimal solution.

There are several notable applications of EC for product innovation, particularly in the domain of topology optimization. EC has been used to evolve models of trusses for bridges, where the models have been physically built using building blocks for testing.[24] The shapes of antennas have been evolved for satellites, which are currently in space.[25] Metals 3D printing has enabled the construction of lightweight doors for aircraft.[26] EC has also been used to generate sculptural forms.[27]

The next section introduces the process of self-assembly, where cubic building blocks are able to construct themselves into structures, in their specific environment. Section 2.3 explains how to evolve self-assembling systems.

2.2. Self-Assembly

Self-assembly is hailed as one of the key areas of nanoscience likely to shape future scientific research.[28] However, self-assembly is not just limited to the nanoscale in chemistry. Self-assembly has also been demonstrated at the macroscale (centimeter and above).[29] This section introduces a set of cubic components, which can be held in the human hand. The significance of these components is that they are the first example of self-assembly in three physical dimensions,[17] which are an extension and physical instantiation of a foundational, mathematical model of self-assembly in two physical dimensions.[30]

The components use shape and magnetism to self-assemble. The body of a component is fabricated using 3D printing. The components are purely mechanical and do not have embedded electronics for controlling interactions/communication between components.

The base shape of a component is a cube. Each face of the cube can have one of three shapes assigned to it, flat, key, or lock (Fig. 5). A flat face acts as a neutral site, where it is not possible for other components to self-assemble. Key and lock shapes are complementary. Keys and locks are such that they permit rotations (360°, 180°, and 90°). Five permanent

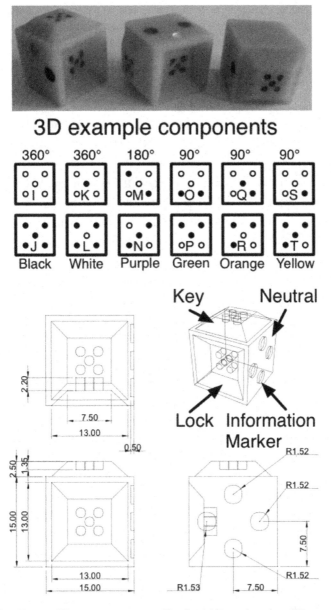

3D example components

Fig. 5. 3D self-assembling component specifications (dimensions in millimeters), where solid black circles represent magnetic north and outlined black circles represent magnetic south in the 5-magnetic-bit patterns (the orientation of the planar magnetic formations are shown in reference to the front face, see Fig. 3).

Table 1. Key and lock designations for the 5-magnetic-bit patterns (zero and one represent magnetic south and north respectively, and magnetic information is represented linearly from left to right as center, bottom right, bottom left, top left, and top right). Φ represents the temperature (i.e., shaking speed) of the environment.

Key/lock	5-magnetic-bits	Label	Fits rule	Breaks rule
Lock	00000	I	I fits$_{360}$ J → I + J	Φ_2 breaks I + J → I; J
Lock	10000	K	K fits$_{360}$ L → K + L	Φ_2 breaks K + L → K; L
Lock	01010	M	M fits$_{180}$ N → M + N	Φ_2 breaks M + N → M; N
Lock	10011	P	P fits$_{90}$ O → P + O	Φ_2 breaks P + O → P; O
Lock	00111	R	R fits$_{90}$ Q → R + Q	Φ_2 breaks R + Q → R; Q
Lock	10111	T	T fits$_{90}$ S → T + S	Φ_2 breaks T + S → T; S
Key	11111	J	J fits$_{360}$ I → J + I	Φ_2 breaks J + I → J; I
Key	01111	L	L fits$_{360}$ K → L + K	Φ_2 breaks L + K → L; K
Key	10101	N	N fits$_{180}$ M → N + M	Φ_2 breaks N + M → N; M
Key	01100	O	O fits$_{90}$ P → O + P	Φ_2 breaks O + P → O; P
Key	11000	Q	Q fits$_{90}$ R → Q + R	Φ_2 breaks Q + R → Q; R
Key	01000	S	S fits$_{90}$ T → S + T	Φ_2 breaks S + T → S; T

magnets are placed within the keys and locks. Once rotation is taken into account, there remains six unique pairs of magnetic configurations (Fig. 5). These magnetic configurations can be optimally assigned to keys and locks to prevent key-lock binding errors (Table 1). Only one magnet is placed in each of the five locations in a key, which allows for weak key-key binding. Two magnets are placed in each of the five locations in a lock, which allows for strong key-lock binding.

The components are placed in a jar of mineral oil. The jar is placed on a shaking table (the type of device found in a chemistry/biology lab for mixing contents held in test tubes). The level of shaking can be adjusted using a speed dial. Therefore, a balance in the speed can be reached where weak binding is significantly reduced and strong binding can be maintained. The shaking provides mechanical energy to the system and allows the components to mix. Over time, the components interact with one another and structures are autonomously constructed (Fig. 6).

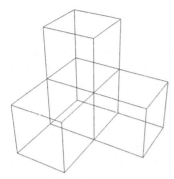

Fig. 6. Target structure (left) and three self-assembled target structures (right).

2.3. *Topology optimization*

Although there are thirty-three choices for each face of a cube (neutral flat face, and six pairs of magnetic keys and locks and their orientations), there are 53,977,737 unique types of components, once rotation and symmetry are accounted.[18] Determining an appropriate set of components that can self-assemble into a target structure — even in this relatively simple system — is extremely challenging. EC can be used to solve this problem.

The content presented in this section is based on a canonical GA, with fitness proportionate selection, sexual crossover, three mutation operators (addition, deletion, and point), and elitism. The parameter settings for the GA used to evolve self-assembling systems is provided in Ref. [17].

An individual's genotype representation is a variable length list of genes (where a gene consists of string of six characters representing the faces of a cube). At least two genes define a genotype (since this is the minimum for self-assembly to occur). An individual's phenotype is the resulting set of self-assembled structures. A single genotype representation may have more than one phenotype representation, depending on the set of components and assembly steps. As a worst-case example, a genotype that consists of n components with information I on all faces and n components with information J on all faces would result in at most $2n!$ phenotypes.[18] Consequently, it is not practical to test all the resulting phenotypes corresponding to a large genotype. Therefore, each individual (genotype) is evaluated three times, at each generation, to help determine the fitness of an individual.

A multi-objective fitness function is used to evaluate each individual. The eight objectives, chosen by design, can be categorized into evaluating a general and refined solution (Fig. 7). The general solution has six objectives, (1) volume (V), (2) surface area (S), (3) mean breadth (B), (4) Euler (E), (5) z-axis, and (6) matches. The volume, surface area, mean breadth, and Euler (connectivity of a shape) are calculated using Equations 2–5, where n_3 is the number of cubes (components), n_2 is the number of faces, n_1 is the number of edges, and n_0 is the number of vertices. Together, these six general objectives are sufficient to describe the three-dimensional shape of the target structure. The volume, surface area, integral mean curvature, and Euler are calculated using 3D Morphological Image Analysis.[31] The second moment of inertia in the z-axis[32] is calculated to identify either identical structures or different structures that have similar reflected features. To distinguish between reflected structures, the number of matching components between a self-assembled structure and a target structure is calculated. A refined solution is accounted for by using two objectives, (7) locations and (8) error. A refined solution is considered as one that minimizes the number of remaining open assembly locations (for the creation of closed target structures), and potential assembly errors (due to magnetic interactions). Errors in magnetic interactions are applied to all potential two-component key–lock and key–key (all five magnet positions are considered in key–key errors and partial interactions are not accounted for) in a system. The potential magnetic error is calculated as the sum of the scores in Table 2, where each cell in the matrix is the sum of errors occurring between two pieces of information in all four orientations. The combination of these two objectives also reduces the number of unique components required, as well as favoring 5-magnetic-bit patterns with higher rotational freedom.

$$V = n_3 \tag{2}$$

$$S = -6n_3 + 2n_2 \tag{3}$$

$$B = (3n_3 - 2n_2 + n_1)/2 \tag{4}$$

$$E = -n_3 + n_2 - n_1 + n_0 \tag{5}$$

Table 2. Magnetic error interactions matrix (in reference to Table 1), where the numbers are the sum of all error between information in the four orientations (using the number of magnets, i.e., two or one, in each of mismatched location), and where N/A is in reference to lock–lock interactions not being possible.

	I	J	K	L	M	N	O	P	Q	R	S	T
I	N/A	—	—	—	—	—	—	—	—	—	—	—
J	0	0	—	—	—	—	—	—	—	—	—	—
K	12	32	N/A	—	—	—	—	—	—	—	—	—
L	N/A	8	0	0	—	—	—	—	—	—	—	—
M	N/A	36	N/A	24	N/A	—	—	—	—	—	—	—
N	36	24	24	24	6	16	—	—	—	—	—	—
O	24	24	36	16	24	24	16	—	—	—	—	—
P	N/A	24	N/A	36	N/A	24	21	N/A	—	—	—	—
Q	36	24	12	32	36	16	24	24	12	—	—	—
R	N/A	24	N/A	12	N/A	36	24	N/A	27	N/A	—	—
S	12	32	36	24	24	24	16	36	20	30	12	—
T	N/A	12	N/A	24	N/A	24	36	N/A	30	N/A	27	N/A

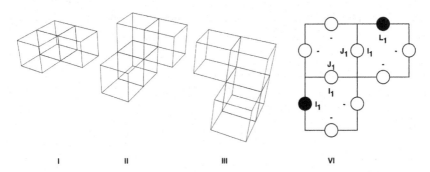

Fig. 7. Fitness objective example. Structure I ($n_3 = 3$, $n_2 = 16$, $n_1 = 28$, and $n_0 = 16$). Structures II and III have the same moment of inertia. The number of matches between structures II and III, which have similar reflected features, is 3. The number of open locations is 2 (indicated using black circles in IV; two-dimensional top view) The potential error score in IV is 8 (Table 2).

Each objective is normalized using the highest and lowest fitness scores from the current generation.[33] This method has been shown to be an effective way to calculate multi-objective fitness.[34] For objective *i*, where $i \in \{1, 2, 3, 4, 5, 6\}$ the average normalized objective (ANO_i) over three evaluations is calculated and compared to the target objective (TO_i) value. For objective seven, the normalized average over the three evaluations (ANO_7) is calculated. For objective eight, the normalized objective (NO_8) is calculated with respect to a genotype. The average is not used with objective 8 as the error is based exclusively on a genotype and does not vary over the three simulation evaluations. The objectives are then weighted and summed to give a final fitness score F (Equation 6).

$$F = \left(0.15 \sum_{i=1}^{6} \left| TO_i - ANO_i \right| \right) + 0.05 \left(ANO_7 + NO_8 \right) \tag{6}$$

3. Creating Creativity

Section 2 presented how EC can be used for topology optimization, as a means of product innovation. In contrast, this section presents how the process of self-assembly itself can be altered as an example of process innovation. First, an example of complex structure shows how staged development of a body plan can be used to leverage a limited set of rules.[18] In particular, component interaction rules can be leveraged by reintroducing previously used component information at later time intervals. Second, the author discusses how EC can be applied to staged self-assembly to create more sophisticated structures. Third, the author explores how the process of self-assembly can enable subprocess, such as cycles, through a thought experiment.

3.1. *Staged self-assembly*

One of the practical challenges facing the creation of self-assembling systems is being able to exploit a limited set of fixed components and their binding mechanisms. The method of staging divides the self-assembly process into time intervals, during which components can be added to, or removed from, an environment at each interval. Staging addresses the challenge of using components that lack the plasticity of biological cells or the programmability of robotic units by encoding the construction of a target structure in the staging algorithm itself and not exclusively in the design of the components. Here, the interplay between component physical features is used to stage the self-assembly process, during which components can only be added to their environment at each time interval. The following example demonstrates, as proof of concept, that staging enables the self-assembly of more complex morphologies not otherwise possible.

Figure 8 shows a target structure that resembles the shape of a dog, which requires six pairs of 90° rotational patterns. However, only three

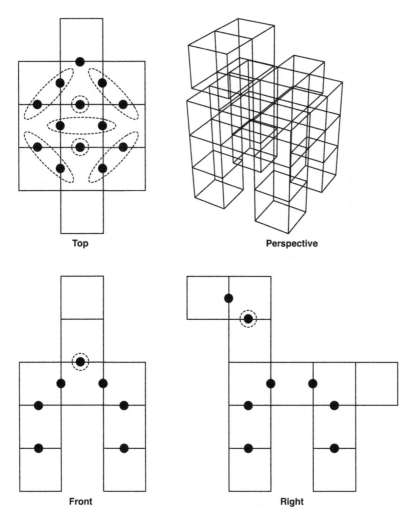

Fig. 8. Dog target structure. Black filled circles indicate an assembly point. Dashed ovals indicate a symmetry group.

90° pairs are present in the 5-magnetic-bit encoding scheme. To overcome this deficiency in the number of 90° rotational patterns, staging can be used to

- reintroduce previously used component information at a later time intervals,
- use the morphology of a substructure from the dog substructure (at an intermediate stage during the self-assembly process), where neighboring components are used to emulate a 90° rotational pattern using the 180° rotational pattern, and
- reduce the number of 90° rotational patterns required when constructing only a single target structure (in contrast to multiple target structures), since the orientation of the overall dog target structure during its construction (i.e., head versus tail facing forward) is not important.

The dog target can use all three types of rotational interaction information in a single structure. Table 3 lists the 5-magnetic-bit-patterns assigned to key and lock shapes that are better suited to create the dog target structure. In this designation, the worst possible mismatch error between component information is a 3-out-of-5 positional match, which is the same as the worst-case scenario between complementary 90° rotational patterns.

Using this new 5-magnetic-bit encoding scheme arrangement, a single dog structure can be made using six time intervals (Fig. 9). In this case, the time interval ψ_1 is used to determine the orientation of the head and tail.

The second and third time intervals are used to create the main body and to determine the orientation of the head and neck and direction of the head. The fourth and fifth intervals are used to build the legs and neck. The sixth interval is to build the head, feet, and tail. This staged process takes advantage of using similar component types in the same time interval and shows the benefits of symmetry within a time interval for parallel self-assembly. Furthermore, the rotational information Q used in the time interval ψ_0 is reused in the time interval ψ_3 (Fig. 9).

Table 3. 5-magnetic-bit encoding scheme to create the dog target structure, where the difference between the encoding scheme used for the original designations (Table 1) are represented in bold. Φ represents the temperature of the environment.

Key/lock	5-magnetic-bits	Label	Fits rule	Breaks rule
Lock	00000	I	I fits$_{360}$ J → I + J	Φ_2 breaks I + J → I; J
Lock	**01111**	L	L fits$_{360}$ K → L + K	Φ_2 breaks L + K → L; K
Lock	01010	M	M fits$_{180}$ N → M + N	Φ_2 breaks M + N → M; N
Lock	**01100**	O	O fits$_{90}$ P → O + P	Φ_2 breaks O + P → O; P
Lock	**11000**	Q	Q fits$_{90}$ R → Q + R	Φ_2 breaks Q + R → Q; R
Lock	10111	T	T fits$_{90}$ S → T + S	Φ_2 breaks T + S → T; S
Key	11111	J	J fits$_{360}$ I → J + I	Φ_2 breaks J + I → J; I
Key	**10000**	K	K fits$_{360}$ L → K + L	Φ_2 breaks K + L → K; L
Key	10101	N	N fits$_{180}$ M → N + M	Φ_2 breaks N + M → N; M
Key	**10011**	P	P fits$_{90}$ O → P + O	Φ_2 breaks P + O → P; O
Key	**00111**	R	R fits$_{90}$ Q → R + Q	Φ_2 breaks R + Q → R; Q
Key	01000	S	S fits$_{90}$ T → S + T	Φ_2 breaks S + T → S; T

The disadvantage of the previous staged self-assembly process is that it cannot be used to create multiple dog target structures simultaneously, as it would then be possible to create dogs with either two heads or two tails in the time interval ψ_1. To solve this problem, at least one pair from each of the three 90° rotational patterns is required in the time interval ψ_1 (Fig. 10). However, this results in an insufficient number of pairs of 90° rotational patterns to create the corner parts of the dog target structure.

The 180° rotational pattern can be used, due to the spatial relationship of the neighboring components to the corner components of the main body substructure of the dog target structure (Fig. 10). As with the staged self-assembly process to create a single dog target structure, the staged self-assembly process to create multiple dog target structures also uses six time intervals and uses the rotational information Q in the time interval ψ_0 again in the time interval ψ_3 (Fig. 10).

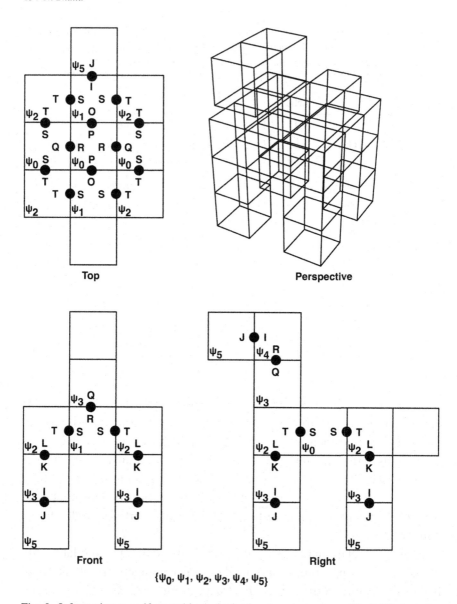

Fig. 9. Information to self-assemble a single dog target structure. Black filled circles indicate an assembly point. Letters correspond to Table 1. Blocks corresponding to a specific time stage are indicated by ψ.

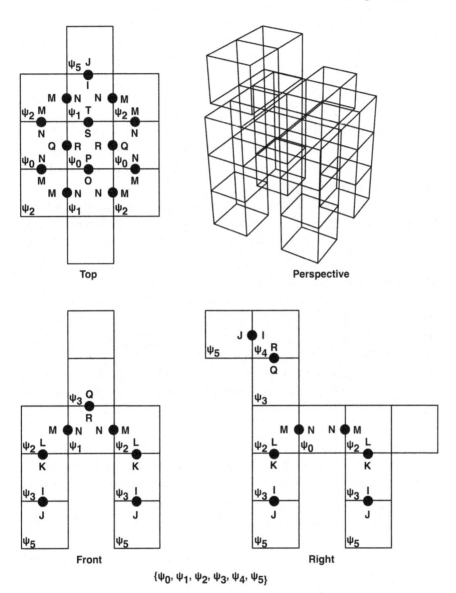

Fig. 10. Information to self-assemble multiple dog target structures. Black filled circles indicate an assembly point. Letters correspond to Table 3. Blocks corresponding to a specific time stage are indicated by ψ.

3.2. *Evolving staged self-assembling systems*

In Section 2.3, a worst-case example was provided, describing how a single genotype representation may have more than one phenotype representation. In the non-staged case, a genotype that consists of n components with information *I* on all faces and *n* components with information *J* on all faces would result in at most 2*n!* phenotypes. The worst case in the staged case is more dire. Extending the original worst-case example, if there are ψ_m stages ($m \in N$, where $m = 0$ is used to start the staged self-assembly process), would result in at most $(2n!)^{m+1}$ structures.[18]

Just as before, EC can be applied to staged self-assembly problems. Building upon the genotype representation provided in Section 2.3, only a simple extension to the genotype is required to account for time (Fig. 11). Segmenting the genotype is one method to specify the components that belong to a particular stage.

The same fitness function (Equation 6) can be used in this simple extension. However, a new crossover and additional mutation operators are needed. Although exchanging, expanding, and contracting stages would be beneficial, these operations could also be a hindrance to evolving staged self-assembling systems. The possibility of convergence is reduced as more and more information is captured in the genotype. Therefore, careful attention to the parameter settings is needed.

One technique for evolving systems with a large amount of differing information is referred to as the island model.[35] In the island model, subpopulations are able to evolve independently of each other in parallel. On occasion, individuals from one subpopulation are introduced into another subpopulation. For example, if one was to also try to evolve the information designation of rule sets (as shown previously with adjusting the rule set for the dog target structure), it could be beneficial for different subpopulations to follow specific rule sets. The same argument can apply to extending the number of component shapes, the number of magnets and their positions, and the number of environmental conditions.

[(I, I, -, P, Q, -) (-, L, -, S, N, I)] [(M, -, -, -, T, S) (M, N, Q, -, T, T)] [(-, L, -, S, N, I)]

Fig. 11. Genotype for evolving staged self-assembling systems.

3.3. *Thought experiment*

The previous section discussed how to evolve staged self-assembling systems in the context of the 5-magnetic-bit rule set. But what if we considered a very different class of components, made from different materials? The original components were inspired by simple proteins. What if instead the set of components included specialized catalysts, capable of complex interactions with other components, that were inspired by enzymes (highly evolved proteins that act as biological catalysts that accelerate and regulate chemical reactions in cells).[36]

Figure 12 shows a schematic of these types of components and their interactions and two scenarios. The interactions of self-assemble and self-disassemble are two common enzyme actions.[37] In Scenario A,

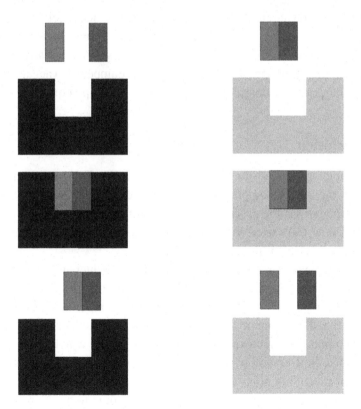

Fig. 12. Self-assembly (left, Scenario A) and self-disassembly (right, Scenario B).

the enzyme binds together two components (substrates) to create a new, assembled structure. In Scenario B, a second enzyme is added to the system, which is capable of disassembling the assembled structure.

Scenario A can be thought of as an example of both product innovation and process innovation. EC could be used to generate the designs (topologies) of the enzyme and the other components cooperatively. A secondary measurement of the system would be the rate of reaction (the speed of producing assembled components), to determine the impact of the process of catalysis.

Scenario B can also be thought of both product innovation and process innovation. Again, EC could be used to generate the designs of the two enzymes and the other components cooperatively. However, making additional measurements about the self-assembly and self-disassembly processes is considerably harder. The reason is that Scenario B is an example of a complex system.[38] One of the defining characteristics of complex systems are feedback loops, where changes in a variable result in either amplification (positive feedback) or in dampening (negative feedback). The design of complex systems via AI is an open question.

4. Conclusion

This chapter presented the use of AI, specifically EC, to automatically generate the set of components that could construct themselves into a target structure via the process of self-assembly. Furthermore, the chapter explored how GAs used for product innovation (topology optimization) could be extended for process innovation.

One the common attributes of using AI for product and process innovation is the need for constraints to guide the design process. The difference between product and process innovation is temporal. This difference enables the development of complex systems. One attribute that was touched upon and not explored in-depth is noise, which is of critical importance. Self-assembly is inherently a noisy process. However, AI is useful for traversing noisy fitness landscapes.

Although self-assembly is not necessarily going to be the revolutionary construction process of the fourth industrial revolution, this nascent field of research does offer interesting lessons to innovation management in the abstract. Industry 4.0 involves cyber-physical systems. Computers and connected devices will make decentralized decisions, without human intervention. The design of these complex systems will define the smart factory of the future. As shown in this chapter AI can be applied to designing complex systems and automating innovation.

References

1. K. Schwab and N. Davis, *Shaping the Future of the Fourth Industrial Revolution: A Guide to Building a Better World*, First American ed. New York: Currency (2018).
2. M. Hammer, Deep change: How operational innovation can transform your company. *Harvard Business Review* (2004).
3. D.E. Nye, *America's Assembly Line*. Cambridge, MA: The MIT Press (2013).
4. A. Nevins and F.E. Hill, *Ford*. New York: Scribner (1954).
5. J. Rifkin, *The Third Industrial Revolution: How Lateral Power is Transforming Energy, the Economy, and the World*, 1st edn. New York: Palgrave Macmillan (2011).
6. Y. Monden, *Toyota Production System: An Integrated Approach to Just-In-Time*, 4th ed. Boca Raton, FL: CRC Press (2012).
7. J.W. Davis, *Lean Manufacturing: Implementation Strategies That Work: A Roadmap to Quick and Lasting Success*. New York: Industrial Press (2009).
8. S.J. Russell and P. Norvig, *Artificial Intelligence: A Modern Approach*, 3rd ed. Upper Saddle River, NJ: Prentice Hall (2010).
9. T.M. Mitchell, *Machine Learning*. New York: McGraw-Hill (1997).
10. T. Wuest, D. Weimer, C. Irgens, and K.-D. Thoben, Machine learning in manufacturing: Advantages, challenges, and applications, *Production & Manufacturing Research*, **4**, 23–45 (2016).
11. M. Mitchell, *An Introduction to Genetic Algorithms*. Cambridge, MA: MIT Press (1996).
12. C. Darwin, *On the Origin of Species Species*. Cambridge, MA: Harvard University Press (1966).
13. G.M. Whitesides and B. Grzybowski, Self-assembly at all scales, *Science*, **295**, 2418–2421 (2002).
14. P. Ball, *The Self-Made Tapestry: Pattern Formation in Nature*, Reprint ed. Oxford UA: Oxford University Press (2004).

15. L. Wolpert, *Principles of Development*, 3rd ed. Oxford, New York: Oxford University Press (2007).
16. N. Bhalla, Designing self-assembling systems via physically encoded information. University of Calgary, Department of Computer Science, xvi, 246 leaves (2011).
17. N. Bhalla, P.J. Bentley, P.D. Vize, and C. Jacob, Programming and evolving physical self-assembling systems in three dimensions, *Natural Computing*, **11**, 475–498 (2012).
18. N. Bhalla, P.J. Bentley, P.D. Vize, and C. Jacob, Staging the self-assembly process: Inspiration from biological development, *Artificial Life*, **20**, 29–53 (2014).
19. P. Bentley and D. Corne, *Creative Evolutionary Systems*. San Francisco, CA/ London: Morgan Kaufmann (2002).
20. P. Bentley, *Evolutionary Design by Computers*. San Francisco, CA: Morgan Kaufmann (1999).
21. L. Adleman, Q. Cheng, A. Goel, M.-D. Huang, D. Kempe, P.M. de Espanés, P.W.K. Rothemund, *et al.*, Combinatorial optimization problems in self-assembly, in *Proc. of Conference Combinatorial Optimization Problems in Self-Assembly*. Association for Computing Machinery, 23–32 (2002).
22. A. Rogers and A. Prugel-Bennett, Genetic drift in genetic algorithm selection schemes, *IEEE Transactions on Evolutionary Computation*, **3**, 298–303 (1999).
23. A. Hussain and Y. S. Muhammad, Trade-off between exploration and exploitation with genetic algorithm using a novel selection operator, *Complex & Intelligent Systems*, **6**, 1–14 (2020).
24. P. Funes and J. Pollack, Computer evolution of buildable objects, in *Proc. of Conference Computer Evolution of Buildable Objects,* 358–367 (1997).
25. J.D. Lohn, G.S. Hornby, and D.S. Linden, An evolved antenna for deployment on NASA's space technology 5 mission, in *Proc. of Conference An Evolved Antenna for Deployment on NASA's Space Technology 5 Mission* (2004).
26. L. Trautmann, Product customization and generative design, *Multidiszciplináris Tudományok*, **11**, 87–95 (2021).
27. K. Ounjai and B. Kaewkamnerdpong, Growing art: The evolutionary art tools, in *Proc. of Conference Growing Art: The Evolutionary Art Tools*, Berlin, Heidelberg, 126–136 (2012).
28. J.A. Pelesko, *Self Assembly: The Science of Things That Put Themselves Together*. Boca Raton, London: Chapman & Hall/CRC (2007).

29. R. Gross and M. Dorigo, Self-assembly at the macroscopic scale, in *Proc. of the IEEE*, **96**, 1490–1508 (2008).
30. P.W.K. Rothemund and E. Winfree, The program-size complexity of self-assembled squares (extended abstract), in *Proc. of Conference the Program-Size Complexity of Self-Assembled Squares (Extended Abstract)*. Association for Computing Machinery, 459–468 (2000).
31. P. Soille, *Morphological Image Analysis: Principles and Applications.* Berlin, New York: Springer Verlag (1999).
32. F.P. Beer, *Vector Mechanics for Engineers: Statics and Dynamics*, 7th edn. Boston: McGraw-Hill Higher Education (2004).
33. P.J. Bentley and J.P. Wakefield, Finding acceptable solutions in the pareto-optimal range using multiobjective genetic algorithms, in *Proc. of Conference Finding Acceptable Solutions in the Pareto-Optimal Range using Multiobjective Genetic Algorithms, London*, 231–240 (1998).
34. D.W. Corne and J.D. Knowles, Techniques for highly multiobjective optimisation: Some nondominated points are better than others, in *Proc. of Conference Techniques for Highly Multiobjective Optimisation: Some Nondominated Points Are Better than Others*. Association for Computing Machinery, 773–780 (2007).
35. G.R. Duarte, A.C. de Castro Lemonge, L.G. da Fonseca, B.S.L.P. de Lima, An island model based on stigmergy to solve optimization problems, *Natural Computing* (2020).
36. R. Chowdhury and C.D. Maranas, From directed evolution to computational enzyme engineering — A review, *AIChE Journal*, **66**, e16847 (2020).
37. P.K. Robinson, Enzymes: Principles and biotechnological applications, *Essays Biochem*, **59**, 1–41 (2015).
38. M. Mitchell, *Complexity: A Guided Tour*. Oxford: Oxford University Press (2009).

Chapter 7

Artificial Intelligence as a Strategic Innovation Capability

Françoise de Viron* and Benoit Gailly[†]

UCLouvain, Louvain School of Management
Place des Doyens, 1, 1348 Louvain-la-Neuve, Belgium
*francoise.deviron@uclouvain.be
†benoit.gailly@uclouvain.be

Mobilizing a knowledge-based perspective of the firm, this chapter outlines how artificial intelligence (AI) technologies can be seen as new innovation capabilities allowing firms to learn from existing and new knowledge assets. This approach allows managers and scholars to adopt a strategic perspective regarding the development of their AI assets and capabilities. We identify in particular four types of organizational learning strategies, considering whether to build analytic capabilities (both technical and organizational) on the one hand to best exploit the knowledge embedded in their existing data assets and on the other hand to explore — identify and capture — new sources of knowledge.

1. Introduction

While artificial intelligence (AI) has emerged during the last decades as a general-purpose technology, how it affects firms from a strategic point of view remains confusing and subject to dense debates, from the skeptics seeing it as "another buzzword" to the "messiahs" announcing the dawn of a disruptive era. In this context, the objective of this chapter is to discuss how AI and its related technologies can be integrated in the strategic management thinking of a firm, using the lenses provided by the knowledge management literature.

In particular, this chapter outlines how AI might be integrated into a strategic management approach as a powerful tool to extend firm resources. Our theoretical reflection is based on our knowledge and experience in innovation management and knowledge management, combined with a general know-how in AI. This experience is both academic, as we conduct teaching and research in these fields, and practice-driven, as we have been actors in these fields and are still consultants and board members in various international companies.

When analyzing AI as a knowledge-based innovation capability, our vision of innovation is aligned with Ref. [1], considering both innovation as a process and as an outcome: "Innovation is production or adoption, assimilation, and exploitation of a value-added novelty in economic and social spheres; renewal and enlargement of products, services, and markets; development of new methods of production; and establishment of new management systems."[1] Let us stress that from this firm-level perspective, the innovation outcomes can be very diverse, including a new product, a new service, a new technology, a new form of organization or a new business model. As a consequence, in line with many authors,[2–4] we consider innovation as essentially a knowledge-based process, aiming at creating new knowledge, a process which is extremely dependent on the availability of existing knowledge.

In this chapter, we use the term AI in wide acceptance of the related technologies, i.e., a system's ability to perform autonomously tasks that usually would call for human intelligence.[5] Or more precisely, a system's ability *to correctly interpret complex and unstructured external data, to learn and adapt from such data, and to use those learnings to achieve specific goals and tasks.*[6] Our broad vision of AI therefore not only includes advanced data analytics and intelligent algorithms[7] but also traditional AI symbolic systems, such as expert systems or language generation systems.[5]

Taking a firm-level perspective, we consider how these technologies can be adopted and implemented by individual firms in order to boost their competitiveness. We outline in the following section the conceptual logic connecting innovation to knowledge assets and therefore its link to data as a form of embedded knowledge. We then discuss in the following section how AI can be seen as a set of technical and organizational capabilities, allowing firms to both exploit and explore knowledge assets. We conclude with a discussion of the managerial implications, limitations and perspectives related to our approach.

2. Theoretical Background

2.1. *Innovation management, knowledge and data*

In our approach, we see innovation both as a process and an outcome, whose main determinants as determined by Ref. [1] are leadership, managerial levers and business processes. In particular at the firm level, beyond an explicit innovation strategy, these authors highlight as key drivers a learning environment, promoting individual and organizational learning, as well as knowledge management systems, including different tools allowing knowledge creation, discovery and sharing, both internally and externally.

Organizational learning has indeed long been known to be an important aspect of innovation.[8–10] Identifying, evaluating and capturing innovation opportunities requires firms to engage in various types of knowledge-seeking activities, both across and outside their organizational boundaries.[11–13] Conversely, organizational learning fosters the identification of innovation opportunities,[14] be it regarding markets, technologies, regulation or business models.

As a consequence, the ability of an organization to learn at individual, team and organizational levels[15] will play a key role in its ability to innovate, both regarding the management of innovation opportunities and the identification of new ones.

In the knowledge management literature, learning is usually viewed as a way of developing and maintaining knowledge assets. Organizational learning therefore implies that knowledge is stored in or used by individuals, groups, and the organization. It is also continually evolving.[16] In their proposed integrated socio-technological approach, it implies a focus on the two facets of knowledge: knowledge as a stock and knowledge as a flow, actual or potential.

One way knowledge can be stored and flow is as knowledge embedded in data (see, for example, Ref. [17]). However, for many years, as pointed out in Ref. [18], the definitions of data and knowledge, as well as related concepts, such as information and wisdom, vary according to the adopted perspective. For the purpose of this chapter, we propose to combine both the information systems and knowledge management perspectives.

Data can be seen as a set of symbols[19] and signal readings,[20] a set of discrete objective facts or observations about events, traditionally described as structured records of transactions.[21] Data is also defined in terms of what it lacks: data can lack meaning or value when it is unorganized and unprocessed.[18] When data is organized and structured for a specific purpose of context, it can be seen as information, for example, as a document, an audible or visible communication[21] or a flow of messages.[22]

On the other hand, knowledge can be seen as a mix of organized and processed data (information) and of understanding, capability experience, skills and values.[18] It is therefore a fluid mix of framed experience, values, contextual information and expert insights that provides a framework for evaluating and incorporating new experiences and information.[21] From this perspective, knowledge can be seen as personalized information[23] and relate to facts, procedures, concepts, interpretation, thought, observation and judgment.

In a firm, knowledge derives from workers' minds, including their practice, experience, expertise, and competencies. But knowledge could also be embedded in a firm's documents, knowledge repositories, organizational routines, patents, copyrights, processes and software, usually referred to as the structural component of the intellectual capital supporting innovation.[24] As Ref. [18] underlined many years ago, in this perspective, explicit knowledge is nothing more than information: organized and processed data.

For Ref. [20], however, in a more constructivist perspective, knowledge is all at once knowing what (the cognition or recognition), knowing how (the capacity to act) and knowing why (the understanding). Knowledge is less a commodity that individuals or organizations may acquire, but knowledge is an activity, something they do, related to their capacity to act and which could be described as a process of knowing.[25]

It follows from these two perspectives that the classical hierarchy between data and knowledge as proposed by Ref. [19], where all knowledge is based on data, should be reconsidered, as already suggested many years ago in Ref. [18]. In line with recent developments,[26] we therefore consider data and knowledge as overlapping sets: knowledge is more than data, as it is also built up from experience, education, and practice. Conversely, data does not always contain knowledge, but is one of the important knowledge "reservoirs" of the firm.[27]

As a consequence, the knowledge assets of a firm include but go beyond the knowledge which is embedded in data, i.e., stored in or derived from data.[28]

2.2. *Knowledge as a strategic resource for innovation*

If we recognize that knowledge is a key resource for innovation, it becomes *de facto* a strategic resource for innovative firms. Knowledge has indeed long been recognized by scholars as a strategic resource, in particular when it is valuable, rare, imperfectly imitable, and non-substitutable.[29,30]

This knowledge-based view (KBV) of the firm establishes the knowledge possessed by organizations as their most essential resource to achieve sustainable competitive advantage.[31,32] Knowledge refers to individual and organizational knowledge, including competencies and resources to mobilize them, and might be in the form of stocks or flows as described earlier. Being recognized as a significant resource, knowledge (including — but not limited to — the knowledge embedded in data) becomes an ingredient of the firm strategy formulation.[33]

A way to link knowledge and strategy in a KBV approach is proposed by Ref. [34], via the notion of knowledge strategy, i.e., the competitive strategy built around a firm's intellectual resources and capabilities. The knowledge strategy focuses on the way knowledge can become a strategic asset and consists of two steps: first an inventory of the intellectual resources of the firm, recognizing its importance and its content followed then by an analysis of these resources in order to identify which knowledge is critical, i.e., valuable, rare and inimitable,[16,35] and why. This inventory and analysis allow the firm to identify the knowledge that develops its competitive advantages or strengthens its position towards its customers, stakeholders and markets.

One way of conducting such knowledge strategy is for the firm to map its own critical knowledge assets along a Johari window, as proposed by

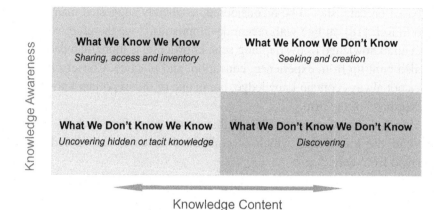

Knowledge Content

Fig. 1. Mapping strategic knowledge assets (based on Ref. [36]).

Ref. [36]. In such a "knowledge map," the firm needs to consider on the one hand the status of various knowledge contents (the know-how, the know-what, the know-why and the know-who), in particular the available data, and on the other hand its awareness regarding that knowledge (see Fig. 1). Let us stress that this analysis can be completed by the firm itself, but that it can also be beneficial to involve third parties able to provide an outside-in perspective.[37]

It distinguishes in particular the knowledge the firm is aware of and has access to (and can therefore purposefully use) versus the knowledge it is not aware of and/or it does not have access to, and the resulting knowledge-related activities: sharing, seeking and creation, uncovering and discovering. In line with the perspective outlined above, those various knowledge contents and activities include, but are not limited to, knowledge embedded in the data the firm owns or has access to.

Such a mapping of critical knowledge assets can help firms strike the right balance between learning strategies focused on exploitation and exploration.[38–40]

In this context, it means on the one hand building the capabilities to exploit available knowledge assets, in particular the knowledge embedded in the available data ("learn from" — top-left quadrant), and on the other hand building the capabilities to explore new knowledge assets ("learn about"), in particular through the use of new data sources. Such exploration includes not only capturing identified missing knowledge assets (top-right quadrant) but also identifying new ones the firm actually has already captured (bottom-left quadrant) or could capture (bottom-right quadrant).

Having highlighted from a theoretical point of view the link between innovation and knowledge assets, the role of data as a source of embedded knowledge, and the resulting challenge of balancing exploitation or exploration organizational learning strategies, we discuss in Section 3 how AI-related capabilities can help firms become more effective in the implementation of these organizational learning strategies, in particular those related to knowledge assets embedded in data.

3. AI Fostering Organizational Learning

In this section, we review how AI-related capabilities (as defined above) can be used as ways to foster both the exploitative and explorative organizational learning strategies outlined above. We discuss first the cognitive capacities of AI allowing firms to more effectively learn from — exploit — the knowledge embedded in their available data. We then discuss how firms can also use AI to learn about — explore — new knowledge assets, leveraging both available and new sources of data.

3.1. *Exploitation: AI as a new way to learn from available data*

We first consider the top-left quadrant of the knowledge map presented above (Fig. 1), i.e., what firms know they know, for example, in terms of product profitability or process performance. On the basis of the synthesis proposed by Ref. [41], identifying the fields of technological development of AI and the techniques used, we outline in the following the related cognitive capacities of historical and current AI technologies. Table 1 illustrates this range of AI cognitive capacities and the tools supporting or developing these capacities.

Mobilizing the cognitive capacities of AI on its known knowledge assets (for example, data from its Enterprise Resource Planning and Customer Relationship Management systems or from its patent database) can indeed help firm grow the value of those assets.

Table 1. AI cognitive capacities, AI technology fields and used technologies (derived from Ref. [41]).

Capacities	Technology field	Example of used technology
Reasoning	Knowledge processing	Expert systems, knowledge graphs, knowledge representation systems, cognitive maps, etc.
Learning	Machine learning	Neural networks, deep-learning evidence-based methods, rule-based methods, decision trees, statistical techniques
Perception	Image and video processing	Pattern recognition, image recognition, video analysis
Communicating	Natural language processing	Language generation, language understanding (text, speech), text mining, semantic search, content analysis
Planning and optimizing, simulation	Data analysis and prediction	Predictive analytics, prescriptive analytics

While this use of AI by a firm as a way to foster its exploitative organizational learning strategy might seem straightforward, one should not underestimate the underlying operational challenges. These include not only attracting or developing the talent required to master the related technologies and software but also developing the organizational capabilities required to identify, integrate and maintain the relevant knowledge assets throughout the firm (data governance, data quality, etc.).

The knowledge management literature (see, for example, Ref. [42]) indicates that developing and maintaining the right organizational capabilities and talent is often a much bigger challenge than developing and maintaining the right technological capabilities, as it can affect the values, power structure, culture and governance of the organization[43,44] and is therefore also a change management challenge, not simply a technology challenge.

3.1.1. *Exploration: AI as a new way to learn from (new) data*

While the cognitive capacities of AI provide firms with new ways to learn from their existing data (as discussed above), they also provide firms new

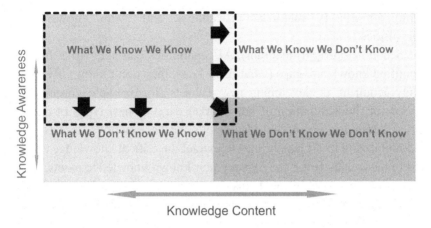

Fig. 2. AI as a way to extend known knowledge.

ways to learn by uncovering new knowledge embedded in existing data and/or by leveraging new data. The resulting options in terms of explorative learning strategies are illustrated in Fig. 2.

First (bottom-left quadrant), AI capabilities can help firms extract valuable knowledge embedded but "hidden" in their existing data (what firms don't know they know). This includes in particular the knowledge held by employees, in their mind or practices, often referred to as human capital of intellectual capital, and not considered as data-embedded knowledge.

AI capabilities can help firms learn, interpret, precept these existing data not yet exploited in order to detect phenomena and extract new knowledge. For instance, in order to identify customer behavior in a shop, data collected via surveillance cameras could be used to identify the routes most used or weak signals on customer behavior and, on this basis, develop new assortments. Or in order to strengthen the safety management plan and identify the pattern of operations leading to nearly missed incidents, AI could help in precepting and interpreting videos of expert practices in manufacturing or in machine maintenance.

Let us stress that this was already the case for AI applications in the 1980s when firms developed expert systems to support decisions or to assist operators or to monitor operations or when they developed cognitive maps or natural language interfaces to speed up the consultation and the filling of quality manuals, procedures, and "who knows what" repositories.

Second (top-right quadrant), AI capabilities can help firms fill their identified knowledge gaps (what firms know they don't know). By proactively acquiring or developing new datasets (for example, through new sensors or the acquisition of new market data) or new types of datasets (images, movies, noise, and also smells, tastes, emotions, moods, etc.), and mobilizing its AI capabilities to extract the critical knowledge embedded in these data, firms can expand their known knowledge assets.

As an example, some firms are now considering how extracting knowledge embedded in new data assets such as weather or traffic data could help them anticipate specific market needs. As another example, the monitoring of the noise or vibration of an equipment can sometimes be used to anticipate failures or accidents.

Third (bottom-right quadrant), the mobilization of AI capabilities can allow firms to discover unexpected knowledge embedded in new data. In this case, the firm is not aware of what it does not know, but explores through experimentation.

This includes trial-and-error approaches, such as the A/B testing implemented by online retailers, or data mining approaches, such as the rapid-throughput research methods used by laboratories to test a wide range of molecules and genes. Again, this approach can be associated with older techniques such as cluster analysis, where researchers try to uncover hidden patterns or properties.

Let us stress that in these three cases, the mobilization of AI capabilities to extract knowledge embedded in new datasets actually enlarges its knowledge assets (what it knows it knows), as illustrated by the dotted line in Fig. 2. As a consequence, it provides opportunities both to identify and better manage innovation opportunities. In Section 4, we discuss some managerial implications of using AI as a way to grow the knowledge assets of a firm.

4. Managing AI as a Strategic Innovation Capability

Taking a knowledge-based perspective on AI as a differentiating capability for innovation management allows us to draw specific managerial implications. In particular, this perspective focuses on distinguishing the critical knowledge assets allowing the firm to develop competitive advantages and deploying innovation capacities.

We highlighted in particular that AI capabilities can allow firms to grow their knowledge assets by expanding what "they know that they know" and inviting innovation managers to have a fresh look at the knowledge assets of their firm. If we consider these knowledge assets as strategic, this means that firms must consider both their knowledge assets (in particular, the knowledge embedded in their data assets) and its capability to extract knowledge embedded in these data assets. We will discuss these dimensions hereafter.

The first key dimension relates to the datasets and data-embedded knowledge that is accessible to a firm versus those that are not currently accessible. Accessibility of data relates in particular to the datasets for which a sufficient volume of data of acceptable quality can be processed by a firm (see, for example, Ref. [45] for a classic discussion of the dimensions of data quality). While some datasets (for example, those related to financials, SKUs or employees) can often easily be accessed by most firms, there are multiple technical, legal, organizational and competitive hurdles which can prevent firms to access valuable datasets, including operational, market, competitive or environmental data.

In particular, building operational "data-lakes" required as a prerequisite by many algorithms has been repeatedly identified as one of the biggest challenges faced by organizations trying to leverage AI,[46] in particular as "Big Data" is not always "better data."[47] As a consequence, analyzing and understanding which valuable datasets are currently accessible, which ones could be accessible through available technical and organizational processes and finally which ones are probably definitely out of reach is a prerequisite for managing AI as a source of competitive innovation management.

The second key dimension relates to the analytic capabilities the firm currently masters[48] and how it can best combine them.[49,50] While most organizations have the talent and skills required to run simple statistical analysis using widely available office tools, only a few truly master cutting-edge algorithms and even less can combine these algorithms with the in-depth technical and business expertise required to on the one hand select and pre-process the right data ("garbage in, garbage out") and on the other hand carefully interpret the results provided (avoid running a "black box"). These analytic capabilities include the ability to use dedicated approaches to analyze not only complex datasets but also the accumulated learning embedded in the algorithms themselves (in particular, in neural networks).

As a consequence, analyzing and understanding where the current analytic capabilities of the firm are adequate, where they need to — and can be — improved and where they could become cutting edge and therefore differentiating is also a prerequisite for managing AI as a source of competitive innovation management.

Consideration of these two key dimensions (knowledge embedded in data assets and AI capabilities) leads to four organizational learning strategies calling for distinct managerial approaches to AI as an innovation enabler (Fig. 3). These are outlined in the following.

In the first organizational learning strategy ("Exploit"), the focus of innovation managers should be to identify "low hanging fruits," opportunities to leverage existing datasets and analytical capabilities to better identify, evaluate and capture innovation opportunities. This strategy is the first step for many firms active in traditional industrial sectors.

In the second organizational learning strategy ("Extract"), innovation managers need to build or acquire the technological and organizational talent, culture and skills required to better extract valuable knowledge from accessible datasets. This strategy is leading firms not only to hire new "data talent" but also to improve their "data governance," in

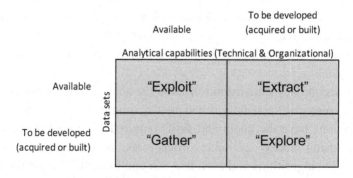

Fig. 3. AI as an enabler for innovation — Four strategies.

particular regarding the handling and integration of multiple data sources across the organization.

In the third organizational learning strategy ("Gather"), innovation managers should focus on leveraging their internal and external resources (such as partnerships) in order to identify and acquire or build new knowledge-rich datasets. This strategy ("data as the new oil") has long been exploited in the consumer space by "digital champions," such as Google or Facebook, but is now increasingly applicable to new (in particular, B2B) industries and sectors.

The fourth and last organizational learning strategy ("Explore") focuses on the design and implementation of cheap experiments (internally or in collaboration with start-ups or research centers) in order to uncover hidden knowledge embedded in data. This means exploring both existing or new types of data and new ways to exploit them. Examples of such strategies include firms exploring the capabilities of quantum computing or firms trying to extract valuable knowledge from individual protein and genetic profiles to develop personalized nutrition or personalized medicine offers.

Let us stress that these organizational learning strategies are not exclusive, as an innovation manager could choose (or need) to combine more than one of them to remain competitive.

5. Conclusions, Perspectives and Limitations

In this chapter, we illustrated how a knowledge-based approach can be mobilized in order to highlight some strategic challenges and opportunities related to AI for innovation managers.

In particular, we highlighted the need for innovation managers to focus not only on sophisticated algorithms but also on existing and new knowledge-rich data assets as well as on existing and new analytical capabilities, both from organizational and technical points of view. We derived four organizational learning strategies that innovation managers could consider and potentially combine.

From a research point of view, we also highlighted how concepts derived from the knowledge-based view of the firm could be mobilized in order to develop a better understanding of the impact and implications of AI for innovation.

Taking a strategic perspective on AI allows in particular scholars to view it as a core capability of the firm rather than (only) a source of technology disruption. This endogenous perspective opens new avenues for research, in particular regarding how data-based knowledge assets can be best combined with other corporate resources and how competitive dynamics (first mover advantages, network and scale effect, alliances, etc.) affects the emergence and competitiveness of specific data-based knowledge assets.

On the other hand, revisiting knowledge management under the lenses of AI also opens new avenues for research regarding on the one hand the interplay between data and knowledge and on the other hand the nature of observable[51] (or accessible) knowledge within a firm.

As an illustration of this blurring distinction between tacit and explicit knowledge, if an AI tool identifies inexplicable patterns of good or best practices simply by observing specific organizational behaviors or processes (for example, in the case of A/B testing), does the result count as tacit or explicit knowledge? A potentially interesting track might be to consider knowledge not according to a tacit/explicit dichotomy, but as a continuum in which the degree of the complexity of knowledge changes depending upon the amount of tacitness involved, as suggested by Ref. [33].

The approach adopted in this chapter is by nature conceptual, which is in itself a limitation. Other limitations one should consider include important contingencies related both to the firm (e.g., its size, culture, age, or the nature of the innovations it pursues) and the nature of the knowledge involved (in particular, the balance and interplay between data-embedded and non-data-embedded knowledge). Different organizations could extract different knowledge from the same data. The organizational culture of the firm or the emotional state of its members are examples of important aspects that cannot be easily reduced to data. We were also not able to take into account important factors related to the environment the firm faces, for example, in terms of regulation or competitive intensity. Finally, there are important leadership and ethical challenges related to the use of AI by firms, which should definitely be taken into account, but these fall beyond the scope of this chapter.

We however hope to have contributed to a better understanding of some strategic implications of AI as an innovation capability and inspired new ways forward both for innovation managers and scholars.

References

1. M.M. Crossan and M. Apaydin, A multi-dimensional framework of organizational innovation: A systematic review of the literature. *Journal of Management Studies*, **47**(6), 1154–1191 (2010).
2. J. Tidd, J. Bessant, and K. Pavitt, Chapter 1: Key issues in innovation management. *Managing Innovation: Integrating Technological, Market, and Organizational Change*, 3rd ed. England: John Wiley & Sons (2005).
3. M. Du Plessis, The role of knowledge management in innovation. *Journal of Knowledge Management*, **11**(4), 20–29 (2007).
4. J. Tidd (ed.), *From Knowledge Management to Strategic Competence: Assessing Technological, Market and Organisational Innovation*, Vol. 19. World Scientific Publishing Company; London: Imperial College Press (2012).
5. J.P. Mueller and L. Massaron, *Artificial Intelligence for Dummies*. Hoboken, NJ: John Wiley & Sons (2018). Available at: https://www.wiley.com/en-us/Artificial+Intelligence+For+Dummies-p-9781119467656.
6. N. Bhalla, H. Blackbright, B. Gailly, and S. Tanev, Innovation Management in the Age of Artificial Intelligence, *Whitepaper presented at The ISPIM Innovation Conference — Innovating in Times of Crisis, Virtual* (2020).
7. T.H. Davenport and R. Ronanki, Artificial intelligence for the real world. *Harvard Business Review*, **96**(1), 108–116 (2018).
8. D. McKee, An organizational learning approach to product innovation. *Journal of Product Innovation Management*, **9**(3), 232–245 (1992).
9. R. Stata, Organizational learning-the key to management innovation. *MIT Sloan Management Review*, **30**(3), 63 (1989).
10. J. Tidd, Complexity, networks & learning: Integrative themes for research on innovation management. *International Journal of Innovation Management*, **1**(1), 1–21 (1997).
11. A.F. De Toni and E. Pessot, Investigating organisational learning to master project complexity: An embedded case study. *Journal of Business Research*, **129**, 541–554 (2020).
12. P.N. Figueiredo, H. Larsen, and U.E. Hansen, The role of interactive learning in innovation capability building in multinational subsidiaries: A micro-level study of biotechnology in Brazil. *Research Policy*, **49**(6), 103995 (2020).
13. S.S.V. Tambosi, G. Gomes, and M. Amal, Organisational learning capability and innovation: Study on companies located in regional cluster. *International Journal of Innovation Management*, **24**(6), 2050057 (2020).
14. Q. Xiang, J. Zhang, and H. Liu, Organisational improvisation as a path to new opportunity identification for incumbent firms: An organisational learning view. *Innovation*, **22**(4), 422–446 (2020).

15. C.H. Lin and K. Sanders, HRM and innovation: A multi-level organisational learning perspective. *Human Resource Management Journal*, **27**(2), 300–317 (2017).

16. D. Vera, M. Crossan, and M. Apaydin, A framework for integrating organizational learning, knowledge, capabilities, and absorptive capacity. *Handbook of Organizational Learning and Knowledge Management*, **2**, 153–180 (2011).

17. M.W. Chun and R.A.M.I.R.O Montealegre, The problems of embedded information systems and embedded knowledge: Implications for systems integration and knowledge management. *Journal of Information Technology Management*, **18**(2), 38–64 (2007).

18. J. Rowley, The wisdom hierarchy: Representations of the DIKW hierarchy. *Journal of Information Science*, **33**(2), 163–180 (2007).

19. R.L. Ackoff, From data to wisdom. *Journal of Applied Systems Analysis*, **16**(1), 3–9 (1989).

20. A. Liew, Understanding data, information, knowledge and their interrelationships. *Journal of Knowledge Management Practice*, **8**(2), 1–16 (2007).

21. T.H. Davenport and L. Prusak, *Working Knowledge: How Organizations Manage What They Know*. Boston, Massachusetts: Harvard Business Press (1998).

22. I. Nonaka and H. Takeuchi, *The Knowledge-Creating Company: How Japanese Companies Create the Dynamics of Innovation*. New York, Oxford: Oxford University Press (1995).

23. X. Lin, Review of knowledge and knowledge management research. *American Journal of Industrial and Business Management*, **9**(9), 1753 (2019).

24. M. Subramaniam and M.A. Youndt, The influence of intellectual capital on the types of innovative capabilities. *Academy of Management Journal*, **48**(3), 450–463 (2005).

25. M. Polanyi, *The Tacit Dimension*. London: Routledge (1967).

26. X. Tian, Big data and knowledge management: A case of déjà vu or back to the future? *Journal of Knowledge Management*, **21**(1), 113–131 (2017).

27. L. Argote and P. Ingram, Knowledge transfer: A basis for competitive advantage in firms. *Organizational Behavior and Human Decision Processes*, **82**(1), 150–169 (2000).

28. W.H. Chen, S.H. Tsai, and H.I. Lin, Fault section estimation for power networks using logic cause-effect models. *IEEE Transactions on Power Delivery*, **26**(2), 963–971 (2010).

29. J.B. Barney, Firm resources and sustained competitive advantage. *Journal of Management*, **17**, 99–120 (1991).

30. P. Hartmann and J. Henkel, Really the new oil? A resource-based perspective on data-driven innovation. *Academy of Management Global Proceedings*, 142 (2018).

31. K.R. Conner and C.K. Prahalad, A resource-based theory of the firm: Knowledge versus opportunism. *Organization Science*, **7**(5), 477–501 (1996).

32. R.M. Grant, Toward a knowledge-based theory of the firm. *Strategic Management Journal*, **17**(S2), 109–122 (1996).

33. S. Ceylan, *Using Knowledge Transfer Partnership Projects to Reveal Latent Dynamics in the Knowledge-Based View of Strategy*. Doctoral dissertation, Nottingham Trent University (2018).

34. M.H. Zack, Developing a knowledge strategy, in Choo, C.W. and Bontis, N. (eds.), *The Strategic Management of Intellectual Capital and Organizational Knowledge*, pp. 255–276, Oxford: Oxford University Press (2002).

35. A. Cabrera and E.F. Cabrera, Knowledge-sharing dilemmas. *Organization Studies*, **23**(5), 687–710 (2002).

36. S. Drew, Building knowledge management into strategy: Making sense of a new perspective. *Long Range Planning*, **32**(1), 130–136 (1999).

37. G.S. Day, An outside-in approach to resource-based theories. *Journal of the Academy of Marketing Science*, **42**(1), 27–28 (2014).

38. Z.L. He and P.K. Wong, Exploration vs. exploitation: An empirical test of the ambidexterity hypothesis. *Organization Science*, **15**(4), 481–494 (2004).

39. A.K. Gupta, K.G. Smith, and C.E. Shalley, The interplay between exploration and exploitation. *Academy of Management Journal*, **49**(4), 693–706 (2006).

40. H.R. Greve, Exploration and exploitation in product innovation. *Industrial and Corporate Change*, **16**(5), 945–975 (2007).

41. E. Prem, Artificial intelligence for innovation in Austria. *Technology Innovation Management Review*, **9**(12), 5–15 (2019).

42. R.L. Ackoff, Management misinformation systems. *Management Science*, **14**(4), B-147 (1967).

43. D.W. De Long and L. Fahey, Diagnosing cultural barriers to knowledge management. *Academy of Management Perspectives*, **14**(4), 113–127 (2000).

44. F.L. Oliva, Knowledge management barriers, practices and maturity model. *Journal of Knowledge Management*, **18**(6), 1053–1074 (2014).

45. R.Y. Wang and D.M. Strong, Beyond accuracy: What data quality means to data consumers. *Journal of Management Information Systems*, **12**(4), 5–33 (1996).

46. L. DalleMule and T.H. Davenport, What's your data strategy. *Harvard Business Review*, **95**(3), 112–121 (2017).

47. M. Ghasemaghaei and G. Calic, Assessing the impact of big data on firm innovation performance: Big data is not always better data. *Journal of Business Research*, **108**, 147–162 (2020).

48. A. Ferraris, A. Mazzoleni, A. Devalle, and J. Couturier, Big data analytics capabilities and knowledge management: Impact on firm performance. *Management Decision*, **57**(8), 1923–1936 (2019).

49. P. Mikalef and J. Krogstie, Examining the interplay between big data analytics and contextual factors in driving process innovation capabilities. *European Journal of Information Systems*, **29**(3), 260–287 (2020).

50. J. Liu, H. Chang, J.Y.L. Forrest, and B. Yang, Influence of artificial intelligence on technological innovation: Evidence from the panel data of China's manufacturing sectors. *Technological Forecasting and Social Change*, **158**, 120142 (2020).

51. L. Michael, Partial observability and learnability. *Artificial Intelligence*, **174**(11), 639–669 (2010).

Chapter 8

Disrupting the Research Process through Artificial Intelligence: Towards a Research Agenda

Mikael Johnsson*, Christopher Gustafsson†, and Peter E. Johansson‡

Mälardalen University, School of Innovation Design and Engineering
Box 325, 631 05 Eskilstuna, Sweden
*mikael.johnsson@mdh.se
†christopher.gustafsson@mdh.se
‡peter.e.johansson@mdh.se

This chapter explores how Artificial Intelligence (AI) will potentially disrupt how Innovation Management (IM) research will be conducted. In the recent decades, the research process has remained virtually unchanged, i.e., a structured, stepwise process. Recently, AI has shown new opportunities that affect this process. AI applications have been developed supporting researchers for specific tasks to ease their work, for example, database searching, transcribing and data management. For example, an autonomous literature review (i.e., database search, selection, analyzing, concluding, and writing) has been conducted by AI, vastly exceeding what human research could achieve in the same time frame, which paves the way for interesting reflections on how AI applications affect research from here on going forward. As we have explored AI techniques and AI applications and discussed their potential for conducting research, three themes emerged regarding how future research might be conducted: simplification thorough the use of computational power, augmentation of a researcher's capabilities, and replacement by automation: Three critical questions are identified: (1) The future use of AI applications in research; (2) Exploring the trust in AI — The black box dilemma, and; (3) Benefits and limitations of AI applications. These topics are discussed, paving a way towards a research agenda.

1. Introduction

An important part of the development of Innovation Management (IM) practice is IM research. The research process of IM, or any social science, has looked largely the same for decades. Of course, there has been some progress regarding certain aspects of the research process, for example, software that supports different kinds of empirical analysis, such as SPSS[1] for statistical analysis and Nvivo[2] for qualitative analysis, and the availability of published publications through an ever-growing number of databases. Yet, major parts of the research process in social sciences remain the same and are characterized by manual labor and, as such, heavily rely on researchers' expertise in conducting research, e.g., conducting literature reviews to identify relevant research questions or analyzing large amounts of empirical data, both of which are key parts of the research process.

In a growing number of areas of working life technologies that can be labeled AI are about to significantly impact how work is conducted.[3] For example, related to innovation management, AI has been used to change how we invent things, i.e., developing the methods of inventing,[4] which means that the outcome of what AI generates is not affected by human impact (except for the fact that humans still develop the code that AI applications use).

This ongoing transformation of working life through the adoption and integration of AI will most likely also be the case in academia and social science research. Following this, in this chapter, we will discuss how the emergence of AI applications may disrupt the highly manual research process as we know it today and, in doing so, potentially radically change the role of innovation management researchers in the future. Based on the discussion, we will pose some critical questions that form the basis of a future research agenda. The following topics are discussed and elaborated in Section 4:

- The future use of AI applications in research.
- Exploring the trust in AI — The black box dilemma.
- Benefits and limitations of AI applications.

2. Approaches in Innovation Management Research

Research on innovation management (IM) practice is largely positioned in the social science research domain, which in its most general sense entails the study of human society and social relationships. The research objects in IM research are many and varied, depending on the discipline to which the researcher belongs. Thus, a diversity of research approaches and methods are used in IM research, suggesting that how research is conducted in practice is highly dependent on the researcher's scientific approach.

In IM research, it is possible to distinguish between three major scientific approaches adopted by researchers: the deductive, the inductive and the abductive.[5] The deductive approach is based on formal logical reasoning and aims to "derive logically valid conclusions from given premises,"[5] in which an essential quality of the researcher is to have the ability of logical reasoning. This approach is highly theory driven,[6] in which formulating and testing hypotheses is a common practice which, in turn, requires a research design suitable for testing hypotheses, such as quasi-experimental design or comparative design. The second approach, inductive, aims "from a number of observations to draw universally valid conclusions about a whole population,"[5] in which the ability to master statistical analysis is to be regarded as an essential quality of the researcher. In this approach, generating large empirical datasets is a common practice. The third and final approach, abductive, aims to "interpret and recontextualize individual phenomena in a conceptual framework or a set of ideas,"[5] in which creativity and imagination are highlighted as important qualities on the researcher's part. In this approach, which is often phenomenon driven,[6] case studies are a common research practice of providing a rich set of data and in-depth insights.

Given the differences between the three scientific approaches, this will significantly impact on the decisions made during the research process: from the start of the process when framing the research problem to the end of the process when drawing conclusions and making inferences.[7]

However, even though most social science research activities depend on the researcher's scientific approach, the research process still comprises a number of generic steps. Examples of research guidelines can be easily found by searching online, including university websites.[8] Even though the nature of the research process is highly iterative, below are five generic and critical steps of the research process and the core activities of each step.

(1) *Identifying and framing the research problem.* Selection of appropriate research questions and research design. A second generic step is to select an appropriate research question followed by a research design and research methods for conducting the research study. Case studies or comparative studies are a common practice, while experimental designs are less frequent in IM research.

(2) *Data collection.* IM research comprises methods such as surveys, interviews and observations. While surveys can be conducted both manually and digitally, interviews and observations typically require social interaction with the respondents. Depending on the type of data being collected, the compilation of data varies.

(3) *Analyzing the data.* In social science research, a common distinction is made between Quantitative analysis and Qualitative analysis.[9] To support data analysis, several computer-based tools have been developed over the years — for example, SPSS for supporting quantitative analysis and Nvivo for supporting qualitative analysis.

(4) *Drawing conclusions and making inferences.* The final step of the research process is when the researcher draws conclusions based on their analysis, which then forms the basis for publishing the results in scientific publications.

2.1. Research ethics

All research requires ethical considerations to be made. There are two main areas of research ethics: internal and external ethics,[10] i.e., how the research has been conducted, referring to the quality of the craftsmanship (internal ethics); and, the impact of the results on the object studied or on society at large (external ethics). For this reason, norms and rules have been developed, for example, the Vancouver Rules published by the International Committee of Medical Journal Editors (ICMJE),[11] which are supposed to be observed by the research community. The norms and rules are basically about the researcher's reliability, honesty, respect, and accountability. However, in practice, ethical aspects are not always taken into account. The website Retraction Watch[12] has continuous updates about research misconduct, for example, falsification and fabrication. In 2020, the most retracted articles were related to COVID-19, during the year that the pandemic started. By the end of the year, nearly 40 articles had been retracted.[13] In most cases, these articles were related to fabrication and falsification. However, in some cases, articles were retracted by the researchers' themselves. They understood that they had jumped to conclusions, as the conclusions had been drawn at the beginning of the pandemic, when the outcome was still unknown.

Regarding AI, the European Commission has published ethical guidelines specifically developed for AI applications. The guidelines describe three aspects for an AI to be considered trustworthy: (1) lawful, the AI application should respect all applicable laws and regulations; (2) ethical, the AI application should respect ethical principles and values; (3) robust, the AI application should be robust from a technical perspective while also taking the social environment into account. This paves the way for further work on AI and research ethics. Will we see fewer retractions on, for example, the Retraction Watch as AI is obliged to follow set rules?

3. Introduction to AI and Applications

In this section, we will take a holistic view of AI and its applications, in everyday life, industry, and in research specifically, in order to frame future opportunities and challenges. In order to share our insights, we refer to examples of AI applications currently available. The reference list contains links to websites.

3.1. *AI technologies*

AI can be divided in five main technological categories: search and optimization, logic, probabilistic methods for uncertain reasoning, classifiers and statistical learning methods, and neural networks. All of them comprise sub technologies, specific characteristics and utilities, as can be seen from the other chapters in this book. Here, in Table 1, computational technologies with sub technologies and examples of applications are summarized,[14–17] followed by examples of, but not limited to, available applications for practical use.

3.1.1. *Search and optimization*

There are three main areas in the field of search and optimization: search algorithm, mathematical optimization and evolutionary computation. A search algorithm is an algorithm that solves a search problem, i.e., which is to retrieve information stored in a data structure, for example, a database.[14–17] This technique is used in search algorithms, for example, to optimize workflows,[18] monitor specified keywords[19] and create graphs or structures.[20] Mathematical optimization or mathematical programming is about selecting the most optimal component of a criterion from a set of available options[15–17] used, for example, to see how algorithms work with the data provided.[21] Finally, evolutionary computation is a family of algorithms for global optimization inspired by biological evolution, meaning a family of population-based trial and error problem solvers with a metaheuristic or stochastic optimization character.[14,15] This is found in applications that control, for example, network connections,[22] accelerate simulation-driven design,[23] pattern recognition,[24] and data mining and classification.[25]

3.1.2. *Logic*

The field of logic has two main areas, namely, logic programming and automated reasoning. Logic programming is a programming paradigm based on formal logic in which a program is written in a logic programming language, for example, Prolog or Datalog, which is a set of sentences in a logical form that expresses facts and rules about a problem.[14–17] Tools that use logic programming include real-time data analytics,[26] automated decision-making and processes,[27] and data annotation and programming.[28] The other main area, automated reasoning, is a metalogic

Table 1. Computational technologies for AI and applications.

Computational technologies for artificial intelligence		Examples of applications
Search and optimization	Search algorithm	Choosing the best move to make next (e.g., games such as chess), optimization of industrial processes (e.g., MES4), and record retrieval from a database (e.g., Algoroo, VISUALGO)
	Mathematical optimization	Applied problems in medicine, manufacturing, transportation, supply chain, finance, government, physics, economics, and mathematics (e.g., MATLAB)
	Evolutionary computation	Traffic control (e.g., NetLimiter), design (e.g., Altair Inspire), pattern recognition (e.g., PRTools), and data mining (e.g., KEEL)
Logic	Logic programming	Relational database management systems (e.g., Ingres, Actian X), natural language processing (e.g., IBM Watson), and education (e.g., Python)
	Automated reasoning	Formal logic (e.g., Logictools), mathematics and computer science (e.g., GeoGebra), and software and hardware verification
Probabilistic methods for uncertain reasoning	Bayesian network	Document classification (e.g., BAYES SERVER), information retrieval, semantic search (e.g., Google), image processing (e.g., OpenCV), and spam filter (e.g., SolarWinds MSP)
	Hidden Markov model	Speech recognition (e.g., Otter), speech synthesis (e.g., eSpeak), part-of-speech tagging (e.g., TEXTINSPECTOR), and handwriting recognition (e.g., Handwriting OCR)
	Kalman filter	Guidance, navigation and control of vehicles (e.g., Space X), time series analysis (e.g., NCSS), and robotic motion planning and control (e.g., RobotStudio)
	Particle filter	Image processing and understanding (e.g., Neptune), video and target tracking (e.g., Filmora), and predicting economic data (e.g., Moody's Analytics)
	Decision theory	Investments in research and development, planning, and scheduling (e.g., Airfocus, FlowForma)

(Continued)

Table 1. (*Continued*)

Computational technologies for artificial intelligence		Examples of applications
	Utility theory	Decision making, economics, finance and marketing, and mathematics (e.g., R)
Classifiers and statistical learning methods	Statistical classification	Computer vision (e.g., CUDA), recognition of things (e.g., speech, handwriting, patterns), classification of documents, statistical natural language processing, internet search engines, and recommendation systems (e.g., LensKit)
	Machine learning	Brain-machine interfaces (e.g., OpenBCI), data quality, handwriting recognition (e.g., AI Multiple), information retrieval, linguistics, and natural language processing and understanding (e.g., MonkeyLearn)
Neural networks	Artificial neural networks	Sequence recognition (e.g., patterns, gestures, speech, human actions, handwritten and printed text recognition) (e.g., Microsoft Cognitive Toolkit), grammar learning (e.g., Grammarly), predict tasks, data mining, visualization, machine translation (e.g., Google translate)
	Deep learning	Virtual assistants (e.g., Google Assistant, Siri), supercomputing, facial recognition systems and image restoration (e.g., Adobe Photoshop CC)

dedicated to understanding different aspects of reasoning, and which involves knowledge representation.[14–17] In this field, the technique is used in applications to predict or propose formulas, for example,[29] as well as in educational tools for mathematics.[30]

3.1.3. *Probabilistic methods for uncertain reasoning*

The field of probabilistic methods for uncertain reasoning has six main areas: Bayesian network, hidden Markov model, Kalman filter, particle filter, decision theory and utility theory. A Bayesian network is a probabilistic graphical model representing a set of variables and their conditional dependencies via a directed acyclic graph.[14–17] It is used in applications for example, detecting anomalies and calculating risk scenarios,[31] object and face recognition,[32] and tools for data protection.[33] A hidden Markov model is a statistical model, whereas the system being modeled is assumed to be a Markov process with unobservable hidden states. The hidden Markov model assumes that there is another process whose behaviour depends on the modeled system, in which the goal is to learn about the modeled system by observing the assumed process.[14–17] This technology is used for transcribing voice recordings,[34] speech synthesizers from written text,[35] text analysis,[36] and reading handwriting,[37] for example. The Kalman filter is an algorithm that uses a series of measurements observed over time that contain statistical noise and other inaccuracies to estimate a joint probability distribution over the variables for each time frame.[14–17] Here, the algorithms are used in, for example, tools for simulating space navigation,[38] forecasting based on observed data,[39] and virtual offline programming,[40] among other applications. A particle filter is a set of Monte Carlo algorithms used to solve filtering problems in signal processing and Bayesian statistical inference.[14–17] The particle filter is commonly used in applications such as image processing,[41] film editing[42] and forecasting economic scenarios.[43] Decision theory is the study of an agent's choices. Decision theory can be divided into two areas, normative theory, which analysis the outcomes of decisions or determines the most optimal decisions based on constraints and assumptions, and descriptive decision theory, which analysis how agents actually make decisions.[16,17] The technology is used for, for example, to create road maps or product strategies,[44] and optimize processes.[45] Utility theory is a perspective on how people assign value based on their ordering of preferences.[16,17] In this context, the theory is used in applications such as statistical calculations and graphical display.[46]

3.1.4. *Classifiers and statistical learning methods*

The field of classifiers and statistical learning methods has two main areas, namely, statistical classification and machine learning. Statistical classification is about identifying the set of categories to which a new observation belongs, based on a training set of data comprising observations whose category membership is known.[14–17] Examples of applications that use this technology are, for example, computing on graphical processing units by harnessing the power of GPUs,[47] programs for evaluating algorithms,[48] and autonomous systems, for example, autonomous driving cars.[49] Machine learning is the study of computer algorithms that improve automatically based on accumulated experience, for example, training data through supervised, semi-supervised, or unsupervised learning.[14–17] Examples include understanding the electrical activities of a human body,[50] handwriting recognition,[51] and tools for training on data.[52]

3.1.5. *Neural networks*

The field of neural networks has two main areas, namely, artificial neural networks and deep learning. Artificial neural networks, for example, connectionism, are computing systems inspired by the biological neural networks that constitute biological brains, such as human and animal brains.[14–17] This technology is used in various tools. For example, realizing and combining neural network models,[53] as well as improvement to writing and grammar.[54,55] Deep learning is a function that mimics the human brain in processing data used for detecting objects, recognizing speech, translating languages and making decisions.[14–17] Tools that use deep learning are, for example, virtual assistants[56,57] and photo rendering systems.[58]

3.2. *Integrating AI in the research process*

In the context of social science research, there are a growing number of examples of AI applications. However, when doing a brief browse for available applications, most of them are used in the initial phase of the research process: *Identifying and framing the research problem.*

For example, we have seen the transition from physical printed publications to library databases with online search engines.[59,60] The MIT Technology Review[61] describes an AI-based search engine that has been developed to facilitate the finding of information by enabling searches for latent meaning, not only the specific content of a paper. Moreover, Ref. [62] focuses their research on the extraction of key phrases and summarizing papers. Reference [63] takes this research even further by summarizing multiple papers and clustering them into categories.

Furthermore, Springer recently published the book "Lithium-Ion batteries. A Machine-Generated Summary of Current Research,"[64] which is a kind of AI-generated literature review of lithium-ion battery research.[65] Springer chose the topic because lithium-ion batteries are commonly used in electric vehicles, which have developed rapidly over a short time frame. Further, they combined two areas: Chemistry and Materials Science. The book, which is an interesting read in many aspects, limited its review to research on lithium-ion batteries from 2016 to 2019. In this time frame, over 53,000 articles were published. Summarizing such a high volume of articles would have been a challenging task for a human researcher. In order to achieve a high standard, a workflow comprising three steps: document clustering and ordering; extractive summarization; paraphrasing the generated extracts. For this edition, the review comprised 1086 publications identified by keywords and year of publication. Niels Peter Thomas, Managing Director of Books at Springer, says that the company is aiming to shape the future of book publishing:

> New technologies around Natural Language Processing and Artificial Intelligence offer promising opportunities for us to explore the generation of scientific content with the help of algorithms. As a global publisher, it is our responsibility to take potential implications and limitations of machine-generated content into consideration, and to provide a reasonable framework for this new type of content for the future.[66]

Based on Thomas's statement, it is conceivable that even more academic publishers and researchers will follow this path by integrating AI applications as part of the research process. Even though the book in this edition is a bit difficult to read because of being fragmented and references disturbing the readability, it is impressive that all this information was automatically generated and analyzed to eventually become a book. It also shows the potential of identifying relevant research gaps for any given topic, speeding up the research process.

However, there are also examples of novel AI applications that are applicable to other phases of the research process. For example, machine learning has been applied to support qualitative coding in social science.[67] The authors conclude that there are few examples of previous research that explore how machine learning can be used in qualitative research traditions. Furthermore, natural language processing has been used for theoretical framework selection and engineering education research,[68] and machine learning has been used to generate novel hypothesis.[69] To support the empirical analysis of voice-based data, e.g., interviews and observations of meetings, several AI applications have emerged that allow real-time transcriptions, thereby enabling verbal meetings or interviews to be captured and automatically transformed into written text.[34,70]

There are a growing number of AI applications that are applicable to a huge range of business domains. However, due to the limited number of research publications on this topic, research communities in social sciences such as innovation management do not appear to be at the forefront of the adoption and development of new AI applications that can support the research practice.

A general conclusion is that the most accessible AI applications adopted as part of the research process fall in the research praxis of search and select, notes and transcriptions.

However, to our knowledge, minimal research has been conducted on how these new emerging AI applications will impact social science and the researcher's role or the research process in the future, which makes this research relevant.

4. Towards a Research Agenda for the Future of AI in IM Research

The question of the actual impact of AI applications on the role of IM researchers and the way the research process is unfolding in practice is, of course, an open-ended question, to which answers will continuously evolve as new AI applications emerge and become used (or not used) by the research community.

However, we believe that several critical issues can be identified, issues that will impact both the willingness of already established researchers to adopt and use new AI applications as part of the research process and society's acceptance of social science and IM research that is partially generated by AI applications. Below is an account of three areas of concern. In each area, critical research questions for future research have been identified.

4.1. *The future use of AI applications in research*

Given the continuous development of AI applications, it is reasonable to assume that the use and development of AI as part of the research process will evolve radically in the coming years. The adoption and integration of AI applications in IM research are, of course, critical if AI is to have an impact on the research process.[71] From previous research on the diffusion of innovation,[71] we know that there are a number of adoption barriers to be overcome, both technological and social. A researcher's ability to understand and utilize the potential of AI applications is expected to be a consequence of an emerging process, and the assumption is that AI applications will initially be met with skepticism but will then become a natural part of any researcher's toolbox.

Inspired by Ref. [72], the potential impact of AI on the research process and the researcher's role can be divided into three types: simplification through the use of increased computational power, augmentation of a researcher's capabilities, and replacement by automation.

4.1.1. *Simplification through the use of computational power*

Most of the existing AI applications used in IM research or social science research in general could be classified as simplification through the use of computational power, i.e., tools or applications that streamline research and make it easier to perform. Examples of such tools include smart search engines or database applications that provide access to and an easy overview of a high number of published articles. In one respect, these kinds of applications have replaced the heavy manual labor that was previously conducted by researchers when searching in the library databases of physical archives. However, it is still the researchers who are responsible for providing the input to and evaluating the output of the search engines in order to achieve the desired results.

4.1.2. *Augmentation of a researcher's capabilities*

To enable augmentation and automation of the research process, there is a need for a form of AI that functions as an autonomous system, i.e., a form of AI that acts upon or responds to events that are beyond the researcher's mindset or awareness. Augmentation means that humans interact and collaborate closely with AI applications to perform a task.[72] There are several areas of application that can be identified in how researchers and AI could interact in the future as a means of enhancing the researcher's ability to conduct IM research.

One potential future area of application is using AI as a tutor/mentor, a facilitator or knowledgeable other,[73] which provides researchers with continuous training and learning based on the researcher's level of experience. The benefit would be that the AI can provide support when needed. For example, by providing instructions on how to conduct a qualitative analysis of a transcribed interview, the AI application could suggest different approaches on how to proceed with the analysis by creating individualized Q&As based on previous database searches, or by providing tips for keeping on topic in the writing process.

A second potential future area of application is using AI as a research partner — a team mate — that could provide the researcher with alternative perspectives or a different skillset, thereby becoming an active part of the research work. This is how AI applications could provide continuous work-integrated learning. Fully operational and autonomous AI applications may augment the researcher by, for example, suggesting new/relevant publications to read, apply for funding, or contact new research partners to approach collaboration. Consequently, in its role as research partner, AI could augment the researcher in parts of the research process, such as suggesting alternative research gaps, research design, collecting data, highlighting when conclusions are not aligned with the research design, and proof writing sentences or paragraphs in order to streamline articles. As in industrial applications of AI, a potential future development could be to create a digital twin of the researcher.

Finally, a third potential future area of application is when AI could serve as a safety net — an AI application which, based on the researcher's interests, monitors the researcher's work and intervenes when the researcher is acting outside pre-determined boundaries. For example, AI could advise the researcher about ethical issues in the research design or suggest research relevant to what is written but lacks references to strengthen the content. Further, AI could suggest relevant conferences/journals for publication of articles, identify special issues and offer advice on the parts of the manuscript that need improvements to meet the selected conference/journal's standard.

4.1.3. *Replacement by automation*

The third type of AI application, automation, refers to software or autonomous machines taking over a human task and consequently replacing some parts of the research process previously performed by humans.

The AI generated Springer book previously referred to in this chapter is an honest attempt to automate critical parts of the research process by summarizing a huge amount of data in order to explain the current state of — in this case — ion-lithium battery research. In the book, the publisher is transparent about how the research was conducted and that further areas will be explored similarly. Thus, we take the standpoint that AI has the potential to independently generate scientific output, probably of good quality, too.

However, if it is properly developed, research conducted by an AI application should be obliged to comply with regulations and standards for AI ethics. Automated research comes with a risk as not all authors are as transparent as Springer. There are multiple AI applications available for generating fraud papers, just for the fun of it.[74] In a recent example, five papers were retracted from a conference because they were computer generated.[75] To prevent these frauds, programs have been developed that publishers use to detect computer-generated papers.[76] This is supported by Springer, which has retracted more than 100 computer-generated papers.[77]

Based on the above-mentioned possibilities, the following critical research question needs to be addressed in the future: *What progress has been made in the use and development of AI applications in IM research?* A second critical research question is to be addressed: *How can AI applications become an integrated part of the research process?*

4.2. *Exploring the trust in AI — The black box dilemma*

In social sciences, the question of trustworthiness and validity is key when it comes to research quality, which is heavily dependent on the researcher's ability to provide accurate and transparent accounts of each of the five steps taken in the research process, as mentioned above. For example, by providing detailed descriptions of how the analysis of the empirical data has been conducted in order to draw conclusions. A critical concern about AI applications is the extent to which it is possible to provide accurate and transparent accounts of how the analysis has been carried out, referred to as the black box dilemma, meaning the difficulties in understanding how decisions are made.[78]

However, to be fair, as a researcher — or as a human being in general — it is very difficult to account for the decisions that have been made and to fully describe the process by which a conclusion has been drawn, or to understand the following consequences from what has been concluded fully. This can be further illustrated with decisions made as part of the literature review process, which is a key part of identifying research gaps but is very time-consuming and generates a vast amount of data. One common practice for conducting a literature review is to search for relevant papers manually. In the paper by Ref. [79], the authors demonstrated their work: The authors first started by defining keywords to search in a selection of databases. Then, based on the search hits, they read 835 titles, and from this, they extracted 150 abstracts, which they then read. Based on the abstracts, they both snowballed and down-selected the papers, ending up with 113 papers, which they used in their research. Their work contained, for example, clustering research streams, prioritizing and selecting papers, analyzing and interpreting texts and extracting keywords. The final step was to loop the sequence again to summarize the papers into a coherent narrative. Anyone who has conducted a literature review will know that it is impossible to read all the available research. Thus, leading to questions as "how much relevant research was missed or overlooked because of a lack of resources?"

Furthermore, the challenges in developing AI applications that are considered trustworthy and valid probably also depend on the scientific approach adopted by the researcher: deductive, inductive or abductive.[4] Given the different characteristics of the research approaches, it is reasonable to conclude that AI applications can be more easily developed and adapted for the two first research approaches: deductive and inductive, as they are based more on formal logical reasoning and primarily rely on statistical analysis, while the third research approach — abductive — requires thinking process that are more subtle and rely on the researcher's imagination and ability to abstract. For example, inferences made by so-called abductive reasoning require the ability to see something — e.g., the empirical observation — as something else,[4] which is a thinking process that requires a highly developed ability to form associations.

Consequently, the following critical research question needs to be addressed in the future: *What part or parts of the research process, if any, can trustfully be replaced by AI applications?*

4.3. Benefits and limitations of AI applications: The pedagogical dilemma

A critical part of teaching Ph.D. students or junior researchers to become independent researchers is participating in the different phases of the research process. For example, when conducting a state-of-the-art literature review, not only does a researcher generate new knowledge in a given field that can be used to frame research problems, they are also continuously learning and developing their own conceptions and understanding in the area of research. It is also reasonable to assume that a researcher's ability for critical thinking is nurtured in the process of reading, analyzing and writing-up previous research into a literature review. If this is the case, what happens if software conducts the literature review, not the researcher? If a researcher is replaced by AI applications with regard to critical tasks in the research process, this will most likely create a pedagogical dilemma and, in the long term, risk impacting the entire researcher community's ability to conduct research.

However, by following the line of reasoning from,[72] it is not necessarily an either-or situation. Instead, we argue that there is a need for AI applications in research that can both provide the output — e.g., an automated literature review or a qualitative analysis — while also augment the researcher by including them in the research in order to facilitate a learning process.

Consequently, a critical research question to be addressed is: *What are the potential benefits and limitations of AI applications as an integrated part of the research process?* Also, a final critical question is: *What are the potential benefits and limitations of AI applications on the professional development of junior researchers?*

5. Contribution

Overall, this research provides new insights into the potential future of the research process in social sciences and IM research. More specifically, it highlights important questions concerning both practical and ethical issues related to AI applications as part of the research process and how researchers might conduct research in the future. To the IM community, this is as relevant as any other research field.

We have explored multiple AI technologies and examples of AI applications currently in use. Some of them are used for research although researchers are currently not using most of them. Researchers will probably experience a significant transformation regarding how future research will be conducted: simplification through the use of computational power, augmentation of a researcher's capabilities, and replacement by automation. This calls for new questions to explore. In our discussion, we have identified three areas for further research:

- The future use of AI applications in research.
- Exploring the trust in AI — The black box dilemma.
- Benefits and limitations of AI applications.

We need to understand how and what can be altered from a researcher's perspective and explore what potential applications can be developed at different phases of the research process. In this chapter we have just scratched the surface. There is a need for further research in this area. The suggested research directions span multiple disciplines and demonstrate the need for multidisciplinary research initiatives.

5.1. Practical implications

The results of our research study provide a basis for researchers planning new research projects or re-analyzing previous data sets using AI applications for research. For senior researchers teaching or supervising Ph.D. students, courses can be developed on building AI resources, capabilities and tools enabling the systematic use of AI in research. For practitioners, a new profession in teaching researchers in AI applications may develop.

5.2. Potential directions for future research

The exploration of the current and future impact of AI-based tools on social science research in general, and how it might influence the role of innovation management researchers in particular, requires a mixed-methods approach. Based on our analysis we can identify two potential directions.

First, in order to enhance our understanding of the current state of AI applications in research, we will investigate researchers' conceptions of AI applications for research and the types of AI applications that are currently available for social sciences. We will conduct surveys and in-depth interviews with researchers representing different research traditions — e.g., by including researchers with a positivistic approach together with researchers with a hermeneutic approach — as well as other social science research fields, in addition to innovation management research. The reason we believe it is essential to include researchers from different research traditions and research fields is that the different approaches to the research process will most probably affect the applicability of AI applications.

Second, the survey data and in-depth interviews will be iterated with a focus on identifying the potential AI applications that could be used in the different phases of the research process, and defining the necessary design requirements for disrupting the research process. This will also allow to visualize the research process and its different phases, identify the critical tasks across different phases, and examine whether there are (and the type of) potential AI applications that could support or replace the researcher.

In parallel, in both research directions described above, AI applications and their use in the research process will be continuously mapped to visualize ongoing developments and identify opportunities for potential implementation.

References

1. https://www.ibm.com/analytics/spss-statistics-software, retrieved February 24, 2021.
2. https://www.qsrinternational.com/nvivo-qualitative-data-analysis-software/home, retrieved February 24, 2021.
3. N. Haefner, J. Wincent, V. Parida, and O. Gassmann, Artificial intelligence and innovation management: A review, framework, and research agenda. *Technological Forecasting & Social Change*, **162** (2021). Available at: https://www.sciencedirect.com/science/article/pii/S004016252031218X.
4. B. Danermark, M. Ekström, L. Jakobsen, and J. Karlsson, *Explaining Society. Critical Realism in the Social Sciences*. London and New York: Routledge (2013).
5. G. Schwarz and I. Stensaker, Time to take off the theoretical straightjacket and (re-)introduce phenomenon-driven research. *The Journal of Applied Behavioral Science*, **50**(4), 478–501 (2014).
6. J. Sandberg and M. Alvesson, Ways of constructing research questions: Gap-spotting or problematization? *Organization*, **18**(23), (2011).
7. https://guides.lib.usf.edu/c.php?g=291297&p=2104188, retrieved November 13, 2020.
8. S. Merriam and E. Tisdell, *Qualitative Research. A Guide to Design and Implementation*. Hoboken, New Jersey: John Wiley & Sons Inc. (2016).
9. K. Säfsten, K. Gustafsson and R. Ehnsjö, *Research Methodology: For Engineers and Other Problem-Solvers*. Lund: Studentlitteratur (2019).

10. http://www.icmje.org/news-and-editorials/new_rec_aug2013.html, received August 24, 2020.

11. https://retractionwatch.com/, retrieved January 15, 2021.

12. https://retractionwatch.com/2020/12/15/the-top-retractions-of-2020-mostly-but-not-all-covid-19/, retrieved January 15, 2021.

13. https://ec.europa.eu/digital-single-market/en/news/ethics-guidelines-trustworthy-ai, retrieved January 15, 2021.

14. N. Nilsson, *Artificial Intelligence: A New Synthesis*. San Francisco, CA, US: Morgan Kaufmann (1998).

15. G. Luger and W. Stubblefield, *Artificial Intelligence: Structures and Strategies for Complex Problem Solving*, 6th ed. Boston: Pearson, Addison Wesley (2009).

16. D. Poole, A. Mackworth, and R. Goebel, *Computational Intelligence: A Logical Approach*. New York: Oxford University Press (1998).

17. S.J. Russell and P. Norvig, *Artificial Intelligence: A Modern Approach*, 2nd ed. New Jersey: Prentice Hall (2003).

18. https://www.festo-didactic.com/int-en/learning-systems/mps-the-modular-production-system/mes4.htm?fbid=aW50LmVuLjU1Ny4xNy4xOC41ODU uNTM3NjA, retrieved January 15, 2021.

19. https://algoroo.com/, retrieved January 15, 2021.

20. https://visualgo.net/en, retrieved January 15, 2021.

21. https://se.mathworks.com/products/matlab.html, retrieved January 15, 2021.

22. https://www.netlimiter.com/, retrieved January 15, 2021.

23. https://www.altair.com/inspire/, retrieved January 15, 2021.

24. http://prtools.tudelft.nl/, retrieved January 15, 2021.

25. https://sci2s.ugr.es/keel/links.php, retrieved January 15, 2021.

26. https://www.actian.com/data-management/actian-x-hybrid-rdbms/, retrieved January 15, 2021.

27. https://www.ibm.com/watson, retrieved January 15, 2021.

28. https://www.python.org/, retrieved January 15, 2021.

29. http://logictools.org/, retrieved January 15, 2021.

30. https://www.geogebra.org/m/McEqwQNb, retrieved January 15, 2021.

31. https://www.bayesserver.com/, retrieved January 15, 2021.

32. https://opencv.org/, retrieved January 15, 2021.

33. https://www.solarwindsmsp.com/, retrieved January 15, 2021.

34. https://otter.ai/, retrieved January 15, 2021.

35. http://espeak.sourceforge.net/, retrieved January 15, 2021.

36. https://textinspector.com/help/tagger/, retrieved January 15, 2021.

37. https://vidado.ai/handwriting-ocr/, retrieved January 15, 2021.

38. https://iss-sim.spacex.com/, retrieved January 15, 2021.
39. https://www.ncss.com/software/ncss/time-series-and-forecasting-in-ncss/, retrieved January 15, 2021.
40. https://new.abb.com/products/robotics/robotstudio, retrieved January 15, 2021.
41. https://neptune.ai/blog/best-image-processing-tools-used-in-machine-learning, retrieved January 15, 2021.
42. https://filmora.wondershare.com/filmorapro-video-editor/, retrieved January 15, 2021.
43. https://www.economy.com/, retrieved January 15, 2021.
44. https://airfocus.com/, retrieved January 15, 2021.
45. https://www.flowforma.com/, retrieved January 15, 2021.
46. https://www.r-project.org/, retrieved January 15, 2021.
47. https://developer.nvidia.com/CUDA-zone, retrieved January 15, 2021.
48. https://lenskit.org/, retrieved January 15, 2021.
49. https://www.intellias.com/autonomous-driving-adas/, retrieved March 5, 2021.
50. https://openbci.com/, retrieved January 15, 2021.
51. https://research.aimultiple.com/handwriting-recognition/, retrieved January 15, 2021.
52. https://monkeylearn.com/#monkeylearn, retrieved January 15, 2021.
53. https://docs.microsoft.com/en-us/cognitive-toolkit/, retrieved January 15, 2021.
54. https://grammerly.com, retrieved January 15, 2021.
55. https://translate.google.com/, retrieved January 15, 2021.
56. https://assistant.google.com/, retrieved January 15, 2021.
57. https://www.apple.com/siri/, retrieved January 15, 2021.
58. https://www.adobe.com/se/products/photoshop.html, retrieved January 15, 2021.
59. https://the.iris.ai/, retrieved February 2, 2020.
60. https://www.omnity.io/, retrieved February 2, 2020.
61. https://www.technologyreview.com/s/542981/academic-search-engine-grasps-for-meaning/, retrieved February 10, 2020.
62. C.D.V. Hoang and M-Y. Kan, Towards automated related work summarization, in *Coling, Poster Volume*, 427–435, Beijing (August 2010).
63. J. Jayabharathy, S. Kanmani, and N. Sivaranjani, Correlation based multi-document summarization for scientific articles and news group, *International Conference on Advances in Computing, Communications and Informatics, ICACCI'12*, Chennai, Tamil Nadu, India (August 3–5, 2012).
64. B. Writer, *Lithium-Ion Batteries A Machine-Generated Summary of Current Research*, Switzerland: Springer Nature (2019). ISBN 978-3-030-16800-1.

65. https://group.springernature.com/in/group/media/press-releases/springer-nature-machine-generated-book/16590134, retrieved February 2, 2020.
66. https://www.springer.com/gp/about-springer/media/press-releases/corporate/springer-nature-machine-generated-book/16590126, retrieved February 2, 2020.
67. N-C. Chen, M. Drouhard, R. Kocielnik, J. Suh, and C. Aragon, Using machine learning to support qualitative coding in social science: Shifting the focus to ambiguity. *ACM Transactions on Interactive Intelligent Systems*, **8**(2) (2018). DOI:10.1145/3185515.
68. C.G.P. Berdanier, C.M. McComb, and W. Zhu, Natural language processing for theoretical framework selection in engineering education research. *IEEE Frontiers in Education Conference*, 1–7 (2020). DOI:10.1109/FIE44824.2020.9274115.
69. A. Sheetal, Z. Feng, and K. Savani, Using machine learning to generate novel hypotheses: Increasing optimism about COVID-19 makes people less willing to justify unethical behaviors. *Psychological Science*, **31**(10), 1222–1235 (2020).
70. https://www.descript.com/, retrieved February 24, 2021.
71. E. Rogers, *Diffusion of Innovations*. New York: The Free Press (2003).
72. S. Raisch and S. Krakowski, Artificial Intelligence and Management: The Automation–Augmentation Paradox. *Academy of Management Review*, 46(1), 192–210 (2021).
73. L. Vygotskij, *Mind in Society: The development of Higher Psychological Processes*. Cambridge: Harvard University Press (1978).
74. https://pdos.csail.mit.edu/archive/scigen/#about, retrieved March 1, 2021.
75. https://retractionwatch.com/2021/02/17/publisher-retracting-five-papers-because-of-clear-evidence-that-they-were-computer-generated/, retrieved March 1, 2021.
76. https://gricad-gitlab.univ-grenoble-alpes.fr/labbecy/scidetect, retrieved March 1, 2021.
77. https://retractionwatch.com/2014/02/24/springer-ieee-withdrawing-more-than-120-nonsense-papers/, retrieved March 1, 2021.
78. R. Yu and G.S. Alì, What's inside the black box? AI challenges for lawyers and researchers. *Legal Information Management*, **19**(1), 2–13 (2019).
79. R. Gould, M.P. Lagun, C. Bratt, and G. Broman, Why choose one sustainable design strategy over another: A decision-support prototype, in *Proc. of the 21st International Conference on Engineering Design (ICED17)*, Vol. 5: Design to X. Vancouver, Canada (August 21–25, 2017).

https://doi.org/10.1142/9781800611337_0010

Chapter 9

The Potential of AI to Enhance the Value Propositions of New Companies Committed to Scale Early and Rapidly

Stoyan Tanev*,‡, Tony Bailetti*,§, Christian Keen†,¶, and David Hudson*,||

*Technology Innovation Management Program
Sprott School of Business, Carleton University
1125 Colonel By Drive, Ottawa, ON K1S 5B6, Canada
†Faculty of Business Administration, Université Laval
2325, rue de la Terrasse, Québec, QC G1V 0A6, Canada
‡stoyan.tanev@carleton.ca
§bailetti@sce.carleton.ca
¶christian.keen@fsa.ulaval.ca
||dhudson1014@rogers.com

A newly developed value proposition is the best expression of a company's innovative capacity — its ability to coordinate the combination of resources to develop new products and services, and shape valuable market offers to address specific customer needs. How a new company can use artificial intelligence to innovate by enhancing its value propositions for customers, investors and other stakeholders is not well known. To address this question, we systematically reviewed the value proposition development, business ecosystems, and the artificial intelligence business value literature streams and used the results to develop 182 assertions — statements about what a new company should do to scale its value early and rapidly. We then applied topic modeling to examine the assertions and produce a framework for value proposition development in the context of a new company that wishes to scale its value early and rapidly. Finally, we made explicit the link between a new company's resources and capabilities in artificial intelligence and the seven elements of the framework. The results suggest that resources and capabilities in artificial intelligence can be used to enhance stakeholders' value propositions, improve foreign market entry performance, increase customer base, and continuously improve individuals, operations, and infrastructures of new companies. The chapter provides a guide of the business value that AI can offer a new company committed to scale early and rapidly.

1. Introduction

New companies that wish to scale early and rapidly need to acquire resources and capabilities in artificial intelligence (AI) and value proposition (VP) development which are different from those required by established companies with small or moderate growth objectives. Adopting a multiple stakeholder perspective on AI and VP development can help new companies enhance their scaling performance.

The objective of this chapter is to develop a corpus of actionable insights about VPs relevant to new companies that wish to scale early and rapidly, examine the results of topic modeling the corpus, use these results to suggest a VP development framework, and propose a link between resources and capabilities in AI and the elements of the VP development framework. Reference [1, p. 227] defines an actionable insight as a context specific and pragmatic heuristic that prescribes actions often with the following syntax: "to achieve X in situation Y, something like Z will help."

This chapter is distinct for three reasons. *First*, it develops assertions that describe actionable insights on how new companies that wish to scale early and rapidly can shape and strengthen their VPs. These insights make explicit how such companies can engage with investors and external stakeholders to access, combine, deploy, and align internal and external resources to deliver significant value to customers; operate across borders; innovate relentlessly; and, ultimately, achieve their scaling objectives.[2]

Second, it uses topic modeling to examine the corpus of actionable insights and suggest a VP development framework. Topic modeling is the process of identifying latent topics in a large set of text documents. It is an example of Natural Language Processing (NLP) method which examines unstructured text data collections to discover topics that are impossible to uncover by human efforts alone. The applications of topic modeling in management research have recently been summarized in Ref. [3]. Its application in the present research study provides an example of how an NLP technique could benefit innovation management research.

Third, our study adopts an AI business value perspective to examine the actionable insights corresponding to the key elements of the suggested VP framework. Thus, the key contribution of this chapter is making explicit the link between a new company's resources and capabilities in AI and VP development. AI is a constellation of many different technologies that were designed to work together in enabling machines to perform tasks with human-like levels of intelligence. A newly developed VP is the best expression of a company's innovative capacity — its ability to coordinate the combination of resources provided by multiple stakeholders to develop new products and services, and shape valuable market offers to address the needs of specific customer target groups.[4] In this sense, the chapter contributes to the broader knowledge domain focusing on the relationship between AI and innovation management.

The chapter is structured as follow. *First*, the results of a comprehensive review of the VP development, business ecosystems, and AI business value literature streams is presented. *Second*, we describe the methodology used in our study. *Third*, we summarize the results from the application of topic modeling on the list of actionable insights, and group them in subsets of activities that could be considered as the building blocks or generative elements of a VP development framework. *Lastly*, we examine each of the actionable insights associated with the emerging VP elements to identify the activities that could be enabled or enhanced by the adoption of AI resources and capabilities.

2. Literature Review

The purpose of the literature review was to identify actionable insights on (i) VP development; (ii) how AI resources and capabilities create value for businesses; and (iii) how business ecosystems can enhance business development. The first two research streams fit quite naturally the objective of our study and are expected to overlap in the near future. The business ecosystem stream provides the conceptual apparatus that could help in dealing with the multiplicity of stakeholders involved in the VP development processes which is typical of new companies interested to scale early and rapidly. The review of these three research streams enabled the development of the corpus of actionable insights that became the basis for the research study.

2.1. Value propositions in the context of new scaling companies

The importance of the VP concept and the multiple issues associated with the development of VPs have been discussed in the literature.[5–7] Nevertheless, the VP concept has often been used casually and applied in a trivial fashion rather than in a more strategic, rigorous manner.[8] A value proposition is the company's single most important organizing principle.[9] Thus, VPs should have a strong influence on key aspects of a business venture such as the acquisition of complementary resources as part of the organization of the value creation process, operations management, inter-organizational structure, and interactions with all relevant stakeholders. The development of VPs should therefore be done from a multiple stakeholder perspective so that the VPs to all relevant actors in the business ecosystem could be reciprocally aligned.[2,10,11] Instead of focusing on trying to predict trends in an uncertain environment, new venture management teams should focus on achieving possible ends through known means[12] thus, designing, developing and implementing VPs that could help them achieve their scaling objectives. If this is accomplished, VPs become one of company's most valuable resources.[2]

Several studies have highlighted the importance given by marketing scholars to customer VPs.[8,11,13] For example, the authors of Ref. [14, p. 472] define a customer VP as, "a strategic tool facilitating communication of an organization's ability to share resources and offer a superior value package to targeted customers." The literature has emphasized the need to articulate the benefits and costs relevant to targeted customers as well as the functional and experiential aspects of the differentiation aspects of the offerings, and of customer experience in particular.[14–16] Although the customer is a key shareholder, it is not the only one and, for many ventures, it might not be even the most important one to deal with. As per the entrepreneurship and innovation literature, ventures tend to focus on the development of their new products and services when the targeted markets are not clearly defined.[17,18] The current literature has also emphasized the importance of proper resource configuration and practices that could enable the delivery of key benefits, resource sharing and integration in the value co-creation process involving key actors in the value chain.[19] Reference [20, p. 144] defines VPs as "promises of value creation that build upon configuration of resources and practices." The authors emphasize the importance of value co-creation with customers as well as of the integration of resources provided by other relevant stakeholders.

However, most studies on the interaction between companies and other stakeholders is still dominated by the focus on VPs related to the venture–customer–supplier triad as well as on established companies whose reality differs significantly from the one of ventures.[11,21] Considering how different actors work together by sharing resources to initiate an offer is key to the development and alignment of a company's portfolio of VPs corresponding to its most relevant business objectives.[2,11,22] The authors of Ref. [12] argue that a VP not only communicates value, but also implies the reciprocal engagement of all relevant actors. However, they do not elaborate on how this reciprocal engagement takes place and in what way exactly it is relevant for a venture. Reference [13] sheds some light on this aspect by suggesting that new ventures interested to grow should shape and align at least two VPs for their business customers: the typical VP based on an innovative offer, and a leveraging assistance VP, which should convey what the customer company will get in return for providing support and resources at this early stage of the new venture's business life cycle. However, the focus remains on the venture–customer duo in a situation where most ventures are struggling to identify who their real customers are. This trend suggests an opportunity to extend the research domain by studying the development of explicit VPs for all relevant stakeholders, such as investors, employees and external resource owners, etc.

There is little knowledge on the factors that enable new companies to scale rapidly and the ways of aligning their portfolio of value propositions with their scaling objectives. Such alignment implies the need to incorporate scale up objectives into companies' business models via the configuration of resources and activities that not only create value for customers, but also allow companies to capture part of that value and distribute it back to key resource owners.[23] Scalability is defined as the extent to which a VP and its corresponding business model can help in achieving the desired value creation and capture targets by increasing the customer base without adding proportionate extra resources.[24] As suggested in Ref. [25], the organizing phase of a venture will have a deep impact on its performing phase that will or will not lead to its potential scale up.

Recent studies have identified an explicit link between the growth orientation of new technology companies and the novelty and attractiveness of their VPs. The authors of Ref. [26] point out that finding new and innovative ways to offer value to customers is important to achieving high sales growth, as well as rapid geographic expansion to new markets. The insights provided in Ref. [27] suggest that companies pursue high growth by: creating new markets, serving broader stakeholder needs, changing the rules of the game, redefining the playing field, and reshaping their VPs. Reference [2] emphasizes that such companies should develop capabilities to access, combine, and deploy resources required to create value and scale, by providing all external resource owners with returns they cannot gain on their own.[28-30] According to Ref. [2], the VPs of new companies committed to scale have two distinctive features: (i) enable a new company and an external stakeholder to directly interact via transactions without the need of an intermediary; (ii) increase investments to create and improve business transactions over time. In addition, three factors that make the portfolio of VPs one of the most valuable resources of a company were identified: (a) it strengthens the company's capabilities to scale; (b) it increases the demand for company's products and services; (c) it fosters investments in the conceptualization, development, maintenance, and refinement of company's VPs.[2] Thus, a properly aligned portfolio of VPs turns into a valuable resource that enables the alignment of other resources, smooths out the interaction of the venture with complementary ecosystem actors and transforms them into preferred stakeholders who could contribute the company scale up process.

2.2. The business value of AI resources and capabilities

Recent research on the business value of AI suggests that AI resources and capabilities could have a significant impact as a value driver for firms and help them get an operational and competitive advantage, even though there is still a significant lack of understanding of how to appropriate value from AI.[31] There is an increasing number of studies that focuses on examining the specific dimensions of value that could be enabled through AI resources and capabilities. For example, the author of Ref. [32, p. 3] defines a firm as "artificially intelligent" if it "deploys classic economic factors of production human labor, capital and land in combination with machine labor in the form of AI agents." He adopts the economic theory of the firm to systematically explore five ways AI could have an impact on it: (i) AI intensifies the effects of economic rationality on the firm; (ii) AI introduces a new type of information asymmetry; (iii) AI can perforate the boundaries of the firm; (iv) AI can create triangular agency relationships; (v) AI has the potential to remove traditional limits of integration.

Other researchers[33] emphasize that businesses should examine the potential value of AI through the lens of business capabilities rather than technologies, and point out that AI can support three important business needs: automating business processes, gaining competitive insight through data analysis, and engaging with customers and employees.

The authors of Ref. [34, p. 36] proposed a strategic framework for using AI to engage customers for different service benefits. AI develops from mechanical, to thinking, and to feeling: (i) mechanical AI could help for cost leadership and standardization mostly at the service delivery stage and when service is routine and transactional; (ii) thinking AI could help for quality leadership and personalization mostly at the service creation stage and when service is data-rich and utilitarian; (iii) feeling AI could help for relationship leadership mostly at the service interaction stage and when service is relational and high touch.[34]

A comprehensive discussion of the role of AI in enhancing sales processes can be found in Ref. [35]. They identified the value of AI systems at each stage of the sales funnel, as well as clarified the role of human intelligence and decision-making at each stage of the AI-enabled sales funnel. According to them, there is a complementarity of humans and AI, and AI, with its enormous information processing capacity, can augment human intelligence or even replace well defined and repeatable human tasks in B2B sales. For example, it could help in building rich customer prospect profiles, update lead generation and lead qualification models via machine learning, personalized and customize communication messages and channels, make contacts via digital agents (e.g., chatbots), enable fast prototyping, curate competitive intelligence, enable dynamic pricing, automate workflows and post-order services, uncover new customer needs etc.

Organizations can explore two major AI value-creation opportunity directions: opportunities in the value chain, and opportunities emerging from the adoption of a multi-stakeholder perspective on benefit analysis.[36] For example, AI could be fully integrated in business value chains and, more specifically, in using replenishment models to manage inbound logistics, robots in operations and order fulfillment, dispatch algorithms to optimize delivery costs, recommendation engines to optimize service levels. The findings in Ref. [36, p. 75] indicate that it could also provide support functions "in human resources to predict the best candidates to hire, in finance to prevent frauds, in procurement to optimize number of suppliers, etc." The second opportunity direction refers to the multiple stakeholder analysis of potential business benefits such as revenue increase, cost savings, risk mitigation or customer experience. Such assessment should help in evaluating how fairly is value divided and if there is any potential conflict of interest between stakeholders such as customers, employees, suppliers, co-innovation partners and society.

AI researchers and practitioners have both dedicated special efforts on instrumentalizing the integration of AI resources and capabilities into business development processes. One example of these joint efforts is the development of canvas approaches to the implementation of AI business value.[37–39] The adoption of AI canvas approaches indicates that the AI field moves into a stage of higher maturity which should inspire even more researchers in contributing to this domain.

2.3. *Ecosystem perspective on VP development*

A new venture requires people with entrepreneurial imaginativeness.[25] The authors of Ref. [25, p. 5] refer to Ref. [40, p. 2266] to emphasize that the act of imaging a new venture is "a cognitive skill that combines the ability of imagination with the knowledge needed to stimulate various task-related scenarios in entrepreneurship." This cognitive skill is essential to move from an idea to identifying an opportunity and creating a venture to exploit it.[25] It implies the shaping of a novel offering[41,42] through the exploitation of resources beyond the ones controlled by the nascent company.[43,44] Such exploitation is the result of a multi-actor process in which different business ecosystem stakeholders are actively engaged.[44–46]

In a globalized world with increasingly complex and interrelated technologies, entrepreneurial innovation ecosystems are vital for ventures that are looking to implement complex VPs.[45,47–49] Every venture committed to scale operates in an environment where different ecosystem actors are actively engaged to complement the value creation process. According to Ref. [45, p. 42] Any such company needs to join a business ecosystem that should provide "the alignment structure of the multilateral set of partners that need to interact in order for a focal value proposition to materialize." The preferred ecosystem partners will be the ones that will be more committed and more efficient than others in enhancing the logic and the alignment of company's portfolio of VPs.[45,46] Securing the commitment (or pre-commitment) of valuable stakeholders can be crucial to the scaling performance of the venture.[12,25,50] Even though the actors of an ecosystem may have certain autonomy in terms of how they design, price, and operate their respective business modules, there is still a need for coordination. An ecosystem defines and provides processes and rules that help to resolve any emerging coordination issues and encourages alignment between ecosystem actors through rules of engagement, standards, and codified interfaces.[51] The modularity of resources and contributions is a necessary but not sufficient condition for the existence of an ecosystem.[52,53] For an ecosystem to emerge and be useful, there must be a significant need for coordination that cannot be addressed by the hierarchy imposed by a focal firm.[48,51] What makes ecosystems unique is that actors "can choose among the components (or elements of offering) that are supplied by each participant, and can also, in some cases, choose how they are combined" (see Ref. [51, p. 2260]).

Reference [51] identified two types of complementarities that can unambiguously characterize the coordination of activities and resource sharing between ecosystem actors. The first type is "unique" complementarity where an activity or component offered by one actor requires the activity or component of another actor, but not vice versa; or two activities A and B of two different actors both require each other. The second type — "supermodular" complementarity — could be described as follows: "more of A makes B more valuable, where A and B are two different products, assets, or activities" (see Ref. [51, p. 2262]). The distinctive feature of ecosystems is that they provide an alignment structure where different actors can engage with each other in value creation through unique and supermodular complementarities, both in production and/or consumption, that can be coordinated without the need for vertical integration. The definition of business ecosystems in such terms offers an opportunity to advance VP research and practice.

2.4. *What is known and what is not known*

The analysis of the literature review leads to several conclusions.

(1) Most of the reviewed literature focuses on established companies.
(2) What is known about new companies relative to what is known about established companies is relatively small.
(3) The literature on the business value of AI is new. However, it is expected to grow rapidly.
(4) There is a gap in the literature on what new companies do to scale their value early and rapidly as well as how resources and capabilities in AI can help a new company scale.

3. Research Methodology

The objective of the present study was to: (i) develop a corpus of actionable insights on how new companies that wish to scale early and rapidly can shape and strengthen their VPs; (ii) apply topic modeling to examine the corpus of actionable insights and suggest a VP development framework; (iii) make explicit the link between a new company's resources and capabilities in AI and its VP development. The key steps of our study are shown in Fig. 1.

In two previous articles we have developed a preliminary set of assertions associated with VP development in the same context.[2,54] In this article we started by expanding the initial set of assertions through a systematic literature review, searching in the Web of Science database for

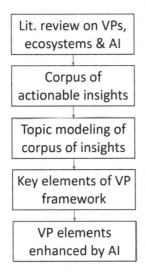

Fig. 1. Symbolic representation of the research steps.

journal research articles containing the "value proposition" in the title, in the abstract or in the author-provided keywords.

The search resulted in 84 articles that were further examined in terms of their relevance to the context of our study. Twelve of the articles were identified as a subset including more comprehensive review sections, VP framework descriptions or actionable insights that could be turned into practical advice for real life companies.[2,7,10,11,13,14,20,22,26,27,55,56] The twelve articles were examined independently by the three authors and used as a basis for the formulation of distinguishable actionable insights that were shaped by following the CIMO logic format as closely as possible. The CIMO logic involves a combination of a Context, for which an actionable insight suggests a certain Intervention type, to produce, through specified generative Mechanisms, the intended Outcome.[57] The VP insights were complemented by insights extracted from selected recent research articles focusing business ecosystems[48,51,56] and AI-based business value.[31–35] The process of developing the actionable insights included feedback from participants in multiple dialogical sessions including entrepreneurs, business mentors, representatives of organizations supporting company growth, and other researchers, to refine the formulation of the assertions and ensure the use of language that is common to executive managers of new firms. The process resulted in a corpus of 182 assertions referring to the development and alignment of the portfolio of VPs of companies interested to scale early and rapidly.

In the next step of our research study, we performed topic modeling analysis[3,58,59] on the corpus of the 182 assertions and identified topics that group the assertions under themes referring to specific VP development activities. We have used an in-house tool based on the most popular topic modeling algorithm — Latent Dirichlet Allocation (LDA).[58] The logic of LDA could be summarized as follows: (i) it assumes that there are k topics across all of the documents; (ii) it distributes these k topics across document m by assigning each word a topic; (iii) for each word w in document m, it assumes its topic is wrong but every other word has been assigned the correct topic; (iv) probabilistically assigns word w a topic based on two criteria — what topics are in document m, and how many times the word w has been assigned a particular topic across all of the documents; (v) it repeats this process multiple times to reach a stable distribution of both topics in documents and words in topics. Figure 2 provides a symbolic representation of process.

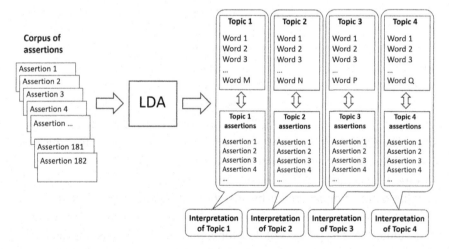

Fig. 2. Symbolic representation of the logic and outcomes of the LDA topic modeling algorithm. The words and the text documents (in our case assertions) associated with each topic are ranked in terms of the degree of their association with the topic.

The LDA algorithm considers every assertion as a text document which is a mixture of topics, and every topic as a mixture of words. Words can be shared between topics and the topics can be shared among assertions. LDA identifies combinations of words that are semantically interrelated and tend to appear together across the different assertions. The combinations of words help the identification of specific themes that are latently present in the corpus. In addition, LDA organizes the corpus by clustering the assertions corresponding to each topic (Fig. 2). The assertions clustered in a given topic are ranked in terms of the degree of their association with it. A closer examination of the topical organization of the assertions enables the interpretation of the overall theme and the labeling of the topics.[3]

The next step in the research process was to examine the consistency of the topics as a whole and the possibility of considering the groups of activities associated with each of them as key elements of a VP development or evaluation framework for companies interested to scale early and rapidly.

The last step in our study was to examine the extent to which the activities suggested by the assertions associated with a given topic could be enabled or enhanced by means of AI resources and capabilities.

Finally, we provide a reflection on the ability of AI to enhance the VPs of companies interested to scale early and rapidly.

4. Topic Modeling of the Actionable Value Proposition Insights

The topic modeling analysis identified seven topics defined by a set of words and a set of actionable insights associated with each specific topic. The words and the insights for each of the seven topics are shown in the Appendix. A close examination of the insights associated with each of the seven topics allowed to label them as follow: value created, stakeholder value propositions, foreign market entry, customer base, continuous improvement, cross-border operations, and company image. The purpose of the labels is to emphasize the thematic distinctiveness of the topics and provide an idea about the overall content of the corresponding topic assertions. The labels should be therefore considered as pointers to the themes emerging from the topics and not as comprehensive content signifiers. It is the specific insights that provide the real content of each topic.

Topic 1 (Value created) refers to the access and combination of complementary internal and external resources for the sake of value creation for all relevant stakeholders. Topic 2 (Stakeholder value propositions) focuses on the various aspects and alignment of the VPs to key stakeholders such as investors, customers, suppliers etc. Topic 3 (Foreign market entry) provides insights related to successfully turning local offers into global ones. Topic 4 (Customer base) focuses on activities that result in engaging and attracting more customers. Such activities are associated with the ultimate goal of a scaling strategy — increasing the customer base in a profitable way. Topic 5 (Continuous improvement) provides insights about improving the value creation process and refining the alignment of company's portfolio of VPs. Interestingly, there is a special focus on improving the cybersecurity of the firm which reflects a focus on online business interactions and global reach. Topic 6 (Cross-border operations) focuses on knowledge sharing and coordination activities across borders as well as to the need for a stronger positioning of the company in cross-border networks. Topic 7 (Company image) refers to the brand identity of the company and its differentiation from competitors.

5. Shaping a Value Proposition Framework

The description of the topics provided in the previous section does already suggest a conceptual framework which is substantiated by the specificity of the actionable insights associated with each topic. We have examined further the potential logical relationship between the seven topics. The insights associated with each topic were conglomerated into seven documents — one corresponding to each of the seven topics — and the cosine similarity values between the seven documents were then calculated. Cosine similarity is a measure that is used to evaluate the semantic proximity of documents or to provide a ranking of documents with respect to a given set of search words, a phrase or a paragraph.[60]

The VP framework is shown in Fig. 3. The numbers on the links between the different topics indicate the normalized cosine similarity

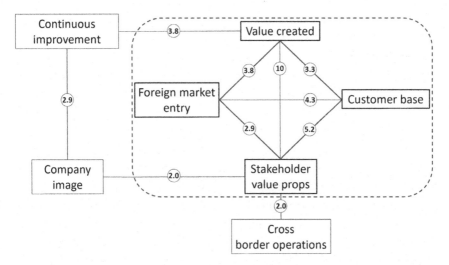

Fig. 3. Value proposition development model showing the textual proximity (or semantic relations) between the seven different topics. Each topic is interpreted as a VP element including a set of actionable insights for new companies interested to scale early and rapidly. Customer base appears as a natural dependent variable for scaling companies.

between the seven documents that were created by including all the assertions corresponding to each topic. The cosine similarity values were normalized by the maximum value that was found to be between Topic 1 (Value created) and Topic 2 (Stakeholder value propositions).

The cosine similarity values shown in Fig. 3 are presented in a 1 to 10 scale by including only the values/links which are equal or greater than 2. It is important to point out that the relationships between the different topics should not be considered in absolute terms. They should be rather considered as a way of using the semantic proximity of the topic assertions as a basis for shaping a VP development framework. The seven elements of the VP framework and the semantic links between them allow to two formulate two key insights.

5.1. *Three VP elements related to customer base growth*

A straightforward interpretation of the graph shown in Fig. 3 suggests that there is a close interrelation between four core VP elements: stakeholder value propositions, foreign market entry, value created and customer base. The claim for a closer relation between these four elements is based on the fact each of these elements relates to the other three. Customer base appears as a natural dependent variable associated with the context of scaling companies. Our framework suggests that a company's customer base is related to: (i) the efficiency of company's value creation processes, i.e., its ability to access, combine and align resources provided by the key actors engaged in their business ecosystem (see assertions associated with Topic 1 in Appendix A); (ii) the attractiveness and the alignment of its VPs for key members of the business ecosystem, i.e., its ability to shape a portfolio of VPs in alignment with its scaling objectives (see assertions associated with Topic 2 in Appendix A); (iii) its foreign market entry strategy, i.e., its strategic plan to penetrate global market locations by transforming its local offers into global ones (see assertions associated with Topic 3 in Appendix A).

5.2. *VP development is a continuously improved process*

The VP framework shown in Fig. 3 suggests that the four core VP elements are continuously enhanced through a positive loop enabled by activities focusing on the continuous improvement of the value creation processes (see assertions associated with Topic 5 in Appendix A), learning based on managing knowledge emerging from cross-border operations (see assertions associated with Topic 6 in Appendix A) and the company brand image (see assertions associated with Topic 7 in Appendix A). This insight helps in emphasizing the dynamic nature of companies' VP development activities in case where they want to scale early and rapidly.

6. Can AI Enhance the VPs of Companies Willing to Scale Early and Rapidly?

This section focus on summarizing the analytical insights about the VP development activities that could be enhanced or empowered by AI resources and capabilities. The aim is to examine the extent to which the

VPs of new companies committed to scale globally could be enhanced by AI. The criteria for the selection of specific assertions were based on the literature.[31,32,34,35] The assertions were selected based on researchers' evaluation of the ability of AI resources and capabilities to enhance VP development activities by

- automating specific business processes
- providing decision-making insights through data analysis
- enhancing engagement or relationship with customers, employees, investors, partners and other relevant stakeholders
- opportunities in the value chain emerging from the adoption of a multi-stakeholder perspective on benefit analysis
- building rich customer prospect profiles, enabling dynamic pricing, automating workflows and post-order services
- uncovering new customer needs and business opportunities.

The list of actionable insights that could be enabled or enhanced by AI resources and capabilities are shown in Fig. 4. Interestingly, they are related to three of the four core VP elements that were discussed above — *stakeholder VPs, foreign market entry* and *customer base*. In addition, it was found that *continuous improvement* (process innovation) is another VP element that could be enhanced by AI. The AI-relevant

Stakeholder value propositions	Foreign market entry	Customer base	Continuous improvement
• Continuously improve VPs to key stakeholders based on business results and feedback	• Measure what worked in one market for use in others (e.g., sales, alliances, interactions with potential customers, job creation, technological breakthroughs, patents, etc.)	• Use analytics to produce insightful information about users, suppliers and customers, improve customer experience	• Continuously improve individuals, operations & infrastructures to deliver a portfolio of innovative offers
• Learn from VPs of companies that have scaled early and rapidly, and use the lessons to differentiate	• Integrate local innovation into global products and services	• Attract web traffic by targeting and retargeting users from search engines, referrals and social media	• Apply processes that make offers easier to understand, produce and deliver
• Track changes in stakeholders' VPs and use the information to realign your VPs	• Insert local actors into global communication systems and learn from multiple local experiences	• Continuously improve the user interfaces and applications that directly influence the entirety of the customer experience	• Invest to improve cybersecurity of the value chain
• Use key stakeholder data to improve competences of the value chain			• Apply processes that continuously improve company cybersecurity, its offers, channels, and resources
• Explain, prioritize, improve and complement existing portfolio of VPs		• Automatically extract the information a user, customer, investor or stakeholder wants	• Use data and artificial intelligence to personalize offers to consumers

Fig. 4. VP assertions that could be enhanced by AI resources and capabilities.

insights associated with *continuous improvement* are: continuously improve individuals, operations and infrastructures to deliver a portfolio of innovative offers; invest to improve cybersecurity of the value chain; apply processes that continuously improve company cybersecurity, its offers, channels, and resources; use data and artificial intelligence to personalize offers to consumers.

What is most interesting in these findings is that the actionable insights associated with companies' *customer base*, or their ability to scale, were associated with the possibility of being enhanced by the adoption of AI resources and capabilities. This is a finding that suggests that the potential of AI to enhance or innovate the VPs of new companies could have a direct impact on their ability to scale early and rapidly.

7. Conclusion

We have used literature on VPs, business ecosystems and AI-based business value to create a corpus of actionable insights, apply topic modeling and suggest a VP framework. The additional analysis of the results suggests that AI resources and capabilities could be used to enhance and innovate the VPs of such companies and help them scale.

The focus and the exploratory nature of our research approach could be benefit from some further elaboration. For example, why focusing on new companies committed to scale? The answer to this question is twofold. *First*, the majority of new firms are facing the scale up challenge. This challenge is not unique to a specific country or geographical region, but it is especially relevant for Canada where, for example, a recent report by the Toronto Board of Trade has recently pointed out that "Canada is a terrific start-up nation but a dismal failure as a scale-up nation."[61] *Second*, the context of new companies committed to scale early and rapidly requires a multiple stakeholder perspective on VP development. Such companies need to design and align a portfolio of VPs to all relevant stakeholders such as investors, suppliers, distributors, partners etc., instead of trying to address the needs of customers alone.[2] The necessity of adopting a multiple stakeholder perspective offers an opportunity to contribute to VP research by enhancing the insights developed by other scholars.[51,56]

One of the key objectives of this study was to articulate actionable insights for new companies interested to scale their value early and rapidly. It should be therefore considered as a contribution to an emerging stream in entrepreneurship research that has called for a stronger focus on the development actionable principles for practitioners. For example, Ref. [62] emphasized the need for the emergence of a distinct body of knowledge consisting of pragmatically oriented actionable principles that could bridge the gap between the causal mechanisms of entrepreneurship theory and the complex realities of entrepreneurial practice. The focus on actionable insights is an expression of our commitment to the applied research cause articulated by Berglund *et al.*[62]

Another contribution of this study is to knowledge on the relationship between AI and innovation management by making explicit the relationship between AI resources and capabilities and specific VP elements such as stakeholder VPs, foreign-market entry, and customer base. Finally, the results indicate that AI resources and capabilities could help in continuously improving companies' operations and infrastructures to deliver their innovative offers; investing in and applying processes that continuously improve company cybersecurity, its offers, channels, and resources; using data to personalize offers to consumers.

References

1. J. Van Aken, Management research based on the paradigm of the design sciences: The quest for field-tested and grounded technological rules. *Journal of Management Studies*, **41**(2), 219–246 (2004).
2. T. Bailetti, S. Tanev, and C. Keen, What makes value propositions distinct and valuable to new companies committed to scale rapidly? *Technology Innovation Management Review*, **10**(6), 14–27 (2020).
3. T. Hannigan, R. Haans, K. Vakili, H. Tchalian, V. Glaser, W. Wang, S. Kaplan, and P. Jennings, Topic modeling in management research: Rendering new theory from textual data. *Academy of Management Annals*, **13**(2), 586–632 (2019).
4. B. Baldassarre, G. Calabretta, N. Bocken, and T. Jaskiewicz, Bridging sustainable business model innovation and user-driven innovation: A process for sustainable value proposition design. *Journal of Cleaner Production*, **147**, 175–186 (2017).

5. J. Anderson, J. Narus, and W. Van Rossum, Customer VPs in business markets. *Harvard Business Review*, **84**(3), 91–99 (2006).
6. P. Frow and A. Payne, A stakeholder perspective of the value proposition concept. *European Journal of Marketing*, **45**(1/2), 223–240 (2011).
7. A. Payne, P. Frow, L. Steinhoff, and A. Eggert, Toward a comprehensive framework of value proposition development: From strategy to implementation. *Industrial Marketing Management*, **87**, 244–255 (2020).
8. M. Lanning, *Delivering Profitable Value: A Revolutionary Framework to Accelerate Growth, Generate Wealth, and Rediscover the Heart of Business.* Cambridge, MA: Perseus Press (2000).
9. F. Webster, *Market-Driven Management: How to Define, Develop and Deliver Customer Value*, 2nd ed. Hoboken: John Wiley & Sons (2002).
10. D. Ballantyne, P. Frow, R. Varey, and A. Payne, VPs as communication practice: Taking a wider view. *Industrial Marketing Management*, **40**, 202–210 (2011).
11. A. Eggert, W. Ulaga, P. Frow, and A. Payne, Conceptualizing and communicating value in business markets: From value in exchange to value in use. *Industrial Marketing Management*, **69**, 80–90 (2018).
12. S.D. Sarasvathy, Causation and effectuation: Toward a theoretical shift from economic inevitability to entrepreneurial contingency. *Academy of Management Review*, **26**(2), 243–263 (2001).
13. M. Wouters, J. Anderson, and M. Kirchberger, New-technology startups seeking pilot customers: Crafting a pair of VPs. *California Management Review*, **60**(4), 101–124 (2018).
14. A. Payne, P. Frow, and A. Eggert, The customer value proposition: Evolution, development, and application in marketing. *Journal of the Academy of Marketing Science*, **45**(4), 467–489 (2017).
15. F. Buttle, The S.C.O.P.E. of customer relationship management. *International Journal of Customer Relationship Management*, **1**(4), 327–337 (1999).
16. H. Holttinen, Contextualizing value propositions: Examining how consumers experience value propositions in their practices. *Australasian Marketing Journal*, **22**, 103–110 (2014).
17. N. Bocken and Y. Snihur, Lean Startup and the business model: Experimenting for novelty and impact. *Long Range Planning*, **53**(4), 101953 (2020).
18. D. Schepis, How innovation intermediaries support start-up internationalization: A relational proximity perspective. *Journal of Business and Industrial Marketing*, Publication ahead of print (2020). https://doi.org/10.1108/JBIM-05-2019-0242.

19. C. Grönroos, A service perspective on business relationships: The value creation, interaction and marketing interface. *Industrial Marketing Management*, **40**(2), 240–247 (2011).
20. P. Skålén, J. Gummerus, C. von Koskull, and P. Magnusson, Exploring value propositions and service innovation: A service-dominant logic study. *Journal of the Academy of Marketing Science*, **43**(2), 137–158 (2015).
21. H. Corvellec and J. Hultman, Managing the politics of value propositions. *Marketing Theory*, **14**(4), 355–375 (2014).
22. Y. Truong, G. Simmons, and M. Palmer, Reciprocal value propositions in practice: Constraints in digital markets. *Industrial Marketing Management*, **41**(1), 197–206 (2012).
23. C. Zott, R. Amit, and L. Massa, The business model: Recent developments and future research. *Journal of Management*, **37**(4), 1019–1042 (2011).
24. J. Zhang, Y. Lichtenstein and J. Gander, Designing scalable digital business model. Business models and modelling. *Advances in Strategic Management*, **33**, 241–277 (2015).
25. D. Shepherd, V. Souitaris, and M. Gruber, Creating new ventures: A review and research agenda. *Journal of Management*, **47**(1), 11–42 (2020).
26. H. Rydehell, H. Löfsten, and A. Isaksson, Novelty-oriented value propositions for new technology-based companies: Impact of business networks and growth orientation. *The Journal of High Technology Management Research*, **29**(2), 161–171 (2018).
27. T. Malnight, I. Buche, and Ch. Dhanaraj, Put purpose at the CORE of your strategy. *Harvard Business Review*, **97**(5), 70–78 (2019).
28. J. Bussgang and O. Stern, How Israeli startups can scale. *Harvard Business Review*, September issue (2015).
29. K. Girotra and S. Netessine, OM forum — Business model innovation for sustainability. *Manufacturing & Service Operations Management*, **15**(4), 537–544 (2013).
30. J.P. Melancon, D.A. Griffith, S.M. Noble, and Q. Chen, Synergistic effects of operant knowledge resources. *Journal of Services Marketing*, **24**(5), 400–411 (2010).
31. A. Mishra and A. Pani, Business value appropriation roadmap for artificial intelligence. *VINE Journal of Information and Knowledge Management Systems*. Publication ahead-of-print (2020). https://doi.org/10.1108/VJIKMS-07-2019-0107.
32. D.N. Wagner, The nature of the artificially intelligent firm — An economic investigation into changes that AI brings to the firm. *Telecommunications Policy*, **44**(6), 101954 (2020).

33. T. Davenport and R. Ronanki, Artificial Intelligence for the Real World. *Harvard Business Review*, **96**(1), 108–116 (2018).
34. M.H. Huang and R. T. Rust, Engaged to a robot? The role of AI in service. *Journal of Service Research*, **24**(1), 30–41 (2021).
35. J. Paschen, M. Wilson, and J. Ferreira, Collaborative intelligence: How human and artificial intelligence create value along the B2B sales funnel. *Business Horizons*, **63**, 403–414 (2020).
36. H. Güngör, Creating value with artificial intelligence: A multi-stakeholder perspective. *Journal of Creating Value*, **6**(1), 72–85 (2020).
37. A. Agrawal, J. Gans, and A. Goldfarb, A simple tool to start making decisions with the help of AI. *Harvard Business Review Online*. April (2018). Available at: https://hbr.org/2018/04/a-simple-tool-to-start-making-decisions-with-the-help-of-ai (last access April 13, 2021).
38. J. Zawadzki, Introducing the AI project canvas. *Medium* (2020). Available at: https://towardsdatascience.com/introducing-the-ai-project-canvas-e88e29 eb7024 (last access April 13, 2021).
39. U. Kerzel, Enterprise AI canvas integrating artificial intelligence into business. *Applied Artificial Intelligence*, **35**(1), 1–12 (2021).
40. A. S. Kier and J. S. McMullen, Entrepreneurial imaginativeness in new venture ideation. *Academy of Management Journal*, **61**(6), 2265–2295 (2018).
41. J.A. Belso-Martinez, F. Xavier Molina-Morales, and F. Mas-Verdu, Combining effects of internal resources, entrepreneur characteristics and KIS on new firms. *Journal of Business Research*, **66**(10), 2079–2089 (2013). https://doi.org/10.1016/j.jbusres.2013.02.034.
42. S. Shane and S. Venkataraman, The promise of entrepreneurship as a field of research. *Academy of Management Review*, **25**(1), 217–226 (2000).
43. G.L. Casali, M. Perano, A. Presenza, and T. Abbate, Does innovation propensity influence wineries' distribution channel decisions? *International Journal of Wine Business Research*, **30**(4), 446–462 (2018).
44. T. Kollmann, C. Stöckmann, and J.M. Kensbock, Fear of failure as a mediator of the relationship between obstacles and nascent entrepreneurial activity — An experimental approach. *Journal of Business Venturing*, **32**(3), 280–301 (2017).
45. R. Adner, Ecosystem as structure: An actionable construct for strategy. *Journal of Management*, **43**(1), 39–58 (2017).
46. S.D. Sarasvathy and N. Dew, New market creation through transformation. *Journal of Evolutionary Economics*, **15**(5), 533–565 (2005).
47. E. Stam and A. van de Ven, Entrepreneurial ecosystem elements. *Small Business Economics*, **56**(2) 809–832 (2021).

48. B. Dattée, O. Alexy, and E. Autio, Maneuvering in poor visibility: How firms play the ecosystem game when uncertainty is high. Academy *of Management Journal*, **61**(2), 466–498 (2018).

49. S. Nambisan and R.A. Baron, Entrepreneurship in innovation ecosystems: Entrepreneurs' self–regulatory processes and their implications for new venture success. *Entrepreneurship Theory and Practice*, **37**(5), 1071–1097 (2013).

50. O. Akemu, G. Whiteman, and S. Kennedy, Social enterprise emergence from social movement activism: The Fairphone case. *Journal of Management Studies*, **53**(5), 846–877 (2016).

51. M.G. Jacobides, C. Cennamo, and A. Gawer, Towards a theory of ecosystems, *Strategic Management Journal*, **39**(8), 2255–2276 (2018).

52. C.Y. Baldwin, Bottlenecks, modules and dynamic architectural capabilities. *Harvard Business School Finance Working Paper.* (15-028) (2015).

53. R.N. Langlois, The vanishing hand: The changing dynamics of industrial capitalism. *Industrial and Corporate Change*, **12**(2), 351–385 (2003).

54. T. Bailetti and S. Tanev, Examining the relationship between value propositions and scaling value for new companies. *Technology Innovation Management Review*, **10**(2), 5–13 (2020).

55. H.S. Kristensen and A. Remmen, A framework for sustainable value propositions in product-service systems. *Journal of Cleaner Production*, **223**, 25–35 (2019).

56. P. Frow, J. McColl-Kennedy, T. Hilton, A. Davidson, A. Payne, and D. Brozovic, Value propositions: A service ecosystems perspective. *Marketing Theory*, **14**(3), 327–351 (2014).

57. D. Denyer, D. Tranfield and J.E. van Aken, Developing design propositions through research synthesis. *Organization Studies*, **29**(3), 393–413 (2008).

58. D. Blei, Probabilistic topic models. *Communications of the ACM*, **55**(4), 77–84 (2012).

59. J. Boyd-Graber, D. Mimno, and D. Newman, Care and feeding of topic models: Problems, diagnostics, and improvements, Ch. 12, in E.M. Airoldi, D. Blei, E. Erosheva and S. Fienberg (eds.), *Handbook of Mixed Membership Models and Its Applications*, 225–254. Boca Raton: CRC Press (2014).

60. M. Anandarajan, C. Hill, and T. Nolan, Ch. 2: Probabilistic topic models, *Practical Text Analytics. Advances in Analytics and Data Science*, 45–59. Cham: Springer (2019).

61. Crane, D. (2019). It's time for Canada to focus on the scale-up challenge. *IT World Canada.* Accessible at: https://www.itworldcanada.com/article/its-time-for-canada-to-focus-on-the-scale-up-challenge/420027.

62. H. Berglund, D. Dimov, and K. Wennberg, Beyond bridging rigor and relevance: The three-body problem in entrepreneurship, *Journal of Business Venturing Insights*, **9**(1), 87–91 (2018).

Appendix A. Topic Modeling Results

Topic 1: Value created: product, service, sale, investor, norm, scaling master plan, benefit, resource.

- Access resources that allow to scale at lower costs by creating benefits for the resource owners that they cannot create alone.
- Allow resource owners to make money using your products and services.
- Align value created from the combination and deployment of external resources with scaling master plan.
- Combine company resources with those of other resource owners to create value that cannot be created by your company alone.
- Make decisions on how to best deploy value-adding combinations external and internal resources, while complying with all relevant cultural, legal, and regulatory norms.
- Establish partnerships that increase the demand for and complement your products.
- Enable your freelance workers to become world class service providers.
- Increase order fulfillment and delivery capacity through partnering with third party service providers and acquiring drop shipping facilities.
- Provide investors with evidence that your business model and target market can generate enough sales for the company to be investable in.
- Provide returns that leave the most important resource owners better off than what they would have if they had not engaged with you.
- Simplify the complementarity of your company products and services.
- Combine two or more resources to create value that exceeds the sum of the value created from each resource separately.
- Provide vendors and suppliers with real-time analytics on sales required to boost their own sales and profits.

- Use company's technical and knowledge expertise to develop prototypes that demonstrate the value of your products and services.
- Demonstrate how your technology, knowledge, and experience contribute to company's scaling master plan.
- Contribute to university research projects and enhance the academic and technical reputation of your team to ensure that your company's proposed technological concept is valid.
- Develop a compelling image of your future company and use it to convince investors to provide funding and resource owners to provide resources needed to scale.

Topic 2: Stakeholder value propositions: value proposition, vision, future, salesperson, path.
- Instill a sense of purpose by articulating and pursuing a compelling vision for the company in the future.
- Provide investors a compelling short-term financial VP and a vision of favorable medium and long-term VPs.
- Develop VPs that enhance employee satisfaction, psychological attachment, and behavioral commitment to your company.
- Continuously improve VPs based on results and feedback.
- Learn from VPs of companies that have scaled early, rapidly, and securely, and use them to differentiate your company on the market.
- Track changes in stakeholders' VPs and use the information to realign your VPs to them.
- Develop VPs for key members of the value chain that align with key members' VPs and improve the competence of the value chain.
- Develop VPs that enhance your customers' and suppliers' outcomes, marketing strategies, and competitive advantages.
- Develop investor VPs describing the path to return on investment in return for investors' funds and confidence.

Topic 3: Foreign market entry: local, prototype, alliance, patent, regulation.
- Develop a replicable formula to repeat what worked in one location in other locations.

- Promote company's achievements to date, e.g., awards, high-profile endorsements from established companies, sales, successful alliances and interactions with potential customers, strength of company's scaling mater plan and the company's potential to create local jobs, contributions to social causes, and advancement of knowledge.
- Enable locals in other locations to succeed because of your company.
- Enter a different geographical market by partnering with or purchasing local companies.
- Improve links, interactions, and shared purpose with locals in each region the company operates in.
- To globalize a local product, develop core product that can be readily disseminated worldwide.
- Integrate local innovation into global themes, products, and services.
- Include local actors into your global communication system and learn from multiple local experiences.

Topic 4: Customer base: customer, stakeholder, user, supplier, loyalty, referral.
- Apply big data analytics to produce insightful information about users, suppliers and customers to enhance shopping pattern analysis, improve customer experience, predict market trends, provide more secure online payment solutions, increase personalization, optimize and automate pricing, and provide dynamic customer service.
- Attract traffic and new customers by targeting and retargeting users from search engines, referrals, adds and social media.
- Engage customers to produce testimonials, reviews and ratings that help new customers to make purchasing decisions with knowledge of other customers experiences.
- Provide rewards that satisfy customer needs for recognition of their loyalty.
- Continuously improve user interfaces and applications that directly influence the entirety of customer experience including personalized content, quality messaging, and the delivery and returns process.
- Implement a stakeholder-centric approach to satisfy stakeholder expectations in all markets.

- Automatically extract the information a user, customer, investor, or stakeholder wants from the vast amount of the available information.
- Build internet-based capabilities to acquire and retain customers during the initial stages of company's lifecycle.
- Define the ideal target customer profiles and engage them relentlessly.
- Use an end-to-end solution that links procurement directly with end customers to eliminate or reduce inventory and the number of intermediaries between the company and customers.
- Enable employees, customers, users, investors, and other relevant parties to automatically extract information from company data for the purpose of decreasing costs and adding value to other stakeholders.
- Establish trust and positive rapport with your customers that lead to long term, mutually beneficial business relationships.
- Adjust to your customers moods and work to find common ground to build familiarity.
- Listen to your customers, take their feedback seriously, and adjust operations as needed.
- Digitize as much of your company as you can to create value for customers, reduce costs, and increase security.
- Deliver better performance on the metrics that customers care about.

Topic 5: Continuous improvement: offer, channel, artificial intelligence, threshold, value chain, data.
- Continuously improve individuals, operations, and infrastructures to advance and deliver a portfolio of innovative offers.
- Apply processes that make offers easier to understand, produce and deliver.
- Invest to improve cybersecurity of the value chain.
- Expand information about the company, its offers, its achievements, and its affiliations.
- Apply processes that continuously improve the cybersecurity of the company as well as its offers, channels, and resources.
- Adapt offers to each market.
- Provide a variety of complementary offers to each market.

- Sell online using a variety of online and offline promotional channels.
- Sell offers the target market perceives better than relevant alternatives.
- Strengthen cybersecurity attributes of offers compared to competitors.
- Use scientific and technological advances to develop innovative offers.
- Broaden company offers to address more customer jobs to be done.
- Unbundle the value chain and the jobs to be done within it to outsource lower value tasks to freelance workers and perform higher value tasks internally.
- Use data and artificial intelligence to personalize offers to consumers.

Topic 6: Cross-border operations: community, founder, regulation, cross border.
- Attain positions in cross-border networks which provide access to privileged information.
- Build operational cross-border capabilities early.
- Coordinate, evaluate and share knowledge between headquarters, cross-border units and among the units themselves.
- Simultaneously develop global learning capabilities, cross-border flexibility, and global competitiveness.
- Build a community where each member supports others rather than building many separate businesses.
- Contribute to the creation of public goods such as open source code, standards, and test beds.

Topic 7: Company image: brand, identity, competitor, competition, ecommerce, price.
- Create a unique brand identity to differentiate from the competition.
- Expand brand coverage and eliminate intermediaries.
- Brand the company and build a brand that has a strong market presence.

- Select and retain a consistent identity for the multiple audiences with which you interact.
- Deploy efficient ecommerce technologies and automation to reduce company costs and lower prices of offers.
- Sell high quality offers at lower prices compared to competitors.

Chapter 10

Fair, Inclusive, and Anticipatory Leadership for AI Adoption and Innovation

Jennifer Barth*, Eurydice Fotopoulou[†], and Chris Brauer[‡]

Smoothmedia Consulting Ltd
41 Great Portland Street, London W1W 7LA, UK
*jenn@smoothmedia.com
[†]eurydice@smoothmedia.com
[‡]brauer@gold.ac.uk

This chapter focuses on the role of management in the process of AI-driven innovation, suggesting that the heart of an AI-enabled organization is the building of a dynamic relationship between leaders and workforce — one based on trust, empathy and participatory relationships. Transformation to digitally and AI-enabled organizations necessitates this dynamic approach. Based on qualitative and quantitative work, we will suggest that today we must become active learners, while leaders need to create inclusive cultures that support and invest in this progressive environment. New relationships between leaders and employees rest on responsiveness, resilience, empathy and an openness to change. This is particularly relevant in overcoming crises, for example, building the type of post-COVID-19 world that heeds its lessons and creates cultures of inclusion and success.

1. Introduction

Artificial intelligence (AI) is set to influence every aspect of our lives. When it is used as a technology platform, it can automate tasks formerly undertaken by humans or create new tasks and activities in which humans can be more productively employed. Taking into account the competitive environment of businesses, with access to enormous amounts of data, while resources remain scarce, companies of all sizes have been inspired to use AI tools. This has become more urgent since February 2020, when the global business landscape started changing due to the COVID-19 outbreak, resulting in significant market gains achieved by leading digital enterprises, hence the requirement for faster, improved decision making by driven by AI innovation[a] and AI adoption.

AI adoption relates to the use of intelligent systems created to use data, analysis and observations to perform certain tasks without needing to be programmed to do so and it enables fast and deep technological development.[1] As such, AI disrupts industries when companies use it to innovate in terms of their business model. AI innovation has recently become the focus of the debate of how companies may preserve their market position, because, just like every innovation and disruptive technology, it can increase market capture, including the creation of new markets and value networks. The existing literature on business model innovation mainly focuses on external antecedents, as companies are forced by competition to adopt AI or innovate using AI to improve their existing business model. The objective of organizations is to establish sustainable competitive advantage by integrating technology into the decision-making process with corporate strategy. Businesses are supposed to be more flexible and responsive to strategic decision-making in the current dynamic environment.[2–5] However, there is a growing body of research that looks how the introduction of AI-driven innovation helps companies to improve their business model with a lasting, transformational effect. See Refs. [3–6] for more examples of technological innovation effects.

So far, driven by market concerns, technological innovation has put limited emphasis on integrating the new tasks where humans can contribute meaningfully, in a way that fosters creativity, as well as a culture of diversity and inclusion. The decision to make AI innovation and adoption more inclusive depends, in part, on organizational leadership; specifically taking a strong lead with a vision for the business and care for the people

---

[a]To avoid confusion, when we refer to AI innovation we mean AI innovation itself, while AI-driven innovation refers to innovation that is enabled by AI.

that make up the business. These leadership qualities are the qualities of leadership that are supportive of technological innovation and that innovation managers should promote in an organization, especially as the workforce and the business operates under the strain of a global pandemic.

It is common for organizations to adopt AI — or indeed any business technology — in only one area of their business, seeking to change a specific process as a discrete aspect of work, drawing from a more traditional approach to innovation management. In this context, each area of business is perceived hierarchically in isolation, not as a dynamic, living enterprise. This may result in the cost optimization of a particular process, while its benefits are primarily felt among the one area where optimizations have occurred. It is also difficult to scale the innovation to other areas of the business — thus limiting the outcomes of both the monetary investment and its scalability.

Recent research suggests that technology adoption needs to be thought of as a broader action — that of digital innovation as a rethink of business strategy where digital transformation is business transformation and the digital journey is a wholesale change in business strategy.[1,2,8–10] With this consideration in mind, technological change is seen as a catalyst for higher impact investment that can scale up.

The technology, then, becomes an enabler for delivering such impact alongside broader organizational cultural change. Asking what business problem needs to be solved and what technology best solves it, provides a starting point. A digital transformation strategy of such a type removes barriers and siloes, while bringing people together by encouraging deeper collaboration, different ways of working together and different practices of engineering and development. Consequently, the focus shifts to thinking about both the technological and the cultural preconditions necessary. Undoubtedly, the technology — including cloud infrastructure, data management processes, and any other science-intensive technological innovation — is the foundation for AI adoption. However, this is not all.

An underlying condition for a holistic AI adoption and innovation management concerns deploying technology efficiently through the social and cultural preconditions including transformational leadership and a culture of dynamic leadership. For instance, the first of the three key shifts necessary a business needs to make to benefit from AI-driven innovation is shifting to interdisciplinary collaboration from siloed work.[11]

While cutting-edge technology and talent are also required, it is equally important to align a company's culture, structure, and ways of working to support broad AI adoption. Leaders as *translators* and *agents of change* of this transformation are crucial in making the shift. The role of ethical leadership is not only important as agents of change, but is also responsible to ensure that organizations use digital technologies to communicate effectively, build stronger relationships and, develop effective strategies.[10] All of which would have a positive and transformational impact on the organizations performance. It is the opportunity of (re-)structuring the organization to be cross-functional and collaborative, thinking about ethics and representation, namely diversity and inclusion, and focusing on both values.

Within this chapter we provide an overview of how thinking about AI as part of a broader digital transformation endeavor can lead to actionable steps for businesses. The chapter first discusses the rationale and theories behind conventional versus innovative approaches to leadership through technological innovation, to illustrate that AI-driven innovation and AI adoption in an organization require a departure from conventional thinking about change management. We then present a case study on competitiveness and economic recovery for the UK, informed by a large survey. The case study demonstrates the importance of inclusive innovation management by business leaders, especially under times of uncertainty or to overcome economic crises, such as the shock to economic activity caused by COVID-19. Finally, we conclude with suggestions on how innovation managers can ensure that AI innovation is adopted successfully within their organization.

2. Leadership for Conventional Technological Innovation

The current COVID-19 crisis and rush to adopt technological innovation brought to the surface many ways that organizations are volatile to shocks. These organizations at times of normal business cycles may exhibit high rates of growth during the high point of the business cycle (when the economy does well booms) — in other words they have the ability to demonstrate competitive business behavior — while at the low phase of the business cycle (recessions-busts) they are hit much harder compared to organizations that did not have as high rates of growth during booms. The weaknesses of this interpretation of standard/typical competitiveness approach in practice lies in the fact that conventional technological innovation focuses on extracting as much value as possible from labor in order to reduce costs — occasionally treating employees as expendable and replacing them with technological solutions. This is driven by the need to account for quantified efficiency and optimization that ignore the role of human workers in the success of a business, leading to less sustainable, short-term gains. The pandemic as a severe shock on the economy, by significantly disrupting economic activity, has exposed the weaknesses of some organizations, by demonstrating that in reality they are not able to continue operating with the same business model. In addition to that, consumers and users of services are increasingly becoming aware of the ethical and environmental implications of their consumption decisions, and are likely to hold such organizations accountable by steering away from them. As a result, organizations following conventional technological innovation are more likely to lose their competitive advantage (due to low labor costs), and take longer to recover.

To understand the economic implications of this type of technological adoption, let us consider it from the productivity effect. The standard approach in Ref. [12] makes the assumption that any advance that increases productivity (value added per worker) also tends to increase the demand for labor, and thus employment and wages (which are necessary for an increase in demand for goods and services, as workers are also consumers). Even when technological progress is acknowledged to partially lead to job loss in some sectors, it is assumed that other sectors will grow and contribute to overall employment and wage growth. Additionally, even if technological progress benefits some workers more than others and increases inequality, the standard approach still predicts that it will tend to raise the labor demand overall, regardless of gender, age, skills, etc. This depends on the way in which the economic impact of new technology is conceptualized — as enabling labor to become more productive in most the activities and tasks that it performs. However, this not only lacks descriptive realism (considering what type of technology makes labor uniformly more productive in everything), but may present a rose-tinted picture of the implications of new technologies.

3. Leadership for AI Innovation

The goal for inclusive leadership in change management and AI adoption and innovation is taking an organization beyond sustainable turnover growth, where organizations strive to maintain a stable upwards-trending trajectory. In this interpretation, competitive edge is achieved by showing resilience due to the existence of underlying organizational and technological structures that ensure that the organization is able to adapt quickly, and scale up with limited costs. For example, such organizations make use of a variety of advanced technologies in multiple (or all) operations, including being fully cloud native and using AI. Besides this, such organizations are able to demonstrate speed to impact as they learn from experience and try out new ways of working by employing technological solutions at pace. For instance, they are likely to transition fully to a new technology fast (usually in a few months), which places them in an advantageous position when it comes to innovate, increase productivity, and ultimately become more competitive. Another key feature of this interpretation is decisive, ethical, caring leadership, which aims to nurture existing talent that is creative and encouraged to innovate, while they contribute not only to economic growth but the culture of the organization, too, making it eventually more dynamic and agile. Ethical leadership[b] is defined in Ref. [14] as "the showcasing of normatively appropriate conduct with the help of interpersonal relationships and personal actions, and employing two-way communication, reinforcement and decision making to promote such conduct to followers." Of course, skilled employees are crucial in this; engineers, scientists, analysts are the nerve system of an organization that wants to be at the forefront of innovation, working in tandem with leadership to create the most fertile conditions. Consequently, organizations that follow this interpretation are likely to be directly concerned with equality, diversity and, notably, environmental sustainability, as this type of innovation adoption has much lower environmental footprint compared to the typical capital-intensive expansions of the past.

---

[b]The responsibilities of an ethical leader for AI adoption are not to be confused with the ethics of AI adoption. An excellent exposition on the matter can be found in Ref. [14].

In this context, we draw our interpretation of inclusive leadership for change management in an organization from political economy, specifically Ref. [15], whereby the notion that social norms constitute distinct frames of reference that coordinate agents' expectations (agents in our case being leaders and employees), and shape the interpretation of the information they receive, thus their behaviors. A particular social norm, such as trust, can persist as a result of the expectation that others will be honest, leading agents to interpret ambiguous signals as still being consistent with honest behavior and thus overcoming occasional transgressions. Conversely, a social norm of distrust would lead to a very different interpretation of the same signals and a less trusting pattern of behavior. This definition of social norms regulates many areas of human interactions and creates self-reinforcing (stable) patterns of behavior, leading to a more positively responsive society, as articulated in Ref. [16]. Nonetheless, norms are not immutable, but emerge and change as a result of social and historical factors, and can also be influenced by leadership, increasing or decreasing cooperation within an organization, which in turn allows it to be more or less agile in the face of sudden change. The agency of leaders stems from their responsibility to focus on what improves dynamism in their teams, ensuring that employees feel appreciated, by providing the space for them to grow in the organization (by retraining or upskilling, and support that takes into account their needs outside the workplace, i.e., childcare), while responding to their concerns and ideas.

This vision beyond "optimization" and towards equitable socioeconomic impact, well established in the literature (for the most influential take on the issue, see Ref. [17]) and in industry, takes economic and cultural investment but provides lasting, sustainable returns. It will positively affect many performance factors of a business, including the ability to launch new value propositions to generate new revenue streams, being adaptable to change, building resilience to changes in the market such as regulatory change, or economic and social impacts (e.g., Brexit and COVID-19), it enables deployment of new technology and value added services, improves operational efficiency and reduces waste, cutting costs, and delights those on the customer end. Most importantly, it creates a culture with desirable working practices, thereby attracting and retaining the best talent, which is essential for continuous innovation in response to external challenges. To illustrate the socio-economic impact, a detailed case study will be considered from our recent research, Ref. [9] in the following section.

4. Case Study

Within the context of the Creating a Blueprint for UK Competitiveness project, we conducted a large survey with 4086 respondents, among whom 2400 were employees and 1617 business leaders (senior managers, general managers, directors, chairmen, chief executives, partners or owners of businesses) from June until September 2020. The survey covered new and more established businesses active in the UK, of all sizes, in all sectors of the economy. The project used mixed methods, utilizing surveys, econometric modeling, data analysis and qualitative interviews.

Under times of increased uncertainty, the Schumpeterian process of creative destruction becomes particularly intense, and in many industries, the choice faced by managers across the world right now is to innovate or die, in all sectors of the economy. Our evidence corroborates this. Companies had to accelerate their digital initiatives out of necessity during COVID-19 because their business-as-usual model has been insufficient. This required fast adoption of remote work and collaboration solutions, at varying degree of sophistication, to ensure business survival, at first, and market capture where opportunities appeared. Whereas leaders previously might not have invested in digital innovation due to a lack of clear ROI or lack of vision, in the pandemic they had to invest in accelerating digital innovation. With cloud technology becoming ubiquitous, the current innovation plan is towards AI innovation as the next enabler. To achieve this, the preconditions — both technological and social — must be met.

The purpose of the survey was partially to understand the engagement of businesses and business leaders with innovation in the UK and how this affects their strategy and plans. From this survey we draw interesting conclusions on the type of inclusive leadership desired to achieve fast and efficient advanced technological innovation. The available statistics on the true size of technological innovation and its impact unsurprisingly lag behind the reality they are meant to explain, which in turn can limit the tools available to assess the impact of technological innovation. As a consequence, the developments in the digital economy have exacerbated the mismatch problem in the economy between real activity and measurement. Measurement is essential in the process, as it will allow businesses to understand the impact of change resulting from technological innovation and create benchmarks against which they can improve social and economic performance of the business. Many attempts have been made to describe the aspects of the digital that need to be measured and to think about *what* precisely should be considered to add value. Reference [13] developed indicators that capture both the upstream and downstream effects, with the long-run aspiration of including them in an index that would measure the digital economy and consequently innovation uptake globally. This is one of the most significant and coordinated efforts to create a uniform way to define what is included in the digital economy and how it can be measured in both developed and developing countries.

Our methodological framework was influenced by Ref. [13] toolkit for measuring the digital economy, and its focus on upstream and downstream aspects of digital transformation including infrastructure, empowering society, innovation and technological adoption and jobs and growth to understand that such measurement at a macro scale considers not only the technology but the people as agents of change too. While this chapter will not focus on Ref. [13], it points to it to note that this combination of social with economic and digital is widely considered as important at a high level, even though such macro policy endeavor is not always reflected in the specific discourse of business and industry at meso and micro level.

> If we look at COVID-19, the people who have been brilliant leaders are those who have been ridiculously inclusive in their input, ridiculously empathetic in their awareness and ridiculously decisive. In a dynamic world, empathy is as important as decisiveness.
>
> Global leader of strategy at consultancy firm,
> interviewed August 2020.

Our findings show that leadership is paramount in creating the circumstances necessary for the flourishing of an organization by strategizing, managing and motivating employees in a caring, inclusive and nurturing manner, while making resources available for the development of new ideas. Confidence in the leadership of a business to adapt and progress is a key determinant of growth. We found that it adds an extra 0.77% to the revenue of a business, if its management is agile, creative, and supportive enough to withstand economic shocks such as this caused by COVID-19.

At times of uncertainty, when agility and resourcefulness is required, a trusted leadership can guide and encourage employees to identify opportunities of growth in the organization, and signpost areas where technological innovation is required. This way employees become stakeholders in change management, take ownership of their work, while contributing to the sense of belonging in the organization. In the survey employee respondents were asked to express how encouraging, responsive and inspirational the leaders of the organizations are. Here is a snapshot of some of the key findings:

(1) *Women felt more heard*: Female employee respondents felt that leaders encouraged their creativity and responded to their ideas and concerns more than male employees.
(2) *Small is beautiful*: Small organizations performed better when it comes to responsiveness of leaders to employees' concerns and ideas. There are several explanations as to why this may happen more in smaller organizations, but this is beyond the scope of this chapter. Responsive leaders are more likely to be in the banking and finance sector, while leaders in retail perform the worst in this metric.
(3) *The unsung creatives*: Leaders who encourage creativity and responsiveness are more likely to be found in banking, marketing, media and product development teams.
(4) *Rare gems*: Inspirational leaders are more difficult to be found, despite the ubiquitous TED speakers. Both male and female respondents are more likely to disagree that their leaders are inspiring them to perform better, regardless of the organizations' size. Inspiring leaders are likely to be found in young organizations (operating for up to 10 years) with low turnover (up to £1m) — these organizations are usually start-ups.

The survey identified a key area for leadership improvement — an inclusive leader who listens, cares and inspires. According to Ref. [18], one of the best ways to achieve an organization's desired outcomes is to adopt the humble mindset of a servant leader. Servant leaders view their key role as serving employees while they explore and grow, providing tangible and emotional support as they do so. They have the humility, courage, and insight to admit that they can benefit from the expertise of others who have less power than them. They actively seek the ideas and unique contributions of the employees that they serve. This is how servant leaders create a culture of learning, and an atmosphere that encourages followers to become the very best they can. The servant leader leadership style highlights that it is the responsibility of a leader to increase the ownership, autonomy, and responsibility of employees — to encourage them to be creative and try out their own ideas- eventually making organizations more dynamic and resilient in the face of disruptions.

The vast majority of leaders in all organizations agree that leadership can produce and promote confident and resourceful workforces through access to a pipeline of culturally and cognitively diverse talent, as is recognizing that people feel more different at work than in any other part of their lives. Nearly all leaders in our survey concur that listening and interpreting the needs of their workforce is a priority. Nonetheless, these responses often do not match the experience of employees, who are less likely to fully agree that their managers show that they feel this way. Clearly here there is a mismatch of expectations and intentions, and the leaders are seemingly failing to do exactly what they claim is important: listen to the needs of their employees.

Leaders during times of crisis have to respond to a number of challenges, and these need to adapt to new information and changes over time. The survey response indicated that March 2020 was, as anticipated, a period that demanded attention to multiple areas of the business simultaneously (Fig. 1). We observe though, that although most priorities remain the same, their urgency has declined. Leaders in our sample flagged two areas that are more concerning in autumn 2020 as opposed to March 2020: redundancies and driving new growth. The combination of these two priorities that experienced an increase may imply that in order to drive

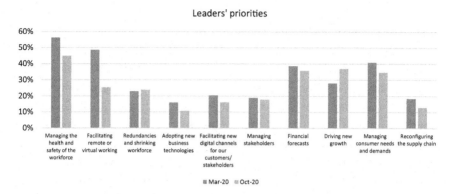

Fig. 1. Business leader's priorities in March 2020 and October 2020 (survey response).

growth up, business leaders as innovation managers may be under pressure to reduce labor costs.

Pressures on costs and increasing efficiency with fewer resources are evident in other ways too. More than half of the leaders responded that they made changes to their existing business model within a month of the COVID-19 outbreak. However, two in five said they are not planning to launch a new model or scrap an existing model in the coming months. This may indicate either that they are adopting a cautious stance, but not risking significant changes, or that the initial changes to the model were sufficient in ensuring the survival of their business.

Besides these concerns about growth and employee well-being, business leaders need to ensure that IT systems necessary for technological upgrade are at a suitable state. In our survey, one in four leaders responded that their organization replaces hardware every three years, regardless of the organization size, turnover or location. However, when it comes to upgrading their operating systems most organizations are likely to be innovation-driven, with one in five leaders of UK based organizations (as opposed to three out of ten non-UK HQ organizations) reporting that they will upgrade their systems when an innovation in an area of interest becomes available. The eagerness to follow innovation in specific areas is a positive sign, ensuring that organizations' operating systems stays safe and efficient, even when having to deal with an unexpected disruption.

In businesses that saw a decline of their revenue by more than 5% in 2020, a key area where leadership in this category seem to be lagging behind compared to other categories is their decision making: the overwhelming majority seems to have decided to change their existing business model within days of the pandemic outbreak, but this did not prevent them from suffering. Drawing from this, it may have been a better strategy to introduce a new model of business/operation in some form after the outbreak and migrate faster to the cloud. However, in order to do so, adaptability, agility and dynamism are necessary, which seem to be missing. The majority of businesses whose revenue declined less than 5% or remain unchanged in 2020 changed their business model within days, and do not expect to launch or scrap an existing model in the near future. The fact that they have managed to weather the storm indicates that the changes made in the early days have proven to be suitable. We also found a strong correlation between business growth in 2020, decisive leadership and fast advanced technological innovation adoption. Companies in the cross-section of these features are more likely to be fast adopters of new technologies, and able to fully transition to a new technology within a year, which is likely to reflect their stronger existing technological infrastructure. We find that organizations that increase their turnover by up to 5% take between 6 and 12 months to fully transition to a new technology, while organizations with turnover increase 5%–10% are likely to need between 3 and 6 months to do so. They are also more likely to have a multi-cloud strategy, using multiple providers, which may contribute to the speed of transition.

Our evidence demonstrates that companies realize now that continuous digital innovation is not so risky after all and is in fact critical to the resilience and future success of a business. Ultimately, to retain and develop further the approach to technological and business change requires a change in behavior at leadership level. The companies that emerge successfully and stronger out of the pandemic will already have these changes in leadership in place. Previously, the relationship between ethics and performance or an organization was viewed through the perspective of corporate identity — the set of interdependent characteristics of the organization that give it distinctiveness: organizational philosophy, values, history, strategy, business scope, and communication, as articulated in Ref. [20]. By focusing on the relationship of innovation management and leadership for successful adoption of AI, we put responsiveness, resilience, empathy and an openness to change in the core of the issue, arguing that it may enhance corporate performance. Leaders with these features play a dominant role affecting organizational productivity and success; a progressive leadership style that shapes organizational characteristics such as technology adoption, strategy, structure, reward system and resources, will also enable workers to exhibit high levels of creativity at work.[21]

Additionally, with the advent of remote work from home, there are indications that the nature of work has changed, we consider how technology, and specifically AI, would improve working life — including increased communication and transparency with leaders on one hand, but also faster, more generic communications where AI implementations are the backbone of email and remote working software. This is a critical area, as over the last year, due to the impact of COVID-19, remote work solutions have been equally praised and blamed for changing the work-life balance and job satisfaction.

We look into the interplay of progressive leadership and innovation management through a number of dimensions that contribute to inclusion, such as performance of businesses that were early adopters of innovation technology, productivity of businesses which prioritize employee well-being, and whether an increase in engagement with the digital in the workplace results in more inclusion of those previously excluded from work in technologically leading areas. Under these conditions, technology that enables humans to maximize their own creative potential, rethinking the way they collaborate, without embedded biases in the design or application of technology, as much as possible, can be thought of "good technology." The findings of the case study strongly support the notion that there is a link between good technology and good leadership. Building a diverse workforce, being inclusive by recognizing the support required for people in working remotely sat hand in hand with the need to increase cloud and speed of technology adoption.

In the autumn of 2020, Ref. [21] focused on a subset group of 26,000 technology suppliers in the UK and applied a similar analysis towards economic recovery, as a follow-up to the original study. Through the pandemic, organizations have been agile and flexible and able to roll out minimal viable products with speed because of the focused attention on agility and change management. The pandemic led organizations seeking to buy technology from these providers to adjust their approach to digital transformation — and this meant really looking at the business problems they had to solve, and fast. Rather than wholesale cloud adoption, they focused instead on where they needed cloud or other solutions quickly and how to achieve maximum security and risk analysis on short timelines. Empathetic leadership ranked high among respondents and willingness to meet employees' needs in areas like training and development, remote working, and communication is directly linked to their ability to offer high quality products, services and experiences. Alongside these aspects are the increased use of cloud and the need to move forward on data analytics and automation — specifically areas where AI enters the conversation. Indeed, as companies find their feet in the transformation afforded by the pandemic, next steps point to AI adoption, acceleration and innovation. Realizing now the connection between inclusive and empathetic leadership and technological advance places these companies, and the people that work for them, in strong positions to excel at speed to impact.

The insights from our case study findings on how empathetic and inclusive leadership can manage change in synergy with technological innovation are not limited to overcoming the impact of COVID-19 on economic activity. They are lessons to be applied when dealing with any severe economic shock that can significantly change market dynamics.

5. Conclusion

This view of innovation and change management thereby opens up insight into the aspects of an organization that need to be in place to best adopt the latest available technology, manage the change and deliver the best results. This chapter explores precisely a changing environment to look at both the role of the technology itself and the role of socio-economic factors in the adoption of AI and continuous innovation. We complement our position with a case study that illustrates these findings. A prerequisite to achieve this for some may be counter-intuitive; adoption of AI and change management requires inclusive leadership that is responsive, resilient, empathetic and creates relationships based on trust, not value.

In practice, this means that for a successful transformation of the organizational culture that will enable it, business leaders need to embark in a reflection journey with open-mindedness to ensure that talent and technology are used in the best way possible to facilitate AI-driven growth. The case study points out that current and future technology adoption should start with an internal digital strategy, followed by an assessment of the managerial and technical skills required to support successful digital transformation with AI. The assessment, in turn, would lead to either a strategy to develop internally or acquire these skills, taking into account the costs and risks involved. Following this, the business leaders should monitor the integration of AI in their business, while being aware of any changes in the scope of the transformation at the benefits/risks emerging from an AI-driven transformation start to materialize. Monitoring the process will increase agility of response. Throughout this process, clear communication and the collaboration between management and other teams within the organization is essential, to mitigate any avoidable costs or misapplication of technology.

Towards this end, the business and transformation strategy that calls for a disciplined focus on people- management synergy can produce the building blocks of an innovative organization. A priority is to formally integrate innovation and an inclusive mindset into the strategic-management agenda of senior leaders. In this way, innovation can be not only encouraged but also managed, tracked, and measured as a core element in a company's AI-driven growth aspirations. A second step is making better use of internal (and often untapped) talent for innovation, without implementing disruptive change programs, by listening and creating the conditions that allow dynamic innovation networks to emerge and flourish.

References

1. J. Lee, T. Suh, D. Roy, and M. Baucus, Emerging technology and business model innovation: The case of artificial intelligence. *Journal of Open Innovation: Technology, Market, and Complexity,* **5**(3), 44 (2019).
2. N. J. Foss and T. Saebi, Fifteen years of research on business model innovation: How far have we come, and where should we go? *Journal of Management,* **43**(1), 200–227 (2017).

3. F. Kitsios, M. Kamariotou, and M.A. Talias, Corporate sustainability strategies and decision support methods: A bibliometric analysis. *Sustainability,* **12**(2), 521 (2020).
4. P. Valter, P. Lindgren, and R. Prasad, Advanced business model innovation supported by artificial intelligence and deep learning. *Wireless Personal Communications,* **100**(1), 97–111 (2018).
5. I.O. Pappas, P. Mikalef, M.N. Giannakos, J. Krogstie, and G. Lekakos, Big data and business analytics ecosystems: Paving the way towards digital transformation and sustainable societies. *Information Systems and e-Business Management,* **16**, 479–491 (2018).
6. M. Garbuio and N. Lin, Artificial intelligence as a growth engine for health care startups: Emerging business models. *California Management Review,* **61**(2), 59–83 (2019).
7. C. Velu, Business model innovation and third-party alliance on the survival of new firms. *Technovation,* **1**(35) 1–1 (2015).
8. J.K. Brock and F. Von Wangenheim, Demystifying AI: What digital transformation leaders can teach you about realistic artificial intelligence. *California Management Review,* **61**(4), 110–134 (2019).
9. C. Brauer, E. Fotopoulou, J. Barth, and A. Ahsan, *Creating a Blueprint for UK Competitiveness.* Microsoft (2020). Available from: https://www.microsoft.com/en-gb/business/uk-recovery/, accessed January 18, 2021.
10. W.L. Lin, N. Yip, J.A. Ho, and M. Sambasivan, The adoption of technological innovations in a B2B context and its impact on firm performance: An ethical leadership perspective. *Industrial Marketing Management,* **89**, 61–71 (2020).
11. T. Fountaine, B. McCarthy, and T. Saleh, Building the AI-powered organization. *Harv Bus Rev,* **97**(4), 62–73 (2019).
12. D. Acemoglu and P. Restrepo, Artificial intelligence, automation and work. *National Bureau of Economic Research,* **15** (2018).
13. OECD G20, *Toolkit for Measuring the Digital Economy.* OECD (2018), Available from: https://www.oecd.org/g20/summits/buenos-aires/G20-Toolkit-for-measuring-digital-economy.pdf, accessed January 18, 2021.
14. C. Green and A. Clayton, Ethics and AI innovation. *The International Review of Information Ethics,* **29** (2020).
15. D. Acemoglu and M.O. Jackson, History, expectations, and leadership in the evolution of social norms. *The Review of Economic Studies,* **82**(2), 423–456 (2015).
16. R. Pucetaite, A. Novelskaite, and L. Markunaite, The mediating role of leadership relationship in building organisational trust on ethical culture of an organisation. *Economics & Sociology,* **8**(3), 11 (2015).

17. R.M. Solow, Neoclassical growth theory. In *Handbook of Macroeconomics,* J. B. Taylor, M. Woodford, and H. Uhlig (eds.), 637–667. Cambridge, MA: Elsevier Science & Technology (1999).

18. D. Cable, How humble leadership really works. *Harvard Business Review,* **23**, 2–5 (2018).

19. P. Berrone, J. Surroca, and J.A. Tribó, Corporate ethical identity as a determinant of firm performance: A test of the mediating role of stakeholder satisfaction. *Journal of Business Ethics,* **76**(1), 35–53 (2007).

20. A.H. Seyal, Examining the role of transformational leadership in technology adoption: Evidence from Bruneian technical & vocational establishments (TVE). *Journal of Education and Practice,* **6**(8), 32–43 (2015).

21. Microsoft, Creating a blueprint for Microsoft UK partner competitiveness. (2021). Available from: https://query.prod.cms.rt.microsoft.com/cms/api/am/binary/RWxudN, accessed March 8, 2021.

https://doi.org/10.1142/9781800611337_0012

Chapter 11

Unveiling the Social Impact of AI through Living Labs

Fernando Vilariño

Computer Vision Center, Universitat Autònoma de Barcelona
European Network of Living Labs
Edifici O, Campus UAB, Bellaterra 08193, Barcelona, Spain
fernando@cvc.uab.es

The Digital Transformation is a human transformation, not just a new industrial revolution, allowing potential access to all human knowledge. Social transformations appear at a pace never witnessed before, with challenges that can no longer be tackled by one organization alone. This makes the flourishing of paradigms of open innovation possible, where the integration of multiple stakeholders around the citizen-centric perspective is a key element. In this context, the impacts that AI will bring to our societies are still to be defined, or more precisely, there is a pending action of unveiling the social impact of AI, and this task has to be done prior to the development of new models in which AI-based automation and automatic decision making will play a fundamental role. Particularly, as an inherent part of the innovation management framework, this will affect strategy, leadership, institutional culture, processes and more — widely beyond the software design tasks. Dimensions such as capacity building, identity(ies), responsibility and creativity are now to be reshaped due to AI. The Living Lab approach appears as a powerful instrument for this mission, and in this chapter we will explore clear examples on how to tackle the unveiling of the impacts on such dimensions.

1. The Digital Transformation as a Human Transformation

The Digital Transformation is not a new industrial revolution, but a human transformation creating a brand-new humankind. The potential universal access to knowledge, enabled by the Internet, creates a new fundamental question of profound ethical relevance posed to every individual. The Internet appears as the democratizing factor of access to knowledge and innovation, and the enabling factor for instant exchange among all human beings too. This expands the vision of the human being as a species (senso laxo), it gives the human being a new extension and functionality, and by doing that, transforms the human being definitively.

I would like to emphasize that from the perspective of potential access to all the available human knowledge (or in other words, since the appearance of the Internet in our history) we are not facing a mere additive contribution of technological innovation: it is a unique event in the historic timeline of humankind that transforms humankind itself.

1.1. *Potential access to human knowledge through the internet*

From a technical perspective, the deployment of Internet is in a very initial stage — on its dawn, we could say with the new human being still in the cradle. For this reason, this transformation must be understood from the perspective of the *potential*: the emergence of the Internet allows access to universal knowledge and interconnection to occur — this was not possible before — and this possibility directly leads to the arrival of a new responsibility against which the individual is faced: *If I have potential universal access to all human knowledge, what am I going to do about it?* Here, the fundamental question is not referring to what to do with the knowledge, but to something with more profound ethical implications: How the fact of having potential universal access to all the knowledge from humankind is repositioning myself as the individual (driver of change). This vision is not to be understood as an optimistic approach, but as a *possibilistic approach*. Whether the universal access to human knowledge and the hyperconnectivity that the Internet provides — potentially — is a better or a worse thing, it is something that will depend, fundamentally, on the implementations that we develop, i.e., on the individual responses that we will give to our new responsibility. From a global vision, this perspective projects the possible answers to the new question of responsibility not in our present, but in the historical future as humankind. In a first approximation, the Digital Transformation will radically lower the social entry cost to accessing and generating knowledge, creating a real opportunity for the personal and collective development of people. At the same time, new areas of expertise and employment will emerge and disappear; the interdisciplinary boundaries will blur, stakeholders borders will fade and this will ultimately trigger profound transformations in the ways that people live their lives.[1]

1.2. *Community development through knowledge and data access: A new open paradigm*

Particularly, direct and profound implications arise at a societal dimension. Decades ago, a group of scientists posed the question "Can a machine think?"[2] and from that question they paved the ground from which Artificial Intelligence (AI) arises. In the same way, the social sciences can now ask a new question: *Is a model of society with democratized access to knowledge and innovation possible?* which reformulates our original question addressed to every individual (what to do with the (potential) access to all knowledge), but from a societal perspective. This prospecting role of the social sciences for the new human being requires environments, laboratories — "labs" — that allow the development and verification of hypotheses, and the channeling of the innovation results from the deployment of such hypothesis. But, fundamentally, it needs from *communities*. In this sense, communities are achieving a capital emerging role, channeling the empowerment of the person with respect to the decisions linked to the societal innovation processes.[3]

Nowadays, experience tells us that we are far from being able to give an answer with practical implications to the fundamental question posed above, and that the necessary condition to demand such an answer — the awareness of the potential for transformation — is not present (yet) for all human beings at a global scale.

On the other hand, it is possible to perceive a stream of skepticism in a broad sector of the population, if not outright opposition, to the development of an idea of a technology-linked human being, and particularly, with specific areas related to AI which challenge traditional approaches to work (robotics and automation), responsibility (decision making and liability) creativity (fake art, fake news, etc.) and identity (digital identities), just to mention a few dimensions. This vision represents the counterpoint of a pendulum movement to the promises aimed at transformations that are not gradual or cumulative, but disruptive. This last term — *disruption* — appears as the Holy Grail of innovation nowadays: The breaking with the "good old fashion" is not only projected as a value in itself but is defined as the differentiating element to participate in the innovation process with the vision of collecting the benefits that innovation generates. This approach has contributed to undeniable economic growth and technical development, though at the same time, to the definition of socio-economic structures, market flows and balance of powers that do not facilitate the configuration of universal knowledge-access structures in an agile way. Thus, innovation processes are mostly limited to a few dominant actors, and globally, the Digital Transformation, despite providing new opportunities to individuals and communities, continues to create digital gaps.

1.3. *Automation, automatic decision making and data*

Embedded in the context described above, we have recently lived an unprecedent growth in the results provided by AI methods and tools, particularly machine learning, and this happened in a large variety of different areas of application. This recent phenomenon has changed the game of innovation based on AI solutions at an accelerated pace. In order to properly understand the roots of this changes, it is worthy to mention: (1) The advances in hardware parallelization (and the distributed character and accessibility of cloud computing infrastructures), (2) The pervasive presence of software tools, freely available software, and training modules in AI for all, (3) The engineering approach to research in Deep Learning boosted by a fast-growing industry, and (4) The universal data sharing (the open and also distributed paradigm through Internet of data accessible for training the new algorithms — the core of Machine Learning methods.

Most directly, we are starting to set the focus of attention on the ethical issues associated to the impact that automation and automatic decision-making technologies can have in the current state of things in industry and academia, in the public sector, and in the day-by-day, the final users, under the concern that such changes are happening too quickly in order to be properly managed, if not, controlled at all. Science fiction and real politics got closer and closer day-by-day, and the tension between the development of innovative AI-based products and services, and the need for a better understanding of the limits that we would like to put to their (yet unknown) impacts in our lives is very present.

Current implementations in the form of apps of our mobile phones are a good metaphor for this: they generate, in many cases, a virtual existence that is opposed to the physical existence, instead of extending it. Our data travels freely over the internet without us having a perception of control over it, our digital identity appears compromised and highly distributed — if not blurred — and everyday situations depend more and more on virtual processes that we do not understand or can even monitor.

However, it is important to say at this point that this is a local vision placed in time and space in our specific moment in life, and also, in the particular types of answers that we are providing for our specific time and historical moment. The universal access to knowledge — and innovation — is a human feature of the new human being, which now is presented only in a state of potentiality. The question, though, is open from a perspective of universal human development, and it introduces, in all its depth, the new human being: What are you going to *do* about it?[3] Beyond a purely theoretical or philosophical issue alone, this fundamental question is having an impact in the innovation management processes, with profound implications at organizational level (institutional culture, responsibility, IP management, …) and social level (identity(ies), learning, creativity, …), as we develop in the following sections.

2. Regulation and Observation: The Missing Action

2.1. *The approach to responsible and trustworthy AI*

One temptation that can arise in order to provide a framework to AI development consistent to the challenges exposed above, is to provide a comprehensive regulatory framework that allows all the stakeholders (scientists, engineers, innovation managers, integrators, final users, and also regulators and public administrators) to have a common reference.

In this context, we can see as a clear example: the European Union AI Alliance.[a] This group represents a Forum open to all the stakeholders, and it has contributed to the White Paper on AI,[4] and the Guidelines for Trustworthy AI.[5] These guidelines are an important effort in spotting the concerns, in order to understand how to potentially address them and how to set up mechanisms for creating AI-based products and services that comply the existing legislation, respect common ethical principles and values, and are robust and sustainable.

The uneasy truth is that this is not an isolated case. In the past months and years, we see how thousands of institutions create similar guidelines and approaches, linked to their own regional or national agendas, aligned among them — or not — and providing a mare magnum of *documentation*. The "Principled Artificial Intelligence" Report[6] is an excellent example compiling (honest) efforts towards a trustworthy approach to AI management, that in parallel reveals one unwanted thing: noise. Why? Fundamentally, because the guidelines and regulations proposed are anticipating unknown impacts.

2.2. *The observatories for ethics in AI: What to observe*

Another example of approach to understanding the different dimensions in which AI is affecting our societies are the numerous initiatives called "Observatories." The European Commission,[b] the OCDE,[c] and eventually countless policy-making institutions are developing such observatories with the aim of better understanding and reporting on the Social Impact of AI, with the sight on an evidence-based policy making. I have the honor and pleasure to be founding member of one of these regional observatories, The Catalan Observatory on Ethics on AI,[d] and it is a big professional opportunity to seat among a variety of experts from diverse disciplines (engineering, science, innovation management, philosophy and ethics, anthropology, policy makers, etc.) contributing to a dialogue in a cross-fertilizing way.

---

[a] EU AI Alliance. https://digital-strategy.ec.europa.eu/en/policies/european-ai-alliance.
[b] EU Observatory for AI. https://www.ai4eu.eu/ai4eu-observatory.
[c] OECD AI Policy Observatory. https://www.oecd.ai.
[d] Catalan Observatory for Ethics in Artificial Intelligence (OEIAC in Catalan). http://smartcatalonia.gencat.cat/en/projectes/tecnologies/detalls/article/OEIAC.

However, not without risk, I usually challenge my own role and the role of my colleagues in the observatory due to one base hypothesis that I do not share: Observatories assume that there is something to observe already out there, and the only thing that we have to do is to *look into* the right direction. This is indeed the case for the astronomic observatories (looking at the evidences provided by the cosmos, by means of telescopes), as well as for the observatories on domestic violence (searching for the roots and consequences of male violence against women, by means of the reporting on factual cases of violence). However, the situation with AI is quite different.

A number of the dimensions of the transformations to happen are most likely already identified (labor, education, mobility, arts, etc.) but those actual impacts are foreseen to take place in a future (both in the mid and long term). From a practical view, we are still in a position of deciding *which* type of impact is going to happen, and to some extent, *how* and *when*.

Thus, we must admit that the adoption of AI-based solutions is taking place at huge speed, and that more than having a concrete scenario to observe, the expected impacts of AI *are yet to be unveiled*. For this particular reason, AI provides an excellent fieldwork to apply action-oriented research, or, in other words, and as will be developed along the rest of the chapter: The innovation managers have the chance to engage in Open Innovation strategies that integrate multiple stakeholders, in order to tackle (unveil) the actual impacts that AI will have in our society. Under the scope of the Digital Transformation, I argue that this can only happen from a citizen-centric approach (understanding the citizen as the core of the community) in a co-creation process with all the stakeholder (as a corollary of the complex-challenge solving approach). In the following paragraphs, I will introduce the concept of Living Labs as powerful tools to unveil the dimensions of the social impact of AI.

3. Open Innovation and Living Labs to Drive the Social Impact of AI

3.1. *Living Labs and the quadruple helix model*

Living Labs are about innovation: User-centric multi-stakeholder innovation ecosystems.[7] On the one hand, the multi-stakeholder approach can be explained through the quadruple helix model.[8] The quadruple helix concept extents the approach of the triple helix,[9] which emphasizes hybrid collaboration between academia, industry and public administrations to provide enabling scenarios for innovation and economic development. The helix plays the role of the propeller of innovation-led growth and each blade represents one necessary component — type of stakeholder — for the innovation process to take place successfully, "The Citizens" can represent not only individuals, but also associations, NGOs, etc., which contribute at a community level, and that can provide the open door for early adopters of new products and services. Citizens are seen as participating in the co-creation process as actors, and not as mere factors from which to obtain ideas or raw data. A multi-helix approach would include elements of sustainable territorial development, further extending the 4-helix model.[10]

3.2. *Main features of Living Labs*

Living Labs share a number of well-known basic features, namely: Real-life setting, Active user engagement, Multi-stakeholder participation, Multi-method approach, Co-creation, and Orchestration.

Real-life setting: Living labs deploy their action in actual real-life settings (hospitals, libraries, streets, shops, etc.), and this endows living labs with the effective transformative power and a dynamic adaptability. The real-life setting allows for the integration of all the stakeholders in a natural scenario for innovation.

Active user engagement: Users (citizens) appear at the centre of the innovation process. Users are not seen here as factors for data gathering but as actual actors (participants) of the innovation process with a clear role in the whole life cycle of innovation. Users are developing natural tasks in the real-life setting, and participate in its process based on the needs and opportunities at the community level.

Multi-stakeholder participation: The diverse natures of the quadruple-helix stakeholders, together with the final users on the real-life arena, facilitates that the innovations can be scaled to a systemic level, by making use of the driving forces of public administrations, the market flows, and the implication for the civil society in the early adoption stage of the provided solutions.

Multi-method approach: There is an intrinsic multi-methodological approach which is inherent to the dynamic adaptability that living labs have. This methodological multiplicity allows for cross-fertilizing oriented to knowledge sharing and (co-)creation tasks.

Co-creation: The co-creation approach appears as the empowerment tool for all the stakeholders in terms of legitimacy of their participation. It implements a whole framework for innovation management in which specific methods and tools are needed, not only in order to understand the processes involved in the generation of an idea and its deployment, but also to have a proper approach to the results obtained, including IP management.[e]

Orchestration: Living labs can be viewed as infrastructures where to develop the role of orchestrator, not only from a project management perspective, but as a bridge for methodological multiplicity. Actually, as the needed translator for the different languages (in the sense of epistemological background) spoken by the different stakeholders.

The approach described provides a number of key principles that permeate all Living Lab operations, namely: value, sustainability, influence, realism and openness.[11] For a survey on living lab methods and tools, the interested reader can consult.[12] For examples on living lab projects, the reader can consult the "Best Living Lab Projects" edited by the European Network of Living Labs every year in Ref. [13]. For a deeper analysis on the emergence of living labs and a starting point for a further literature review, the paper in Ref. [14] is an excellent entry point.

3.3. *Systemic transformation and AI*

The first corollary for the above-mentioned approach to open innovation could be stated as follows: By using living labs as infrastructures around

---

[e]For more details, the interested reader can access the outcomes of the SISCODE EU Project. https://siscodeproject.eu.

which the ecosystem is organized, a systemic innovation process can be tackled. Clearly, the challenges that we are currently facing in the Digital Transformation are not affecting one specific aspect of our lives alone, but the way in which we organize our society. In particular, and in the specific field of AI, this will be affecting aspects such as the way in which we are making our decisions as a society, how we transform our job profiles to new digital challenges, how we move around in our cities and communities, how we understand creativity and it brings open questions that will have to be solved one by one, but *by all involved, not leaving anyone behind.* The responsibility of the innovation manager in this scenario will be to address this (systemic) process in a context that allows for the co-creation actions needed to settle down into sustainable solutions.

I purposely use the word *sustainable* here bringing in two different referents: On the one hand, it refers to the assumption of products, services and processes that are respectful with the territory and the available natural resources. On the other hand, it refers to solutions that do not respond to one single market opportunity, but to a robust offer for a *sustained* innovation stream towards the ecosystem (linking private and public), maintained in time and able to integrate supporting mechanisms.

It is especially in the systemic change where the business opportunities arise at a higher magnitude during the Digital Transformation, and very intensely in AI-related solutions. For instance, urban mobility, with the horizon of autonomous connected car, appears as one paradigmatic example of both the need of infrastructural investments affecting the core of urban design, and also of the transformation of habits that citizens will need to assume in their lives in a long-term framework. In this context of opportunities, the fields of application of AI are immense and fast-growing. From medical imaging analysis, to optimization of logistics, from pervasive document analysis to natural language processing, from security and surveillance to assistive robotics, we can identify a number of shared dimensions in which our societies will quickly change in a near future. In the following paragraphs, I will address common and not so widely spread approaches to such impacts, with the aim of illustrating the action-oriented nature of the unveiling processes.

4. Some Relevant Dimensions of the Social Impact of AI

We have seen that, at the systemic level, AI will have a profound impact in different dimensions of our life. We are now able to advance some of these dimensions, since we are witnessing relevant changes, though it is not clear which types of impacts and the intensity in which these impacts will happen. The proposal of using living labs as exploratory arenas for the user-centric innovation has the objective of the iterative unveiling of such impacts through action research. In the following paragraphs, I will focus on how AI can affect the dimensions of labor, responsibility, creativity and identity, advancing potential impacts.

4.1. *Labor: Capacity building as building block*

The arrival of AI has particularly shaken the perspective of new job profiles in the years to come. Automation and robotics will bring to the production lines a scenario of redundancies, since processes that can be automated will be indeed automated, due to the shrinking of cost and the optimization in the value chain. Without any doubt, this scenario is providing a certain level of social distress, particularly when it is not clear if an alternative can be offered to all the employees.

Strategic capacity building actions appear, therefore, as one of the main priorities to be taken by innovation managers in order to provide the right competences needed in the new job profiles, and also to provide a route for the integration of those people who need to adapt to the new scenario: the scenario beyond Industry 4.0.[15]

Historically, this professional capacity building task has been part of the vocational training schools, universities and centers for specialized studies. Now, the capacity building on AI will tend to cover all the stages of education, with formal, unformal and informal schemes, and in a lifelong learning approach. Different initiatives understand capacity building in digital competences as an act of democratization of the access to knowledge and innovation, for both the urban[f] and rural[g] contexts, with the perspective of including all, not leaving anyone behind. Open courses aiming at AI for all,[h] or training modules boosting the AI-based skills in the context of entrepreneurship in open innovation contexts[i] are providing an entry point for those who are not experts in AI, increasing the digital literacy and better endowing people for the new scenario.

More and more, the catalogue of projects developed in the personal software repositories, such as GitHub,[j] are receiving more attention than the academic qualifications in the CVs during the recruitment processes, and the evidences about what the employees have *done* in the recent past provide a better picture about their profile than the degree diplomas achieved. This is affecting not only the way in which the recruitment processes are considering KPIs, but also most deeply, the way in which the career development plans have to be developed within private and public institutions in order to guarantee a proper positioning and adequate capacity building in AI, to unleash the potential impacts in the new contexts of challenge-solving problems and innovation-led growth.

Finally, the need for capacity building also affects the innovation managers' task from a different perspective, since it becomes essential to be able to explain the changes in the decision-making chain that AI brings in. This mission to tackle explainability — opening the door to the specific topic of Explainable AI — can be approached in two different ways: (1) On the one hand, the ability of the software engineers to give reason on why the algorithms perform in one way or another, using natural language for those explanations. This is a low-level approach to explainability which is intrinsically linked to the machine learning algorithms.

---

[f]Knowle West Media Centre Living Lab actively collaborates with unfavored populations in digital capacity building in Bristol, U.K. https://kwmc.org.uk.

[g]Guadalinfo, Consorcio Fernando de los Ríos actively work in the development of digital literacy and open innovation literacy for rural communities in Andalucía, Spain. http://www.guadalinfo.es.

[h]University of Helsinki and Reaktor: Elements of AI Free Online Course. https://www.elementsofai.com.

[i]AI4ALL Entrepreneurship Course. https://www.ai4all.cat.

[j]Open Software Repository GitHub. https://github.com.

(2) On the other hand, we also need a dimension of interpretability, which relates to the extent to which a cause and an effect can be observed and predetermined, or, in other words, to what extent we will be able to predict a result. In addition, interpretable systems may be ready to generate explanations at either model-level or at individual instance-level, and finally, this brings to the table the need of making interpretability a fundamental criterion at design level.[16]

Since, as argued, the proper deployment of trustworthy and sustainable solutions on AI in our society would need of a proper development of citizen-centric multi-stakeholder approaches, it becomes more and more relevant to understand how to structure the governance models of the 4-helix, how to develop efficient and responsible citizen engagement processes, how to implement co-creation mechanisms with reliable IP management, how to (co-)create new business models for the innovation obtained, etc. The "how" and not the "what" acquires today specific emphasis, since the systems become more and more complex to manage. In this sense, the European Network of Living Labs (ENoLL), the largest and more relevant network of living labs in the world, with members all around the globe, has developed a Capacity Building Program in which the experts of the living labs share their experience as mentors of the Community. As a tool, ENoLL has developed a syllabus on the above-mentioned topics that can be followed online though its Virtual Learning Lab[k]. This also serves as an excellent example to a life-long learning approach to capacity building in open innovation for all.

4.2. Responsibility: Addressing an acceptable perspective to innovation in AI

AI has brought a big debate to our societies about responsibility and what is exclusively human about intelligence. Maybe, the responsible reader has taken the conscientious decision of reading this chapter precisely with the hope of reinforcing the knowledge acquired in the topic of social impact of AI, with the aim of strengthening the reader's position, and in

---

[k]ENoLL Virtual Learning Lab. https://openlivinglabdays.com/virtual-learning-lab/.

order to be able to take decisions in a more responsible way. Indeed, AI can provide us with automatic decision-making, and this dilutes our historical notion of responsibility (both individual and collective) over those decisions.

The concept of responsibility — and at practical levels its juridic sister: liability — is put into stake when it is not the human but the machine who is taking the decision. This naïf approach is embedded in a complex lattice during the whole innovation process, from the moment of inception in the research phase — by the researchers — to the exact instant in which the final user is enjoying the new product. In the specific case of the European Union, a wider framework for Responsible Research and Innovation has been develop during the past years,[17] providing the ethical bases of acceptable and non-acceptable approaches in the whole cycle of research and innovation, and by including different dimensions of such impact from the point of view of awareness, perception and a participative approach.

In this sense, I can bring our experience in the Living Lab to the development and consolidation of this responsible view to AI-based solutions. One example of this is the action ExperimentAI,[l] taking place at the Computer Vision Center's Library Living Lab. In this action, researchers and citizens have the opportunity of testing demos from the latest results of research in Computer Vision together with the researchers, engineers and public servants. We accompanied this action by inviting the master's degree students at the Design School Eina from Barcelona to have a prospective analysis of these demos and propose together potential futures in which the society has been transformed by the effect of the technology (in positive or not so positive directions). This was complemented by a series of debates with philosophers, politicians and representatives from SMEs and large companies explicitly tackling the ethical issues associated to the deployment of such technologies.[m] By including all the stakeholders, we

---

[l]ExperimentAI at Library Living Lab. Artificial Intelligence and Computer Vision with researchers in Public Libraries. http://librarylivinglab.cvc.uab.cat/calendar/experimentai-the-impact-of-artificial-intelligence-in-society/?lang=en.

[m]Artificial Intelligence, Ethics and Citizen Engagement. Series of working focus groups and open debates. http://iabcn.cvc.uab.es/blog/cvc-granted-with-a-la-caixa-palau-macaya-grant-for-public-engagement-of-ai-and-computer-vision/.

guaranteed an educated approach, explicit to the public opinion, using as case study not only current impacts but also the impacts on potential futures — some of them truly dystopic — in which the technology would be the enabler of change, serving as an example of anticipatory testbed for decision making.

The key question, now, is how to move from principles to actions when including the dimension of responsibility towards a trustworthy implementation of AI.[18] This view is now inherent not only to a general public debate about AI in our society, but also to the actual participatory co-design of the potential scenarios or as a social construct. And indeed, this has concrete implications in the development of the new products based on AI-technologies, and affects the whole cycle of production, from the (now co-)design phase to the end-user, changing the way in which the pipeline of the innovation process is managed.

In the same way as public institutions have devoted large amounts of effort into the implementation of guidelines and reference texts for trustworthy AI, global corporations, such as Google,[n] IBM,[o] Microsoft,[p] or Intel[q] have recently paid major attention to the development of guidelines showing the way in which the AI-related innovation process is acceptable for them. As a matter of fact, and as an inherent part the of the innovation management system framework reflected by standards such as ISO 56002[19] and other models, this will affect many shared elements, from strategy, leadership, culture, processes, organization, ecosystem, and more, widely beyond the single software design and coding stage performed by the software engineers.[20] In summary, the institutional culture is affected, and the fluxes are modified within the whole life cycle of the AI-related innovation process, due to the inclusion of the considerations on the societal and ethical issues linked to the social impacts of AI, in a

---

[n]Google's AI Principles. https://www.blog.google/technology/ai/ai-principles/.

[o]IBM's ethics for AI. https://www.ibm.com/watson/assets/duo/pdf/everydayethics.pdf.

[p]Microsoft's guidelines for conversational bots. https://www.microsoft.com/en-us/research/uploads/prod/2018/11/Bot_Guidelines_Nov_2018.pdf.

[q]Intel's AI recommendations & principles. https://blogs.intel.com/policy/2017/10/18/naveen-rao-announces-intel-ai-public-policy/#gs.8qnx16.

process that the innovation managers will have to tackle now *from Plato to Python*.[r]

4.3. *Creativity: Reloading arts, IP and business models*

AI is contributing to the expansion of the concepts of creativity and arts, allowing not only new pathways for cultural enjoyment, but also the co-creation of cultural assets through IA-tools (I use here the word *cultural* not in the restricted context of *tangible or intangible cultural heritage* but in its widest form possible). From an innovation management perspective, it can be useful to differentiate: On the one hand, to what extent the current state-of-the-art is challenging the concept of creativity itself, and on the other hand, how the new paradigm is affecting the potential new business opportunities and the management of the intellectual property (IP) created.

High-level concepts such as aesthetics, artwork, originality, authorship and ownership, previously reserved to humans, are now being challenged by software engineers and machine learning researchers, and machines started a role in the creation of not only optimized processes, but actual culture-related artifacts. A couple of examples will serve as illustration.

Artificial Neural Networks, and particularly Recursive Neural Networks (RNN) have shown very successful results in creating and recreating folk music tunes,[21] just after learning from the folk music databases on the Internet, openly available and contributed by the community of passionate musicians around the world. These tunes are, in occasions, indistinguishable from actual human-crafted compositions, and the

---

[r] *Plato* refers here, of course, to the well-known Greek philosopher (427–347 BC). *Python* is one of the most popular programming languages for AI. This play on words clearly tries to envisage that the ethical issues associated to the development on AI is not something to be tackled during the deployment phase alone, but intrinsically included in the development process of AI-based products and services. This affects all participating people and teams, and therefore must affect the management approaches and the fluxes involved at all levels.

algorithms are so fast in their inception that a virtual parallel universe of new tunes on every second provides our digital cultural heritage with an unsoundable dimension of artificial creativity.[s]

In the image field, Convolutional Neural Networks (CNN) have provided the right tool to make abstraction of the style of panting in order to apply it to a completely different visual context, by using the technique called style transfer.[22] In other words, today it is possible for a machine to learn Van Gogh's style and apply it to the reader's favorite photo[t] — providing a "starry night effect" to the pictures taken last summer while having holidays close to the see in Barcelona.

One of the main consequences of this step forward of AI is that new business models appear associated to this — so far human-specific — feature, and it widens the concept of creativity to a not yet fully explored field. The mentioned AI-based methods and tools are now openly available, and they are easy replicable by just downloading the software models shared in the authors' GitHubs, ready to run in production mode in domestic laptops.

A collateral result of such a fast advance is that the mode of protection of this software engines has become a completely different business in a moment of history in which open access to knowledge is becoming the rule. The industry results are arriving so fast that big corporations are finally assuming that creators cannot hold their knowledge within the institutional borders. Big and small firms are nowadays investing millions in basic research and the big conferences of Computer Vision and AI such as CVPR, ICCV, ECCV, NIPS, just to mention a few, have become the best place for head-hunting top young Ph.D. students with the bait of a 6-figure contract as future managers of the AI or machine learning teams.[u] The approach of investing in research with basic, oriented and applied view, in order to speed-up the widening of the market of AI-based

---

[s] The FolkRNN website allows the curious reader to hear the tunes. https://folkrnn.org.

[t] Deepart.io is a webservice that implements the style transfer technique to personal photos. So now, the reader can Van Gogh-ise his favorite memories. https://deepart.io.

[u] Indeed, the fact of actually finishing the Ph.D. Thesis in these conditions becomes an act of faith, and a prove of true love for since.

solutions, acts as a *de facto* TRL elevator.[23] Here the tension is evident between protecting the IP generated and receiving the community acknowledgment, between showcasing a personal project portfolio and the institutional positioning to attract the right talent (as discussed in the previous section). The open approach is gaining more and more terrain, and initiatives such as AI Commons[v] gathers an ecosystem of AI practitioners, entrepreneurs, academia, NGOs, AI industry players and organizations or individuals focused on the common good. The Wikipedia Commons spirit helps in order to "support the creation of a knowledge hub in AI that can be accessible by anyone, that can help inform governance, policy making, and investments around deployment of AI solutions, and be a catalyst for supporting diversity and inclusivity in how AI is deployed for sustainable development goals."[w]

4.4. *Identity: Exploring our digital dimensions*

In recent years, we witnessed how our data is freely flowing deep into the Internet oceans. Our data is used to provide us with adds tailored to our exact needs (Amazon), but also to project ourselves from different perspectives: professional (LinkedIn), instantaneous information (Twitter), formative (specific YouTube channels), ludic (TikTok), etc. AI algorithms are playing the function of filtering out irrelevant contents, while letting us focus on what is actually of interest to us. As a matter of fact, our profiles are the building blocks of our digital identities.

The concept of identity itself, and the protection of our identity, has become one of the most recurrent topics in the discussion around AI. Particularly, face recognition[24] represents a paradigmatic example. Machine Learning techniques have provided very effective tools to analyze massive data in a pervasive approach. Nowadays, governments and institutions can use this technology for surveillance and security actions, but in the way, our privacy is compromised. In this line, Barcelona municipality is working in the context of the initiative "Cities for

---

[v] AI Commons. https://ai-commons.org/.
[w] United Nations Sustainable Development Goals. https://sustainabledevelopment.un.org.

Digital Rights,"[x] with the specific challenge of working with researchers and citizens towards the acceptable uses of face recognition technologies, the conditions of their development, etc. But the face recognition issue gets complicated when it is not limited to existing entities only, since recent advances in CNNs have made it possible to create fake identities, faces of people that never existed.[25] This fake component of AI directly challenges not only our own individual identities, since it allows to create potential media contents showing real people doing things that never occurred, but the identity itself, since it allows to supplant the faces, voices and gestures of people with completely fabricated images and sounds, but with fully realistic results.

It is necessary, thus, to approach the identity issue from a perspective in which we are able to safely respond to a confusing scenario, and we will use Epica Lab[y] as an example linking the dimension of identity with dimension of creativity explained above. Epica Lab represents a very original approach on how a living lab can explore the new digital dimensions of the human being by using a personalized performing arts-based approach. Founded by one of the most important companies of street arts in the world (La Fura dels Baus), and responsible for years of staging world-acclaimed operas, the participative performing arts is understood in the lab's mission as the vehicle used to challenge the current approaches in a collective work of different creators, professionals, technicians, and scientists who will carry out projects which will later be validated by society through their exhibition. By having the citizen physically and digitally (inter)acting in their performances, the impact provided by the technologies becomes a life experience. This real-life setting, and the life experience of having access the citizen's image, data, facial expressions, etc. allows for the first-person approach and understanding of the implications of having digital identity(ies). The performing arts tool allow to create dynamics mimicking potential futures (as in the case of the Library Living Lab) and this serves as an excellent beta-testing platform for both researchers and developers.

---

[x] "Cities for Digital Rights" initiative joins 46 global cities. https://citiesfordigitalrights.org.
[y] Èpica Lab. https://epicalab.com.

5. Conclusions

The previous paragraphs have provided us with a number of key ideas that can be summarized in the following list:

- The Digital Transformation is a human transformation, not yet another industrial revolution alone. In this context, the Social Impact of AI is yet to be unveiled.
- The challenges that we are facing are of a systemic nature, and they represent the biggest business opportunities. They integrate all the stakeholders, and thanks to the lowering of the social entry cost to accessing and generating knowledge, they create real opportunities in the context of open innovation actions.
- These systemic changes have to be tackled by using both Hard Technologies, among which AI appears as one of the principal market drivers. But, in parallel, they also need the development of a layer of Soft Technologies, which allow for the articulation of the open innovation processes in a citizen-centric approach.
- As examples of such Soft Technologies, Living Labs appear as useful tools to implement the user-centric action research processes associated to multi-stakeholder innovation.
- The innovation process is oriented therefore in a sustainable way, underpinned by a strong capacity building approach, that enables the needed co-creation process to unveil actual impacts.

To conclude this chapter, and as a humble sample of food for thought, I will point out potential action items for those innovation managers willing to engage in the most exciting, thrilling and appalling experience of contributing to the unveiling of the Social Impact of AI.

6. What's Next?

Let us close this chapter with two examples that will serve to state possible actions to be prioritized when holding the multi-stakeholder user-centric approach to unveiling the social impact of AI.

The first example clearly brings the City — its transformation — as the new scenario for open innovation. The concept of Smart Cities is evolving toward a Sustainable Community of empowered citizens, as mentioned in the former paragraphs. Cities around the world are joining efforts within global covenants,[z] mid/-term projects and institutional declarations for action-oriented commitments.[aa] Cities are emerging as arenas for exploring novel paradigms, and the concept of the City as a Living Lab[26] is more evident than ever was. The window of opportunity is there to proactively attract City Mayors and representatives to be aligned in objectives and business models for our actual challenges.

Thus, it becomes more and more necessary to take into account instruments such as public–private partnerships based on Public Procurement of Innovative Solutions (PPI), in which both the SME and the Public partner go on risk regarding the final solution, with a business plan associated to the SME under no-exclusivity of use by the public partner. Particularly, in the context of AI-based solutions, this approach represents a natural link to the unveiling of the expected impacts. For instance, anticipatory scenarios for mobility, such as those provided by the use of simulators for the scenario of implantation of the autonomous and connected car[27] may also represent an opportunity for the development of *in silico* products and services (fundamentally but not only as software as a service — SaaS), together with the community of early and final users. The concept of Digital Twin[28] provides us with a safe sandbox for anticipatory regulation and provisioning, and this brings in, as mentioned before, a competitive advantage in terms evidence-based approach to impact.

The second example develops the idea of a City emerging as an Open Innovation Ecosystem profoundly linked to its territory, and for that reason, there is an enormous opportunity to tackle the rural area development as a living lab too. The whole life cycle from farm-to-fork represents a good chance to re-shape the sustainability of habits regarding food

---

[z] The Covenant of Mayors. https://www.covenantofmayors.eu.

[aa] An excellent example is Living-in.EU (https://www.living-in.eu), a political declaration for city Mayors and stakeholders committing to interoperable solutions for the Smart City.

production and consumption. The shift toward a sustainable green energy production and management approach will need of advanced mechanisms of optimization, decision making, logistic management, etc. AI-based systems will contribute to the change of habits that we, the citizens, will have to co-design. The digital capacitation in rural areas will need from a big effort of all the stakeholders with the aim of building up a completely new scenario of innovation in a field (literally) not particularly easy so far for innovation processes to be assumed by the Communities. In any case, the change is systemic and fully user-centric, affecting, by the end of the day, the way in which we eat and in which we use energy. But AI can help also re-valorize the rural areas by extending the concept of heritage to the sectors of Culture, Tourism, Sports and Nature. We are already used to the optimized tracks for our tours around the land through GPS mapping, but AI-tools can also help us enjoy our territory by identifying cultural heritage sites and its artifacts[bb] or by providing us with information regarding the flora and fauna.[29] The understanding of the Rural Area as the complement of the Smart City allows for the actual comprehension of the community-based approach.

Our two examples are both needing the development strong capacitation in AI, but also the subtract of Social Technologies,[30] such as living labs in user-centric multi-stakeholder contexts. Precisely for that reason, capacity building, both in hard and soft technologies, should emerge as the building blocks and the seed for an actual competitive advantage. Indeed, the first step to the consolidation of the bet on AI as innovation-led driver must be investment in capacity building. This capacity building, as mentioned above, is now injecting the open innovation paradigm in a natural way, and it affects the whole life cycle of the AI innovation process, including the consideration of the societal and ethical issues linked to the impacts from Plato to Python.

Walking the walk would very much likely imply assuming the change of paradigm from ecosystem to community. As a recent example of this, the Catalan government in Spain oriented Catalonia's Artificial Intelligence Strategy towards the development of the *Catalonia.AI Community*, in which different instruments are aimed to connect the Community from

---

[bb] MS AI & cultural heritage. https://www.microsoft.com/en-us/ai/ai-for-cultural-heritage.

different perspectives. The European Digital Innovation Hub (DIH)[cc] is expected to play a role of single-entry point to those SMEs and willing to develop their products and services into their production pipelines. One research centre of AI will be the propelling force for talent, and the Observatory will support an ethical view to the ecosystem.

In summary, unveiling the social impact of AI is a joint effort, which starts in a clear bet for capacity building both in hard and soft technologies, and that envisages our cities and communities as living laboratories of the Digital Transformation. Managing this complex and exciting process in this precise time of our History is one of our main challenge, and also one of the most appealing endeavors.

References

1. ENoLL *et al.*, *The Manifesto for Innovation in Europe* [Internet]. 2018. Available from: https://manifestoforinnovationineurope.org.
2. A.M. Turing, Computing machinery and intelligence. *Mind,* **49**(236), 433–460 (1950).
3. F. Vilariño, What is new in the digital transformation? *La Maleta de Portbou*, [Internet] **28**, 2018. Available from: https://lamaletadeportbou.com/articulos/nuevo-la-transformacion-digital/.
4. European Commission, *White paper on artificial intelligence. A European approach to excellence and trust.* European Commission (2020).
5. European Commission, *Ethics guidelines for trustworthy AI.* European Commission. (2019).
6. J. Fjeld, N. Achten, H. Hilligoss, A.C. Nagy, and M. Srikumar, *Principled Artificial Intelligence: Mapping Consensus in Ethical and Rights-based Approaches to Principles for AI.* The Berkman Klein Center for Internet & Society Research (2020).
7. O. Hernández-Pérez, F. Vilariño, and M. Domènech, Public libraries engaging communities through technology and innovation: Insights from the library living lab. *Public Library Quarterly* [Internet]. 2020. Available from: https://www.tandfonline.com/action/journalInformation?journalCode=wplq20.

[cc] EDIH.   https://ec.europa.eu/digital-single-market/en/digital-innovation-hubs-dihs-europe.

8. L. Höglund and G. Linton, Smart specialization in regional innovation systems: A quadruple helix perspective. *R&D Management*, **48**(1), 60–72 (2018).

9. H. Etzkowitz and L. Leydesdorff, The dynamics of innovation: From National Systems and "mode 2" to a Triple Helix of university-industry-government relations. *Research Policy*, **29**(2), 109–23 (2000).

10. E.G. Carayannis, T.D. Barth, and D.F. Campbell, The Quintuple Helix innovation model: Global warming as a challenge and driver for innovation. *Journal of Innovation and Entrepreneurship*, **1**(1), 4–5 (2012).

11. A. Ståhlbröst, A set of key principles to assess the impact of living labs. *International Journal of Product Development*, **17**(1–2), 60–75 (2012).

12. K. Malmberg, I. Vaittinen, P. Evans, D. Schuurman, A. Ståhlbröst, and K. Vervoort, *Living Lab Methodology Handbook* [Internet]. 2017. Available from: https://doi.org/10.5281/zenodo.1146321#.X9auwfl_NZI.mendeley.

13. ENoLL. Best Living Lab Projects 2019. European Network of Living Labs (2020).

14. S. Leminen and M. Westerlund, A framework for understanding the different research avenues of living labs. *International Journal of Technology Marketing*, **11**(4) (2016).

15. Y. Lu, Industry 4.0: A survey on technologies, applications and open research issues. *Journal of Industrial Information Integration*, **6**, 1–10 (2017).

16. W. Samek, A. Vedaldi, K-R. Müller, G. Montavon, and L.K. Hansen (eds.), *Explainable AI: Interpreting, Explaining and Visualizing Deep Learning*. Switzerland: Springer Nature (2019).

17. R. Von Schomberg, A vision of responsible research and innovation, In R. Owen, M. Heintz, and J. Bessant (eds.), *Responsible Innovation: Managing the Responsible Emergence of Science and Innovation in Society*. Chichester, UK: John Wiley & Sons, Ltd. 13–19 (2013).

18. J. Morley, L. Floridi, L. Kinsey, and A. Elhalal, From what to how: An initial review of publicly available AI ethics tools, methods and research to translate principles into practices. *Science and Engineering Ethics*, **26**(4), 2141–2168 (2020).

19. ISO, ISO 56002:2019 — Innovation management — Innovation management system — Guidance (2019).

20. N.B. Yams, V. Richardson, G.E. Shubina, S. Albrecht, and D. Gillblad. Integrated AI and innovation management: The beginning of a beautiful friendship. *Technology Innovation Management Review*, **10**(11), 5–18 (2021).

21. B.L Sturm, O. Ben-Tal, Ú. Monaghan, N. Collins, D. Herremans, E. Chew *et al.*, Machine learning research that matters for music creation: A case study. *Journal of New Music Research*, **48**(1), 36–55 (2019).

22. L.A. Gatys, A.S. Ecker, and M. Bethge, Image style transfer using convolutional neural networks, in *Proc. of the IEEE Computer Society Conference on Computer Vision and Pattern Recognition (CVPR)*, 2414–2423 (2016).

23. European Cooperation for Space Standardization — ECSS, *Technology readiness level (TRL) guidelines* (2017).

24. G. Hu, Y. Yang, D. Yi, J. Kittler, W. Christmas, S.Z. Li, *et al.*, When face recognition meets with deep learning: An evaluation of convolutional neural networks for face recognition, in *Proc. of the IEEE International Conference on Computer Vision (ICCV) Workshops*, 142–150 (2015).

25. T. Karras, S. Laine, and T. Aila, #StyleGAN — A style-based generator architecture for generative adversarial networks, in *Proc. of the IEEE Computer Society Conference on Computer Vision and Pattern Recognition (CVPR)* (2019).

26. T. Santonen, L. Creazzo, A. Griffon, Z. Bódi, and P. Aversano, Cities as Living Labs — Increasing the impact of investment in the circular economy for sustainable cities. European Commission (2017).

27. Y. Xiao, F. Codevilla, A. Gurram, O. Urfalioglu, and A.M. López, Multimodal end-to-end autonomous driving, in *Proc. of the International Conference on Computer Vision (ICCV)*, (2019). https://arxiv.org/pdf/1906.03199.pdf.

28. C. Koulamas and A. Kalogeras, Cyber-physical systems and digital twins in the industrial internet of things. *Computer,* **51**(11), 95–98 (2018).

29. R. Kwok, AI empowers conservation biology, *Nature Research*, **567**, 133–134 (2019).

30. A. Serra, Etnógrafos y diseñadores culturales en la era de la alta tecnología, in M. Matus, J. Colobrans, and A. Serra (eds.), *Cultura, diseño y tecnología Ensayos de tecnoantropología*. El Colegio de la Frontera Norte, A. C. (2020).

https://doi.org/10.1142/9781800611337_0013

Chapter 12

Innovation Management and Public Procurement of AI

Manuel Noya*,§, Manuel Varela†,¶, and María José Ospina-Fadul‡,||

*Linknovate Science S.L.
Rua das flores, 33 15896, Santiago de Compostela, A Coruña, Spain
†Sidi Consultoría y Gestión S.L., Madrid, Spain
‡Public Health England, London, United Kingdom
§manuel@linknovate.com
¶manuel.varela@knowsulting.com
||mariajoseospinaf@gmail.com

Artificial Intelligence (AI) technologies have an immense potential to transform the way governments work, and the way they innovate, at the local, national and international level. However, in spite of the efforts both from governments and from supranational organizations, uptake of this key general-purpose technology has its limitations. This chapter lays out the advantages of using Innovation Procurement to foster the development and deployment of AI technologies for the provision of public services, while also addressing potential bottlenecks. Overarching socio-ethical challenges are discussed, mainly around privacy and accountability, based on real-world procurements. The use-cases provide examples and inspiration from the Innovation Management perspective, as Innovation Procurement can support the public sector in spurring and scaling collaborative, inclusive and human-centric innovation in AI. In accordance with the practical perspective of this chapter, in the end, the authors provide a series of recommendations that could help in avoiding common pitfalls in Innovation Procurement of AI.

1. The Potential of AI for Governments

1.1. *The world is resetting*

This chapter takes shape at a point in time where all economies and societies around the globe, and the relations between them, are re-shaping. Besides completely disrupting global value chains, pushing well-established industries to the edge of extinction and widening the inequality gap, the COVID-19 pandemic has prompted the digital transition of our society and has made it necessary to overhaul production and interaction models. This has inevitably emphasized the imperative for responsible innovation and for the ethical use of technology. Furthermore, the enormous differences on country-level management and outcomes of this pandemic have yet again highlighted both what a technology-driven society can be capable of when relying on science (e.g., prevention, treatments, remote social connection, climate change, etc.) and which dangers it faces when not doing so (e.g., fake news, lack of interoperability, suboptimal humanitarian disaster management, vulnerability as a result of interdependencies, etc.).

The relevance of Artificial Intelligence (AI) in this challenging context is two-fold. Firstly, AI is at the core of several potential solutions for controlling the pandemic: in fact, organizations responsible for public health surveillance and genome sequencing have been forced to accelerate their analytics' capabilities to navigate this pandemic. Secondly, as AI can act as an enabler for other technologies in various fields (i.e., digital enabler technology), it can unlock the transformation of the wide range of processes in the economy and the society that have not and most likely will not go "back to normal."

In fact, some compare the potential impact of AI to that of the spread of electricity in the 19th century. Electricity had an enabling effect on machinery and industrial processes, which led to further innovation. In the face of COVID-19 these altered processes will well exceed the industrial dimension, going into the public and private sphere, prompting AI to be considered as the key general-purpose technology of our times.

The appeal of AI for governments, in particular, has increased in the current context. Governments can in fact achieve considerable advantages for societies in need of deep transformation by fostering an innovation environment that reduces risk for companies developing AI, while protecting citizens and encouraging their trust in these technologies. Additionally, they can (and already have) improve their response to the challenges of the current pandemic and beyond in policy domains like health, transport and agriculture by procuring, piloting and developing AI solutions in the provision of public services. Incidentally, as we will discuss in the other sections of this chapter, these procurements contribute to the widespread uptake of AI and have an impact in productivity and competitiveness.

1.2. AI for the improvement governments' performance

Because AI is constantly evolving and is a key enabling technology, it is understandable to believe that it can be equally effective across the full range of problems in each policy domain. However, more specifically, AI can readily help whenever the challenge at hand involves machines using statistics to find patterns in large amounts of data and/or when it involves the ability to perform repetitive tasks with data without the need for constant human guidance. As such, three keywords seem to define the value of AI for the government in the short term: patterns, (lots of) data, and repetition.

Using these three concepts, it is possible to identify the areas in which AI can serve the government's purpose by

(1) Providing more accurate information, forecasts and predictions allowing for better decision making and readiness/early intervention. In this sense, AI technologies can enable more accurate and timely medical diagnoses (e.g., AI technology to detect over 50 ocular diseases from a single retinal image, contributing to efficiently preventing sight loss[1]) while they can also help prevent and mitigate natural disasters or accidents.

(2) Simulating complex systems and provide estimates for realistic outcomes. For example, there are several predictive systems for assessing the risk of violence and extremism in adolescents, used to determine

early interventions by social services and schools, such as the Structured Assessment of Violence Risk in Youth (SAVRY).[2]

(3) Allowing policy makers to experiment with different policy options within any specific program, or even across policy domains, in face of challenging social problems, and spot unintended consequences or trade-offs before committing to a measure. For instance, the flood of data that is generated every day from sensors and gauges is monitored and aggregated in NASA's Landsat[3] and now analyzed by complex AI technologies, provides an increasingly accurate picture of how the world's land surface is changing. This allows policymakers to forecast impacts and trade-offs between policies and concrete objectives (such as CO_2 emissions). Other AI systems directly tackle allocation decisions in similar areas of study, such as regional Innovation Procurement project Innovaugas in Galicia,[4] one of Spain's flagship procurement projects in the topic. The initiative relies on big data analysis to offer integrated water management aimed at optimizing resources and planning for variations of different water uses.

(4) Improving public services and tailor them to individual circumstances, while maintaining standards and ensuring legal compliance. For example, several welfare schemes rely on AI systems to efficiently manage benefit claims by aggregating more accurate and detailed information of citizens with similar needs (not one size fits all) and allowing for cross-referencing between databases across the government, when the legal framework allows it, to ensure compliance and welfare maximization.[5]

Just as AI can serve multiple policy dimensions and specific government tasks, its relevance varies greatly across levels of the government. Though competencies at each level differ across countries, a general overview of key policy domains into which AI can contribute at the national, regional and local level is summarized in Fig. 1.

Another application that is relevant across these three levels is that of procurement itself: AI systems can aid all steps of the procurement process in most countries in the world and can help identify and mitigate risk of corruption while increasing value for money (see examples in Fig. 1).

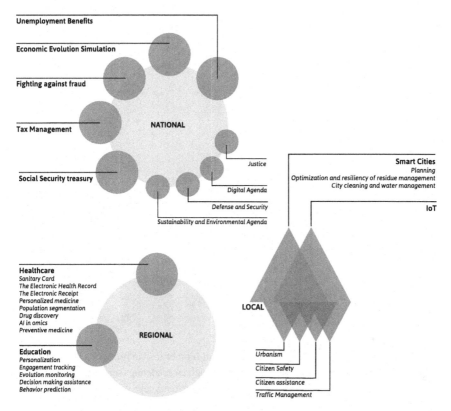

Fig. 1. Key policy domains for the application of AI at different government levels led by public procurement.

AI for transparency in innovation procurement

The smart use of AI and open data can help public organizations to better plan, implement and evaluate the procurement of goods and services. The European Commission, the European Bank for Reconstruction and Development and the Open Contracting Partnership are joining forces to improve the quality and transparency of public tenders in two pilots:

- In **Greece**, it aims at consolidating all databases into a single smart public contract register. This will enable online access for bidders and citizens, improve quality of data and facilitate the use of data-driven analytical tools for monitoring the procurement process.
- In **Poland**, it supports Polish national and local authorities to introduce open data in public procurement and promote automated collection, standardization, and consolidation of procurement data on all tenders.

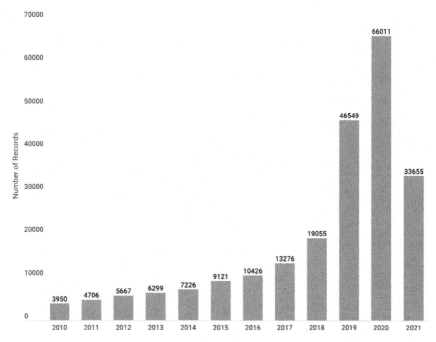

Fig. 2. Exponential growth of "mobile health and biometrics" in recent years, with a plateau in 2020, considering multiple data sources, such as academic (scientific publications, conference proceedings and grants) and industrial (patents and trademarks in USA and Europe) and specialized news.

Source: Linknovate.com.

Governments are in fact already looking into the potential uses of AI, notwithstanding studies that show there is still a lag compared to adoption in the industry. Specific policy domains have been particularly prolific in this sense: policing the internet (e.g., young radicalization, detecting early depression symptoms, etc.), connecting machines in the industry (e.g., predictive analytics, sensors, etc.), new applications in health (e.g., use of biometrics, e-health apps for improving adherence to treatments of chronic conditions, etc.) are examples of this (Figs. 2 and 3).

It's worth noting that applications in the health arena, with stricter regulations, have been more likely to spark concerns in the general public about sensitive and personal information misuse, as well as surfacing bias. The COVID-19 crisis is making uplifting the relevance of this

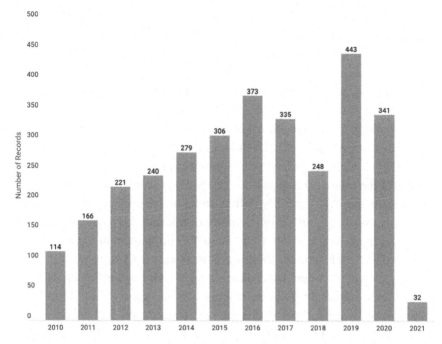

Fig. 3. Same "search" for "mobile health and biometrics" limited to publicly funded grants shows a linear growth in the number of awarded grants over recent years and is stable after 2017. It serves to exemplify how the industry moves and scales faster than public investments and publicly funded R&D alone, when compared to the previous graph. *Source*: Linknovate.com.

debate and this can entail further considerations, and potential obstacles, for the adoption of such technologies, as we discuss in the following sections.

1.3. *Limitations of AI from the government's user perspective*

Forasmuch as public procurement of AI technologies has evident potential to transform all policy domains and all levels of the governments (including procurement itself) there seems to be a mismatch between this potential and the effective deployment AI solutions in governments.[6] This can be attributed to different causes.

First, just as it is useful to raise awareness about the potential of AI to solve challenges, it is also appropriate to clarify the cases in which AI may not (currently) be the right solution: this is a relevant distinction as innovation procurement is most likely to fail when specific solutions are mismatched to needs (even when these are important), as it is presented in the last section of this chapter, affecting the trust in both the solutions and in the innovation procurement, which can be permanently damaged as a policy instrument. In brief, AI's main limitation is related to its capability to present us with general-purpose solutions: rather, AI seems to be more useful (at the moment) for well-defined tasks in narrow application areas. This means that AI is unlikely deliver imaginative and creative solutions, or perform well without a large quantity of relevant, high quality data. On that account, AI-based solutions are harder to implement in scenarios with limited data where critical thinking is necessary to fill gaps with other sources, as well as where it needs to identify cause and effect on its own. In this sense, although decision making can be supported by AI in most public service areas, final decisions (for instance on budget allocation across policy domains) can be supported by AI but should probably be decided in the context of political deliberation. The same seems to be true for decisions in very complex problems that are not iterative and that require the combination of qualitative and quantitative data. Problems of this nature are of indeed high importance in the political agenda and though they can be partitioned into several tasks, some of which can be carried out by AI technologies, in the end human integration appears to be (currently) necessary.

Furthermore, many public organizations face the following problem: highly qualified civil servants (i.e., experts in the field) are unlikely to "easily" find a *pattern* when only looking at the limited available and controlled data. Thus, public organizations expect some type of AI to help solve the problem by detecting patterns humans simply cannot see in higher quantities of more noisy, uncontrolled data. This constitutes one of the most ambitious uses of AI governments are (already) procuring for. However, it is often the case that many corrections, bias detection algorithms and adjustments are needed for the AI system to achieve the *right* insights without human supervision (notwithstanding the challenge of defining of what *right* insights mean). To allow for this, highly complex factors such as unconscious bias and privacy concerns need to be put at the center of procurement processes, that end up becoming more human-centric, causing civil servants and procurers to end up with a whole different (and possibly more complicated) challenge than the one they had a beginning. On the other hand, even if AI can help meet user needs, often times simpler solutions may be more effective and less expensive. For example: optical character recognition (OCR) technology can extract information from scans of passports. However, a digital form requiring manual input might be more accurate, quicker to build, and cheaper. The procurer will need to assess alternative mature technologies thoroughly to check if this is the case and this requires a relatively good knowledge of these technologies.

These are some of the main reasons why public organizations have persistently limited their AI procurements to solve needs for *repetitive, time consuming tasks* that are well known to qualified civil servants. In such cases, public administrations' concern with data privacy and bias are greatly reduced, as the main benefit is not altering the outcomes or even the methodology but reaching the same outcomes in a more efficient way (less use of resources and/or faster). On the one hand, this is positive because it focuses on Innovation Procurements that are very likely to succeed — and to then be replicated and scaled in different departments of the government as well as in the private sector. On the other hand, it is harmful as the reluctance of public organizations to take higher risks and invest in more complex technologies hinders the full potential of innovation procurement as enabler for state-of-the-art AI.

One of the advantages of innovation in public procurement to foster the wider adoption of AI is precisely that, once the government has taken the risk as a launch customer (early adopter), companies are more likely to engage with these technologies, as in a way the technology has been *de-risked*. However, not only are governments naturally risk averse, despite recent efforts to introduce a learn-by-doing and innovation friendly culture, but cutting-edge technologies, like most of the AI under development, have little evidence of the specific long-term social and economic impacts (and, in some cases, of any impacts achieved so far). This is a vicious circle that supranational organizations can help overcome. Table 1 presents an overview of some of the remarkable actions and initiatives from these

Table 1. Global organizations actions and steps on AI principles and observation.

Organization	Description of action	Date of creation
OECD	AI Principles.[7] OECD's Committee on Digital Economy Policy began discussing the need for a Recommendation on AI principles, finally established in 2018 (List of expert group members)[8]	2016 to May 2018
	OECD Policy Observatory on AI.[9] Aims at providing evidence and guidance on AI metrics, policies and practices to implement AI Principles, and constitute a hub on AI policies	February 2020
G7	Common Vision for the Future of AI. In the 2018 meeting in Canada, the leaders of the G7 (Canada, France, Germany, Italy, Japan, the UK, and the US) committed to 12 principles for AI	June 2018
G20	Human-centered AI Principles based on OECD AI principles	June 2019
World Economic Forum (WEF)	Formed the Global AI Council to develop a common understanding among countries: best practice in AI policy. "Empowering AI toolkit" for boards leadership to protect societies and their businesses	May 2019 to January 2020
Nordic-Baltic Region	Promote use of AI, access to data and specific policy to develop "ethical and transparent guidelines, standards, and values" for when and how AI should be used (Nordic Co-operation, 2018)	2018
European Parliament	STOA[10] Panel for the Future of Science and Technology. Launched partnership OECD for future of AI (December 2020).[11] Study: The ethics of AI: Issues and initiatives (March 2020)	2020
European Commission (EC)	Post AI Strategy launch in 2018, the EC appointed a group of 52 experts to advice for its implementation: AI High Level Expert Group (AI HLEG). Open and comprised by representatives from academia, civil society and industry	2018 to June 2020
Inter-American Development Bank (IADB)	Launched fAIr LAC (Latin America and the Caribbean), platform to develop standards and tools that guide a responsible and reliable use of AI in LAC through certifications, algorithmic audits and specific guides. Encourages its responsible adoption, through pilots, and regional hubs	2019

global organizations to foster an inclusive and human-centric adoption, and reduce the abovementioned limitations in its applicability.

2. Overarching Challenges

2.1. *Privacy and transparency*

The General Data Protection Regulation (GDPR) came into force in Europe in May 2018. The GDPR can be considered one of the most ambitious pieces of legislation when it comes to data protection on the globe and it has inspired data protection rules around the world. Brazil now has its own "GDPR legislation," just like Japan, China, Russia and California. A harmonized European legal space in terms of data protection is still in the making, due to the nature of GDPR which is rather non-specific and open to interpretation, and also the capability of data protection authorities (DPAs) to act and enforce the rules. There are three main areas of special attention where innovation procurement can play a strategic role:

(1) Increasing legal certainty for SMEs and working toward incentives for "privacy-first" and "privacy-by-design" innovation.
(2) Application of GDPR uniformly across Europe, and GDPR-like legislation across the globe.
(3) Making sure GDPR and GDPR-like legislation does not hinder innovation.

Privacy-first businesses, as value-driven ventures, often experience tension between adhering to values and generating profits. To retain users, privacy-first companies must also offer a service with all the features the user expects (at least as good as those in the mainstream). Innovation Procurement, in this sense, has the ability to favor:

- Open-source business models, where communities of developers are both clients and key contributors to collaboratively build, use and improve the software and AI systems.
- Trust as a priority. As opposed to data-extractive competitors, "privacy-first" innovators see trust as a priority and core value proposition. This sometimes implies decisions to forgo or delay profit.

> **Privacy-first businesses and public frameworks:** Encrypted email
>
> Key-players: ProtonMail
>
> ProtonMail is an end-to-end encrypted email service founded in 2013 by researchers from CERN. It uses client-side encryption to protect email content and user data before they are sent to ProtonMail servers, unlike other common email providers. Proton Technologies AG received over 2M€ in public funding from EC SME Instrument in H2020 R&D program investment (now EIC accelerator). The company's vision is "building an internet that protects privacy, starting with email." ProtonMail started with an Indiegogo crowdfunding campaign in 2014 that raised 0,5M€. Its main stakeholder is the privacy-conscious community.

In this way, innovation procurement has the chance to favor "privacy-first" and "privacy-by-design" businesses to

- Satisfy the appetite for projects with an ethical approach to privacy and data, despite their (inherent) challenges, which is growing in younger generations that show a greater awareness of privacy than their elders.
- Respond to public administrations interest in privacy tools, as many public institutions use management tools built by large corporations, but more and more countries are demanding alternatives that guarantee data confidentiality and security.
- Push for a changing tech sector: more ethical tech is an emerging trend, exemplified by the movement *Zebras Unite*: Zebras, as opposed to unicorns, are businesses that prioritize sustainable growth and the public interest over market domination.

2.2. Ethical concerns

Automated and algorithmic decision making (ADM) is arguably the most interesting capability of AI for governments. As discussed earlier, AI systems that allow for ADM can contribute to the planning and delivery of public services in areas that go from health and welfare to crime and border control. Nevertheless, its potential to introduce efficiency into each of these dimensions is directly related to numerous ethical concerns that it carries for governments acquiring solutions to support it. When AI systems enjoy a high degree of autonomy in the decision-making process, concerns about accountability and transparency become crucially more important as, through public policy, ADM can have wider societal and economic impacts. In fact, they may endanger safety or breach fundamental rights (such as human dignity, privacy, data protection, freedom of expression, workers' rights, etc.). These systems may make it more difficult for persons having suffered harm to obtain compensation and it might disproportionately and unjustifiably affect specific groups, leading to discriminatory outcomes.

As much as a concern in the deployment of AI systems, discrimination is paradoxically a social challenge of huge proportions and historic roots that many governments now have hope of fixing with objective, unbiased ADM. The same as traffic accidents, with a disproportionate death rate impact in practically every country in the world, any positive effect from AI applications could immediately translate into significant improvements. In other words, we have so far accepted a situation that is clearly flawed and, ideally, an objective software-based approach could be expected to produce significant positive outcomes. This is already happening with automating driving and commuting, as accredited by the EC in 2018.[12] In fact, governments have invested in the development and deployment of technology whose overarching objective is to prevent structural discrimination *using* AI-powered ADM. Below, two use-cases (albeit incipient trends) are presented as examples.

Tackling unconscious bias: AI against biased prosecutors in the United States of America

Key-players: City and County of San Francisco and Stanford Policy Lab

In words of the SF District Attorney (official social media): "Lady justice wears a blindfold to signify impartiality of the law, but it's blindingly clear that our justice system remains biased when it comes to race." The SF District Attorney Office and the Stanford Computational Policy Lab developed a tool to limit the threat of implicit bias in prosecutors' charging decisions, using an AI program that redacts potentially biased information from police reports. This initiative is based on claims that the criminal justice system in California is racist, with far more Afro-Americans and Hispanics being arrested than white people.

However, it is worth noting that several risks linger for the use of these technologies and their potential effect on discrimination. Intended or unintended bias can be present not only on the principles that determine the overall functioning of the AI system, which requires a complex assessment on its own.[13] It can also be present in the data set (was it perhaps developed by people with prejudices that are not accounted for?), in the decision to develop an ADM system (why is this system being designed and is it bound to harm specific groups?), in the presentation/communication of the results (are they poising key stakeholders toward biased positions?) and in the way the governments use these results (is the execution systematically harming specific groups?).

Tackling unconscious bias: Unconscious bias in facial recognition software

Key-players: Brookings Institute, IBM

Biometrics are not free of potential bias either. Common facial recognition training datasets are estimated to be over 75% male and 80% white.[14] Consequently, false positives across certain racial and gender demographics are more probable.

Tech giant IBM abandoned "biased" facial recognition tech, and in their letter to the US Congress, claimed AI systems used in law enforcement needed testing "for bias" and opposed (in words of IBM CEO) the use of "any technology, including facial recognition technology offered by other vendors, for mass surveillance, racial profiling, violations of basic human rights."[15]

In spite of these challenges, now that we have "digital and virtual lives," AI still presents an opportunity, with the right training, quality assurance and guidance to uncover and even cancel out human biases: public procurement of innovation can play a key role, while mitigating the aforementioned challenges.

Most importantly, innovation procurement of such technologies, and PCP of highly innovative and potentially revolutionary ADM, when controlled in a sandbox-style scenario, contributes to focus the ethical debate around useful frameworks on the ongoing developments (instead of very popular, yet less relevant, debates on potential applications of AI), while informing this debate with lessons from real-life scenarios. Whereas regulatory risk might be present in AI applications in the private and productive sector, any decision-making process based on predictions of human behavior and widely affecting society is considerably more crucial for the citizens' trust in AI. Successful procurement of these solutions, as challenging as it might be, can therefore play a critical role in paving the way for their application to less regulatory-complex situations in the productive sector.

Finally, even when AI technologies are proven to be non-discriminatory, the fact that these systems "make" decisions that may seem inscrutable to most eyes and trigger governmental actions for which the rationale cannot be transparently explained, understandably generates distrust in the people whose lives can be radically affected by such decisions and actions. Innovation procurement operations can be designed to account for the very relevant role of civil society involvement by ensuring participation of civil service organizations in the process of co-creation and testing of these solutions. Furthermore, contracts can include additional requirements from providers in terms of communication with civil society and training for members of the civil service that later may be required to operate these technologies.

3. Innovation Procurement, an Instrument for AI Innovation

3.1. *Strategic procurement*

Spending in central governments for AI is expected to grow at approximately 44% growth rate globally through 2022. This means a faster growth rate than AI spending in personal and consumer services.[16] However, in order to bring innovative AI solutions to the market and enabling its introduction to different industrial sectors, well-established production models may be disrupted while corresponding providers for each of the link in the supply chain may be forced to drastically transform or, in many cases, see their business disappear. Potential displacements may also happen at the micro level with tasks and in some cases whole roles (i.e., jobs) taken over by AI-powered systems. Governments who are interested is fostering the adoption of AI as a means to transform their economies may consciously and willingly disrupt local industries to make them tougher and globally more competitive, knowing that there is a learning curve both for the development of providers and for the full deployment of such technologies.

In view of this potentially "hostile environment" for the adoption of AI in traditional industries, innovation procurement provides opportunities for a smooth deployment of such technologies and, notably, for the strengthening of its providers in terms of R&D investment and overall turnover. Although few empirical studies have systematically investigated the impact of public procurement on R&D and innovation activity and broader economic outcomes,[17,18] the evidence shows that firms awarded with government contracts are twice as likely to report R&D expenses in the following year compared with non-awarded firms. In the US, contractors that regularly supply to the federal government are more likely to seek the registration of trademarks in the USPTO (U.S. Patent & Trademark Office), suggesting that firms introduce new goods and services as part of or as a result of their fulfillment of government contracts. Finally, public procurement seems to stimulate demand. Furthermore, firm turnover is positively correlated with past contract obligations (rising by 0.3–0.4% as the value of past contract obligations increases by 10%).[a]

There are many ways in which government contracts might be a more nurturing environment for these firms to grow. For example, when part of a broader innovation or industrial policy, the government may assign a

---

[a] OECD data linkage and analysis of FPDS-NG contract award data (2000–2011) matched to company R&D, performance and USPTO patent and trademark filing data. FPDS-NG data include modifications.

higher value to innovation procurement of AI solutions than the actual contribution to the public service they aim to improve. That is to say, in a strategic procurement effort to foster national industries, some governments might show less resistance to higher costs as these can be perceived as a national industry "premium." There are examples of this kind of policies in Brazil, China and Uruguay.[19,20] The willingness to accept higher costs in the short term, can help reduce the pressure on the learning curve for providers while funnel-structured innovation procurement processes favor co-creation with the final user, allowing providers to develop better adapted solutions that can go on to become plug-and-play for the private sector. *Phased innovation procurement* and *strategic procurement* also allows governments to nurture AI start-ups and SMEs who have early-stage concepts and technologies but are in need of funding to attract and retain researchers, data scientists and talent in general before they become profitable and are able to export their products.

In addition to this challenge, there is the communication challenge. The industrial fabric for emerging tech such as AI can be categorized in three segments: corporates, small-medium enterprises (SMEs, including start-ups) and the research community, which often speak different languages. This means that, for highly complex technologies such as AI, even when the environment is not hostile, adoption is hindered by lack of communication between innovation key players. In contexts where the government has important in-house scientific capabilities and needs — the case of many Asian nations but also increasingly that of multiple public administrations in the West — this obstacle can be mitigated by innovation and strategic procurement. In largely established industries scientists, companies (i.e., providers) and need-owners (i.e., buyers of the public service that can be improved by AI) are used to working together in the pursuit of common objectives, and so formal and informal communication channels are more likely to have been long established.

Even when the governments' needs exceed in-house capabilities, scientists employed by the government can provide valuable assistance in specifying functional requirements for technology providers. They can (should) also aid the process of bid appraisal and in the overall management of the contracts. However, it is worth noting that the complexity of the technology is proportionately related to the difficulty of identifying functional requirements on the governments side: when in-house R&D+i capabilities are low, governments face additional hurdles for innovation procurement of complex AI technologies. They can turn, however, to the (emerging) use of broader challenge/mission-oriented approaches to enable truly innovative proposals.

Innovation procurement and collaborative innovation management

Key-players: Government Technology Agency of Singapore

The Government Technology Agency of Singapore has been introducing a new procurement framework to move towards a collaborative approach for innovation management of AI. GovTech is now looking to co-develop technologies with industry partners, by working together directly in trials to develop tailored solutions for the government.

One of the hurdles it has contributed to overcome is the need to develop new contracts when new or different need are identified in the process of developing and testing a prototype AI technology in the government. In fact, a separate procurement process to implement those ideas adds additional complexity and could end up suppressing their potential. To overcome this, GovTech has released "outcome-based calls for solutions" in which proposals are shortlisted based on preliminary criteria, and selected partners can improve their proposals as they gain better knowledge of the government's need. Different stages can be awarded to different partners but are all part of the same procurement process. This allows for innovation through a trial-and-error approach and makes the process more resilient for technologies that can become obsolete in a matter of months.[21,22]

Another way in which AI technologies can overcome resistance from traditional industrial sectors is by inspiring confidence into the viability and potential benefits of their introduction. Governments can also play a relevant role in this area through public procurement by becoming a particularly pro-active launch-customer. Besides contributing to the co-creation of these technologies and effectively being the reference cos-tumer, innovation procurement contracts can include additional actions from the government in the showcasing of the AI technologies they buy. For instance, actively participating in the provider's communication strategy, by contributing to success stories that can raise the interest of executives and investors. For example, some public institutions in Spain have organized visits to receive other government committees and private companies interested in seeing, first hand, the functioning of a new AI system. In this role governments become the much-needed "AI communicators," showcasing the results of R&D+i to other governments and to the private sector and therefore facilitating technology transfer.

Finally, it is worth highlighting that, although innovation procurement can help overcome the resistance of traditional industrial sectors and favor the consolidation of SMEs that develop these technologies, they might also face somewhat different resistance within governments. This resistance is a consequence of the dynamics of the public sector, in conjunction with the characteristics of these technologies. AI technologies can be especially threatening to various civil servants and public officials specialized in surveillance tasks, data processing, and others. AI technologies may not only displace older technologies ones in specific tasks (e.g., certain database structures, etc.) but, potentially, make certain positions redundant or less powerful, where directly involved officials may end up acting as obstructions for the purchase.

Additionally, in relation to technological dependence, it is also worth mentioning the existing problems in a large part of the public sector, regarding the acquisition of Software-as-a-Service (SaaS) solutions, and how these might increase resistance to the acquisition and deployment of AI technologies in the government. Perhaps due to bad past experiences (derived from the commercial strategy of large multinationals) many governments remain wary of investing in SaaS, as this may mean they would be falling into technological dependence. This is more worrisome as previous experiences have shown that this dependence of a specific provider can lead to a steep increase in public spending, through unfair pricing of related expenses such as maintenance, specific training and extensions. These experiences have led many governments to require extended access or ownership rights over Intellectual and Industrial Property Rights (IPRs) of technology-based solutions, in order to keep the possibility of acquiring maintenance and other services from third parties.

Since the code and algorithms in AI-based solutions, are many times the result of a significant investment in R&D, most solutions are still based on proprietary software, which collides with governments' preference to have extended IPRs over them. This situation creates two problems.

- First, many companies and technology/research centers with advanced AI-based solutions (or with the capacity to develop them) do not bid for public sector tenders because of the IPRs conditions it entails. This reduces the quality of the technologies that can be potentially acquired by the government.
- Second, the public sector ends up acquiring tailor-made tools (that are not heavily guarded as valuable assets), which generates additional problems in the long run, both in terms of interoperability and, above all, evolution and improvement based on the additional data they can get by interoperating with other systems.

In the final section of this chapter, some recommendations are suggested for actions to potentially mitigate these risks.

3.2. *Innovation procurement for AI and IM*

Innovation Procurement of AI serves as a public-private alliance that improves the framework conditions for innovation management (IM) both within the government and in the AI sector as a whole. Innovation Procurement requires identifying the problem (functional requirements) rather than the solution (technical specifications) in the tender. This has shown to be a major disruption to standard-oriented government's procurement culture and, simultaneously, this is the first condition for effective innovation management within public organizations. In effect, reframing procurement in terms of functional attributes rather than specifications is the first hurdle to turning ideas into useful, successful innovations. Whilst in the case of innovation procurement the solutions come from non-public actors, overcoming this hurdle is a relevant internal change in innovation management in the civil service as it sets a precedent for solving problems or improvising the available solutions rather than simply replicating well-established protocols.

Furthermore, in phased processes of innovation procurement of AI, need-owners in the government become active actors in transforming an idea into a successful innovation as they participate in concept development, business plan, solution development, prototype testing and implementation: a culture that supports these processes is one of the final goals of an effective innovation management strategy. Additionally, and particularly in the case of complex technologies like AI, market consultations (a key element of innovation procurement) forces public procurers to engage in future innovation management through the identification of trends and future opportunities and risks. All in all, this process enables the government to participate in innovation networks and leverage external innovation sources and resources, an important ingredient for a successful innovation management strategy. This interaction with potential providers is also beneficial to the chances of success of the procurement itself. In fact, the most successful PPI & PCP calls have counted on the "market push" necessary from established companies since a problem that has not enough interest and capable providers is not a procurement need but a limitation that has to be bypassed by *other* type of innovations.

Furthermore, AI has notably been studied elsewhere (see for example Ref. [23]) as a useful tool to support innovation management in several organizations. The government is not the exception particularly when it acquires these technologies through innovation procurement. With functional requirements instead of rigid technical requirements and an iterative and highly interactive process of co-creation of the solutions, AI technologies are more likely to provide valuable feedback to the initial problem identified and contribute to the discovery of new problems with corresponding (innovative) solutions. For example, by identifying patterns in large sets of data from transportation, AI applications may reveal problems that were not identified by the service providers before, unleashing new processes of innovation that can be in many cases accommodated in subsequent phases of the innovation procurement. In this sense, when procurement results from non-solicited offers (a key element in bottom-up innovation procurement), knowledge-intensive companies are given another channel to influence innovation management within governments by identifying potential solutions to challenges that the government had not identified in the first place. In high-tech fields such as AI, this can easily be the case as the government's limited knowledge of the possibilities of these technologies can be interconnected with its inability to reframe long established limitations as potential problems with emerging solutions.

On the side of AI developers and providers, innovation procurement can also help inform their innovation management strategies. Phased procurement may allow them to identify potential synergies with otherwise competitors, and market consultation can help in the prioritization of the innovation portfolio and R&D roadmap. Furthermore, when coherent policies of innovation procurement led to the establishment of long-term *catalogues of early demand* (see for example Ref. [24]) these documents become beacons for the development of the innovation management strategy and possibly a major part of specific companies' innovation roadmap. From the perspective of innovation procurement as a top-down policy, serious commitment to long-term challenges can also help frame companies' innovation strategy: a clear example of these kind of challenge-oriented procurement are the missions in Horizon Europe,[25] inspired in previous successful, top-down innovation policies like the Graphene Flagship.

Challenge-based procurement to encourage AI: The case of BRE

Key-players: GovTech Catalyst, BRE and BEIS, UK

When facing complex problems with potential for truly innovative solutions, flexible routes to market and requests for proposals have enabled governments to focus on the challenge rather than on a detailed specification of the technology, allowing for the development of better solutions that may have not been foreseen originally. As this is many times the case of procurement of AI-powered technologies, the UK GovTech catalyst, a public fund that pays suppliers to solve public sector problems using innovative digital technology, has developed specific tender templates, model contract clauses and specific procurement frameworks to support challenge-based procurements of AI.[26]

A government department that has successfully relied on these resources is the Better Regulation Executive (BRE). In partnership with the department for Business, Energy and Industrial Strategy (BEIS) they pursued techno-logical solutions to analyze the effect of different sets of regulations on business to inform the government's reform.

Although there was clarity over the need of developing an AI-based solu-tion, there was uncertainty about the specific techniques and software/hardware requirements.

The challenge-based approach gave this project a much-needed flexibility in the procurement process, allowing them to trial different approaches while ensuring that they scoped out the project extensively.

As the BRE had little technical expertise in-house and the whole process was allowed to be open to different ideas and technical specifications, they partnered with BEIS Digital and the experts at the National Archives to improve their decision making, enabling cross-policy and cross-agency innovation management.

See more details in Ref. [27].

4. Common Pitfalls in Innovation Procurement of AI

In this last section we present, from a practical perspective, a series of common pitfalls in innovation procurement of AI and suggest actions to avoid or minimize them.

(1) Fail to define what "success" means when incorporating AI in the government: as mentioned in previous sections, AI has a huge poten-tial to improve public services, but the final results might take a long time to materialize and might be hard to capture. When engaging in innovation procurement of AI, buyers need to reflect on what "suc-cess" means, using the toolkits and AI principles described in previ-ous sections to weigh potential risks and benefits. Whether it means improving the quality of life of citizens or nurturing AI companies (or, ideally, a combination of both), this definition should include clear indicators for success in different stages of the procurement, including but not limited to (leading) impact-indicators, as it makes take several

months and sometimes years before these impacts are materialized. Although these objectives should not be confused with secondary and tertiary objectives that often times take the spotlight, such as political gain or attainment of national or supranational funds, a successful innovation procurement of AI should not disregard these additional objectives (impact key indicators, IKIs) as they are many times enablers (and can also be important impediments) of the procurement process itself.

(2) Insufficient interaction between supply and demand side: as mentioned, many of the benefits that innovation procurement brings to innovation management within the government and within potential provider companies comes from the constant interaction between both sides. This interaction is particularly relevant for a correct definition of the need that justifies the process: while public officials have more knowledge of their own needs, companies and research centers have a better understanding of the State of the Art. The distribution of this knowledge is even more complex in fields where disruptive innovation and changes in the field are more frequent, such as AI — e.g., a specific research center may have identified a challenge solution in the government, as a result of a recent R&D development, that public officials don't recognize as a need as they believe there is no solution to it or no other "way to conduct business" (and therefore, there is no official problem, just an underlying working condition). Since ill-defined needs will most likely lead to failure in innovation procurement, governments must strive to guarantee that this interaction is as fluid as possible, while adhering to the principles of transparency and fair competition. Technology scouting and competitive intelligence, as well as more long-term efforts such as market landscaping and trend monitoring, are the pillars to achieve the right analysis of State of the Art. Preliminary market consultations are also helpful to understand technology and commercial readiness of the different potential solutions. Finally, including research centers, companies and organizations with specialized knowledge, both at regional level and at national and supranational levels, in an External Advisory board could constitute a good practice.

(3) Poor definition of the functional requirements: one of the most frequent mistakes in innovation procurement of highly complex technologies, like AI, is providing too much technical requirement detail in the bid specifications (precision of analysis, response times, data volume, base-technology stack, and others), without a correct definition of the solution from the functional requirements standpoint. This problem often leads to developing what the client wanted, but not solving the government's need. This definition gap can affect proper access to data and fail to guarantee interoperability among solutions. Public buyers, especially in AI and software-related calls, tend to underestimate the importance of standardization, anonymization and revision of data quality, as well as validating the interoperability of the existing system and data flow with the one to be developed, and future integrations. When these concerns arise in the execution of the project, additional barriers need to be sorted (legal obstacles, access to databases, anonymization and encryption, incorrect scaling, etc.) and the time and quality of the development are affected. It is important to hit the right balance between setting minimums from the technical requirements' standpoint and allowing flexibility with the definition of the right functional requirements.

(4) Inadequate funding and "change management" for full deployment and operation: many flagship projects of transformation of a public service using AI are funded by trans-national funds (trans-national in Europe, trans-statal in US, trans-provincial in China, trans-prefecture in Japan, and others), either with direct management (such as Horizon 2020, and the equivalent Horizon Europe for 2021–2027, in the European R&D framework) or indirect (e.g., regional and pluri-regional FEDER funds in Europe). This funding only covers the investment in the development of the project, not in the scale-up, and operation costs. When the scale-up and maintenance costs are not correctly planned projects are not able to overcome the pilot phase. Furthermore, even when funding is available after the pilot stage, resistance to full deployment and operation can understandably come from people and institutions within the government. End-user feedback would reduce the friction and maximized the user experience, but there has to be an exhaustive analysis, evaluation and monitoring

of public processes that are being modified as unexpected behaviors may occur. Change management needs to be in place to ensure support for civil servants and for institutional resilience (e.g., need to alter the system to comply with regulations, specialized training, organizational changes, hiring process).

Acknowledgment

The views expressed in this article are those of the author(s) and are not necessarily those of Public Health England or the Department of Health and Social Care.

References

1. S. Ravindran, How artificial intelligence is helping to prevent blindness. Nature Outlook [Internet]. April 10, 2019 [accessed on February 12, 2021]. Available from: https://www.nature.com/.
2. J. Sijtsema and T. Kretschmer, The structured assessment of violence risk in youth in a large community sample of young adult males and females: The TRAILS study. *Psychological Assessment*, **27**(2), 669–677 (2015).
3. U.S. Geological Survey — USGS [Internet], Washington, D.C.: U.S. Department of the Interior [accessed on April 16, 2021]. Available from: https://www.usgs.gov/core-science-systems/nli/landsat.
4. Augas de Galicia [Internet], Innovaugas 4.0, Gestión avanzada de los recursos hídricos gallegos, Santiago de Compostela: Xunta de Galicia [accessed on April 16, 2021]. Available from: https://innovaugas.xunta.gal/.
5. S. Marsh, One in three councils using algorithms to make welfare decisions. The Guardian [Internet]. October 15, 2019 [accessed on April 6, 2021]. Available at: https://www.theguardian.com/society/2019/oct/15/councils-using-algorithms-make-welfare-decisions-benefits.
6. G. Misuraca and C. Van Noordt, Overview of the use and impact of AI in public services in the EU. *Publications Office of the European Union* (2020).
7. The Organisation for Economic Co-operation and Development. OECD Principles on AI [Internet]. Paris: OECD; [updated June 16, 2019, accessed on April 16, 2021]. Available from: http://www.oecd.org/going-digital/ai/principles/.

8. The Organisation for Economic Co-operation and Development, List of participants in the OECD Expert Group on AI, AIGO [Internet]. Paris: OECD; 2020 [updated June 16, 2021, accessed on April 16, 2021]. Available from: https://www.oecd.org/going-digital/ai/oecd-aigo-membership-list.pdf.

9. The Organisation for Economic Co-operation and Development, AI Policy Observatory: A platform to share and shape AI policies. [Internet]. Paris: OECD; 2020 [accessed on April 16, 2021]. Available from: https://www.oecd.org/going-digital/ai/about-the-oecd-ai-policy-observatory.pdf.

10. Panel for the Future of Science and Technology (STOA), History and Mission [Internet]. Brussels: European Parliament; 2020 [accessed on April 16, 2021]. Available from: https://www.europarl.europa.eu/stoa/en/about/history-and-mission.

11. Panel for the Future of Science and Technology (STOA), History and Mission [Internet]. Brussels: European Parliament; 2020 [accessed on April 16, 2021]. Available from: https://www.europarl.europa.eu/stoa/en/home/news/details/launch-of-stoa-s-partnership-on-artifici/20191209CDT03143.

12. P. Boucher, Artificial intelligence: How does it work, why does it matter, and what can we do about it? *European Parliamentary Research Service*, PE 641.547 (2020).

13. algorithmwatch.org [Internet], Berlin: AlgorithmWatch; c2019 [accessed on April 16, 2021].

14. S. Lohr, Facial recognition is accurate, if you're a white guy. *The New York Times* [Internet]. February 9, 2019 [accessed on February 10, 2021]. Available from: https://www.nytimes.com/2018/02/09/technology/facial-recognition-race-artificial-intelligence.html.

15. bbc.com, BM abandons "biased" facial recognition tech [Internet]. London: BBC; 2020 [accessed on March 10, 2021]. Available from: https://www.bbc.com/news/technology-52978191.

16. Deloitte Center for Government Insights, Government trends 2020 [Internet]. 2020 [accessed on February 10, 2021]. Available from: https://www2.deloitte.com/content/dam/Deloitte/lu/Documents/public-sector/lu-government-trends-2020.pdf.

17. M. Guerzoni and E. Raiteri, Innovative public procurement and R&D subsidies: Hidden treatment and new empirical evidence on the technology policy mix, University of Turin, Working Paper (2013).

18. T. Simcoe and M.W. Toffel, Government green procurement spillovers: Evidence from municipal building policies in California, Harvard Business School, Working Papers No. 13-030 (2013).

19. S. Appelt and F. Galindo-Rueda, Measuring the link between public procurement and innovation, *OECD Science, Technology and Industry*, Working Papers (2016).

20. E. Urraya and D. Moñux (eds.), Spurring innovation-led growth in Latin America and the Caribbean through public procurement, *Inter-American Development Bank*, Discussion Paper No. IDB-DP-488 (2016).

21. M.J. Ospina-Fadul and D. Moñux, Compra pública de innovación en América Latina: Recomendaciones para su despliegue en Uruguay, Inter-American Development Bank, Discussion Paper No. IDB-DP-542 (2017).

22. tech.gov.sg [Homepage on the Internet]. Singapore: GovTech [updated June 7, 2019, accessed on February 8, 2021]. Available from: https://www.tech.gov.sg/media/technews/3-new-ways-to-partner-with-govtech.

23. OECD Observatory of Public Sector Innovation, Embracing innovation in government 2019 [Internet], 2020 [accessed on February 3, 2021], Available from: https://trends.oecd-opsi.org/.

24. N. Haefner and J. Wincent, Artificial intelligence and innovation management: A review, framework, and research agenda. *Technological Forecasting and Social Change*, **162**(1) (2021).

25. ACCIO, *Catalogue of Early Demand: Smart City Expo World Congress 2019*. Barcelona: Generalitat de Catalunya (2019).

26. S. Gerdon and V. Molinari, How governments can use public procurement to shape the future of AI regulation — And boost innovation and growth. Retrieved from www.weforum.org. (June 8, 2020).

27. S. Gerdon, E. Katz, E. LeGrand, G. Morrison, and J. Torres, AI procurement in a box: Pilot cases from the United Kingdom. World Economic Forum, Geneva (2020).

Index

Series on Technology Management

(Continuation of series card page)

Printed in the United States
by Baker & Taylor Publisher Services